THE BLACK BEETLE ™

To my twin soul and lovely wife Lisa.
And to my friends.

THE BLACK BEETLE

IN

"NO OUT"

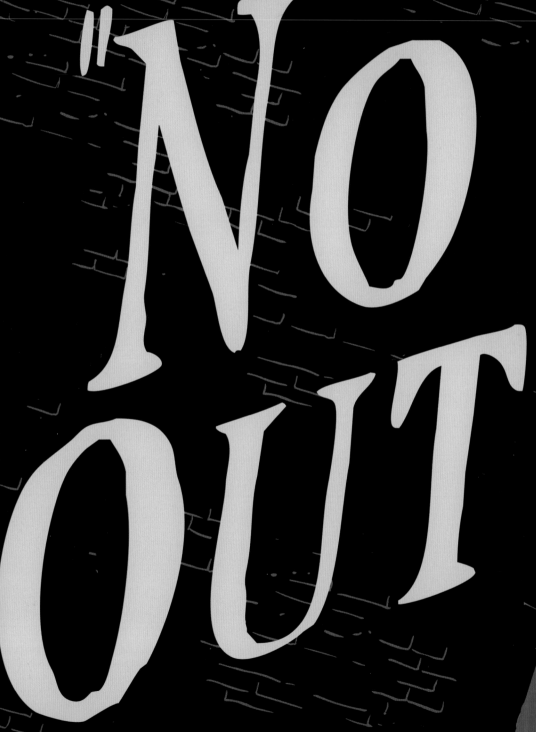

DARK HORSE BOOKS

Lettering by
NATE PIEKOS of BLAMBOT

Covers by
FRANCESCO FRANCAVILLA

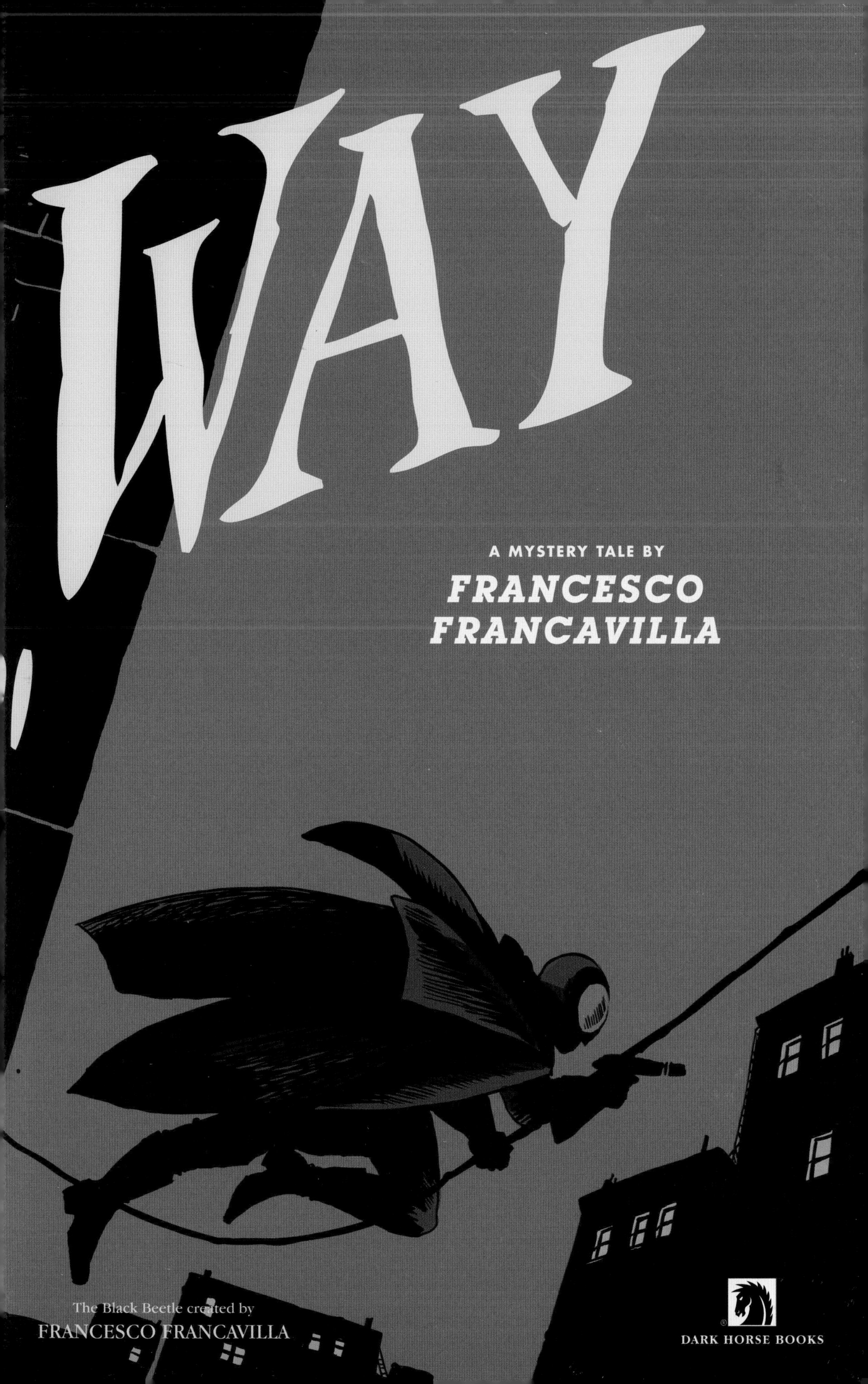
WAY
A MYSTERY TALE BY
FRANCESCO
FRANCAVILLA
The Black Beetle created by
FRANCESCO FRANCAVILLA
DARK HORSE BOOKS

President & Publisher
MIKE RICHARDSON

Editor
JIM GIBBONS

Cover Designer
FRANCESCO FRANCAVILLA

Collection Designers
FRANCESCO FRANCAVILLA
and JUSTIN COUCH

SPECIAL THANKS
Lisa Francavilla, for her invaluable Editorial and Production assistance.

THANKS
Mike Richardson, Darwyn Cooke, Jim Steranko,
Warren Ellis, Gail Simone, Rick Remender, Matt Wagner, Steve Niles,
Rafael Kayanan, Monique McPherson, Sierra Hahn,
Scott Allie, and John Schork.

Published by
DARK HORSE BOOKS
A division of Dark Horse Comics, Inc.
10956 SE Main Street
Milwaukie, OR 97222

DARKHORSE.COM

This volume reprints the comic book *The Black Beetle: Night Shift* #0 and the series *The Black Beetle: No Way Out* #1–#4 from Dark Horse Comics. International Licensing: (503) 905-2377. To find a comics shop in your area, call the Comic Shop Locator Service toll-free at (888) 266-4226.

10 9 8 7 6 5 4 3 2 1
Printed in China

First edition: October 2013
ISBN 978-1-61655-202-2

Neil Hankerson Executive Vice President • Tom Weddle Chief Financial Officer • Randy Stradley Vice President of Publishing • Michael Martens Vice President of Book Trade Sales • Anita Nelson Vice President of Business Affairs • Scott Allie Editor in Chief • Matt Parkinson Vice President of Marketing • David Scroggy Vice President of Product Development • Dale LaFountain Vice President of Information Technology • Darlene Vogel Senior Director of Print, Design, and Production • Ken Lizzi General Counsel • Davey Estrada Editorial Director • Chris Warner Senior Books Editor • Diana Schutz Executive Editor • Cary Grazzini Director of Print and Development • Lia Ribacchi Art Director • Cara Niece Director of Scheduling • Tim Wiesch Director of International Licensing • Mark Bernardi Director of Digital Publishing

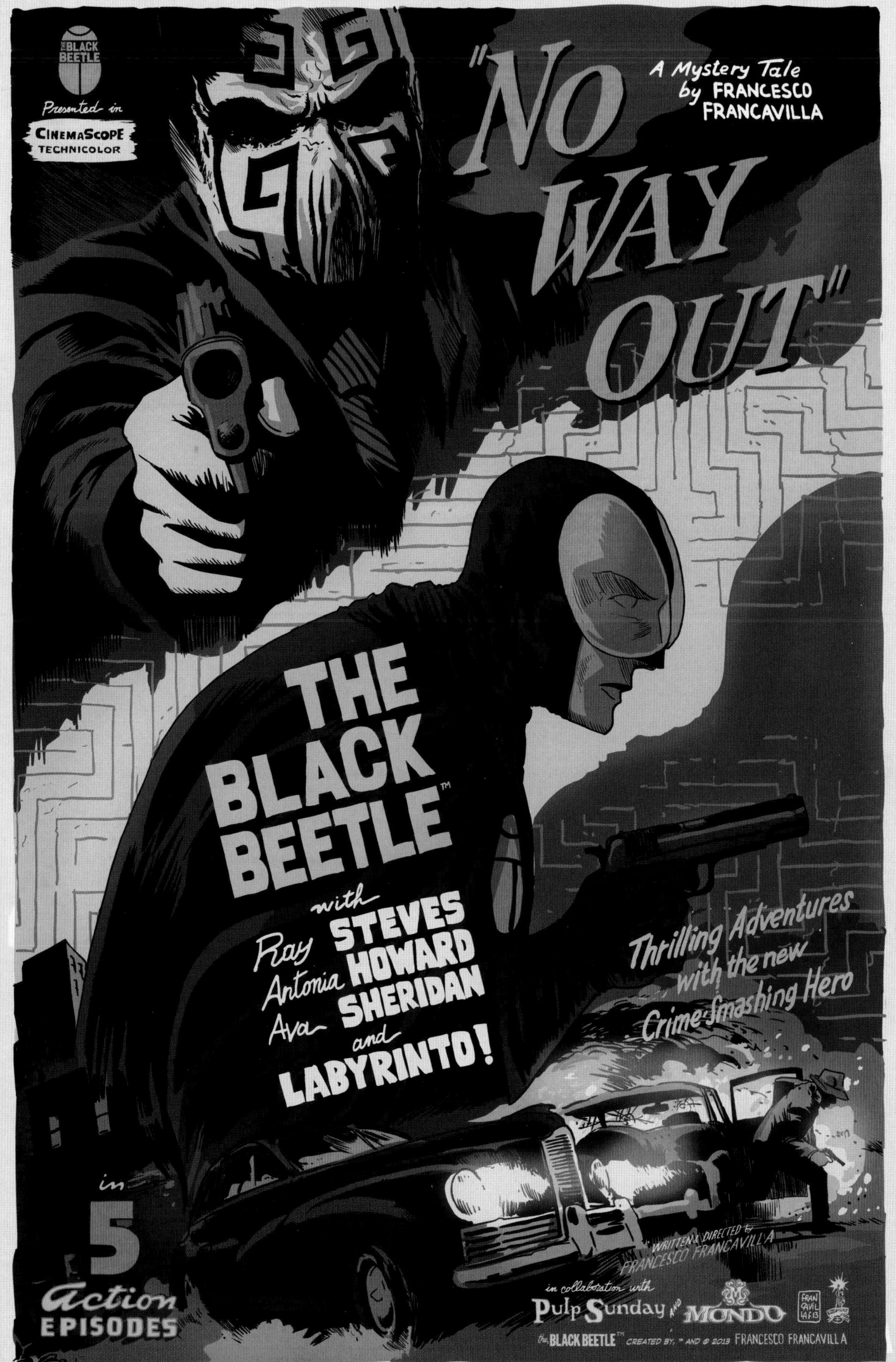
THE BLACK BEETLE
Presented in
CINEMASCOPE TECHNICOLOR
"NO WAY OUT"
A Mystery Tale by FRANCESCO FRANCAVILLA
THE BLACK BEETLE™
with
Ray STEVES
Antonia HOWARD
Ava SHERIDAN
and
LABYRINTO!
Thrilling Adventures with the new Crime-Smashing Hero
in 5 Action EPISODES
WRITTEN & DIRECTED by FRANCESCO FRANCAVILLA
in collaboration with
Pulp Sunday AND MONDO
FRAN CAVIL LA F.13
the BLACK BEETLE™ CREATED BY, ™ AND © 2013 FRANCESCO FRANCAVILLA

FOREWORD

by *DARWYN COOKE*

So a Canadian and an Italian meet in this bar.

No punch line for this one, just my way of explaining what I'm doing here. You go to the conventions across America and you meet people from halfway across the world and you realize you share a deep bond you couldn't possibly have had if it wasn't for American entertainment.

So it was for Francesco and me.

One of the coolest things about American popular entertainment is seeing what happens when it goes abroad and ignites the imaginations of other cultures. I'll cite the British invasion and Hong Kong action films from the nineties as two examples of what I mean.

When I was a boy in Toronto, my friends and I had many local cultural obsessions, but the youth of my generation were probably the first in our country to be seared by the light of the American pop culture machine. This is where I found Jonny Quest, Batman and Robin, Green Lantern, Archie and Betty, and Sergeant Rock. Later it would be Don Siegel, Robert Aldrich, Howard Hawks, Frankenheimer, and John Huston. Then came Jim Cain, Cornell Woolrich, Chandler, Jim Thompson, and my beloved Donald Westlake. By the time I had a chance to try my hand at a big story where I had some control over its direction, I was brimming with two decades of ideas brought forward by voraciously ingesting American entertainment. I can still taste the desire I felt, at the onset of *New Frontier*, to tell a distinctly American story.

And this is how I like to imagine my dear friend Francesco. Far over the ocean in some fertile valley with sun-dappled orchards, his young imagination brimming with images and characters and stories from America. I'm told that, even as a boy of ten, he had his small beard perched below his lip. I picture him on a sunny hill under an olive tree . . . Perhaps his pet goat is there with him. Beside him are stacks of translated pulps and comics: *The Shadow*, *The Spider*, *Doc Savage*, and such. And I like to think that like me, he was dreaming of what he'd do if he could ever tell such a story. When he wasn't guzzling wine and chasing girls, that is. They start young over there.

This book feels like the glorious result of all of that. *No Way Out* and its mysterious hero, the Black Beetle, are like a celebration of everything Francesco ever read or saw in the pages of those bygone pulps and old Republic serials. This, of course, is not a new enterprise, but the freshness comes from Francesco's cultural filters and how they've reshuffled the deck. All the beloved pulp tropes are there: gas guns and deathtraps and cryptic clues. But it's all happening at a very Italian tempo. Tempo is the only word I can manage to describe what I mean. The story splashes forward in bursts and operatic set pieces that make the familiar fresh and exciting. Montage, maps, sheet music, sequence-specific layouts, and even intermezzo scenes are brought forward with confidence and bravura. Nine panel, four panel, vignette, half splash, directional panel composition, and more all work to maximize the action in a sequence. What holds this barrage of approaches together is that tempo I mentioned. Staccato and breakneck, like the bullets from a Thompson.

The other thing I love about *No Way Out* is that it is an unapologetic action story. Often people revisit this genre and use the tropes or action as window dressing for an emotional deconstruction meant to reflect a more modern sensibility. Here the action is the story, and every detail rings period true. Hell, I don't even know who the Black Beetle is under that mask, and I kind of like it that way.

Amazingly, *The Black Beetle* is but a fraction of what this Italian workhorse is creating. If you haven't yet, hit the Google and marvel at the staggering breadth and amount of work by this cat.

Now if you'll excuse me, I'd better get my ass back to work. This guy is starting to make me look lazy.

Darwyn Cooke
East of Colt City, 2013

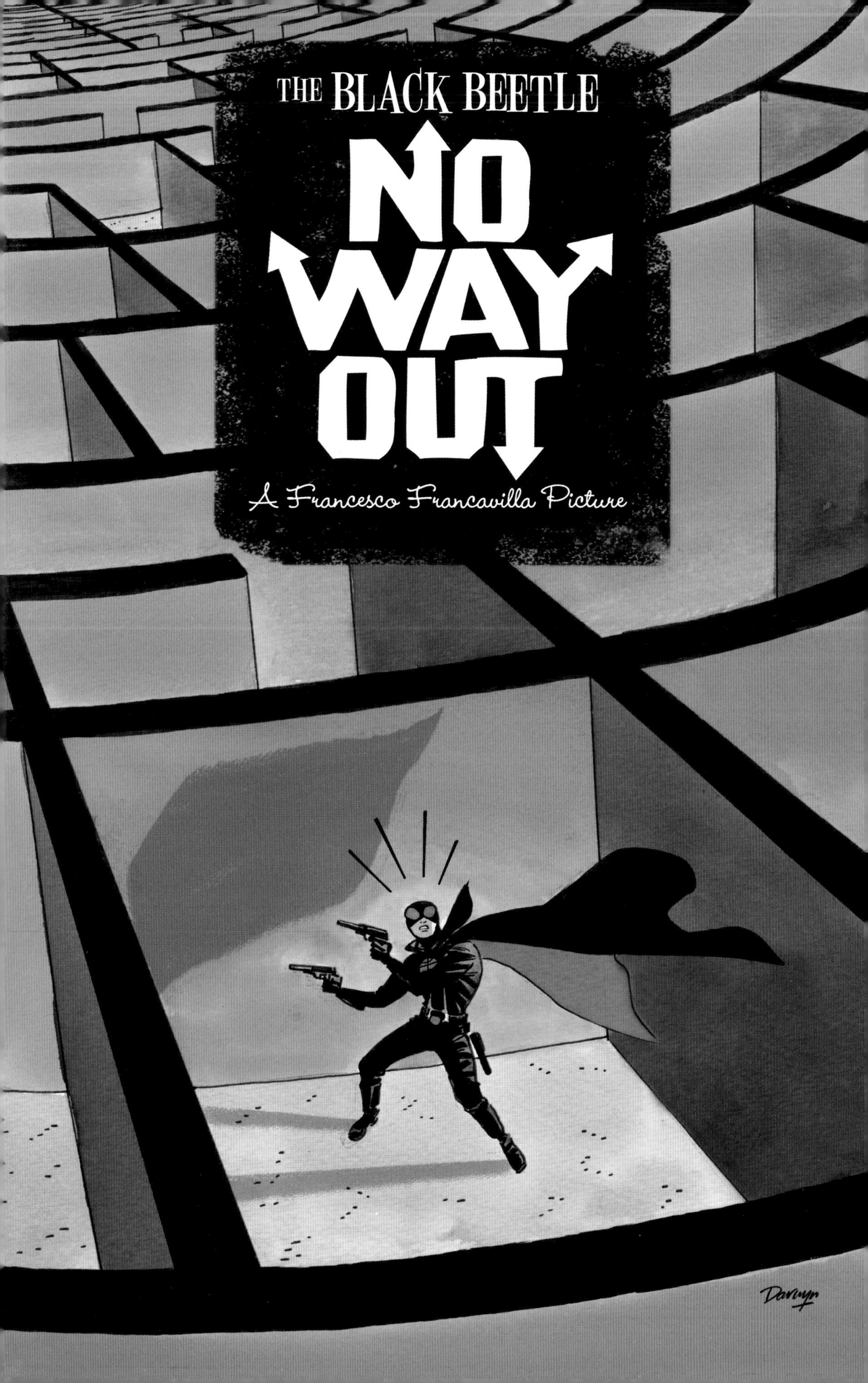
THE BLACK BEETLE
NO WAY OUT
A Francesco Francavilla Picture
Darwyn

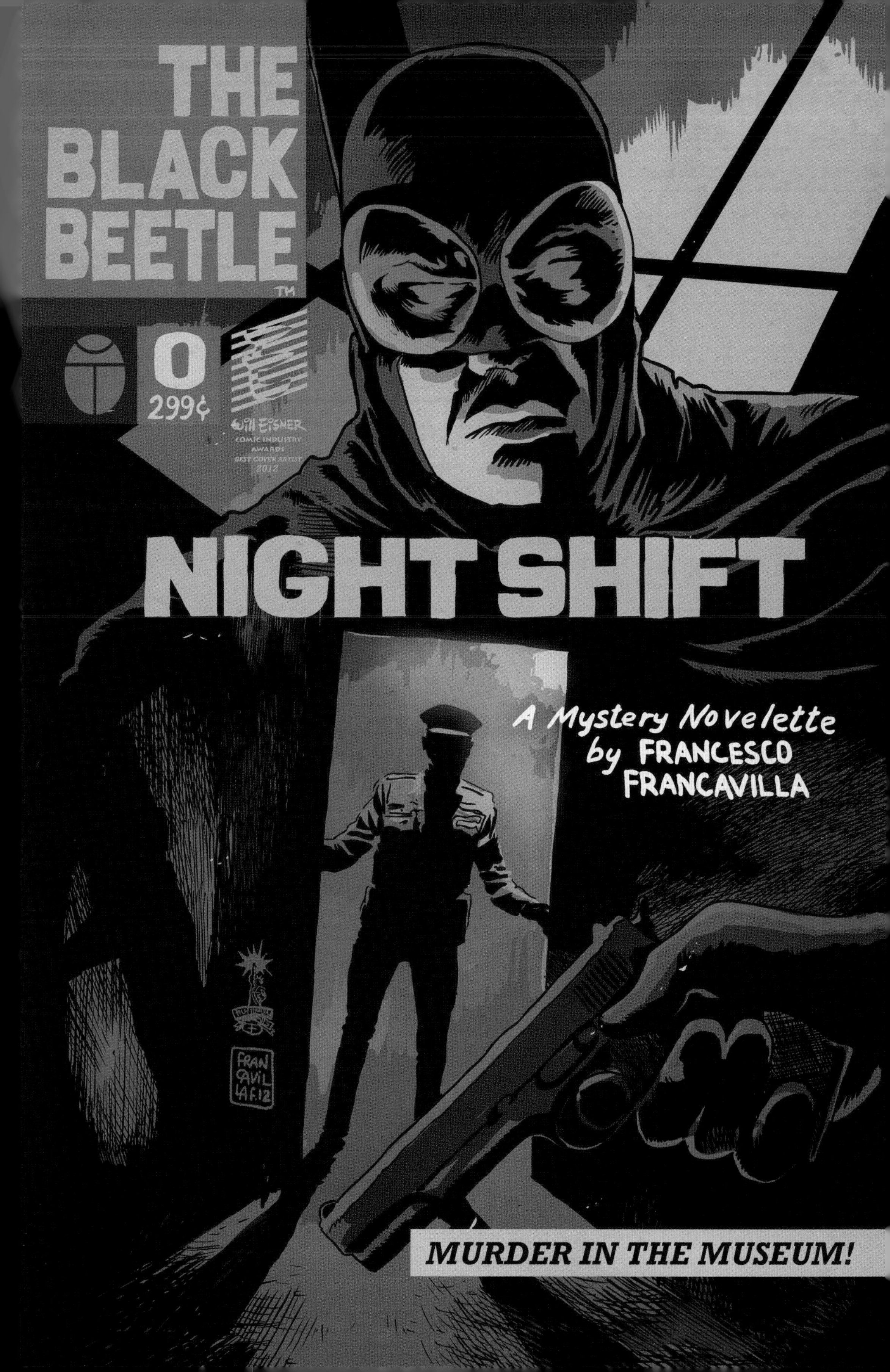
THE BLACK BEETLE
TM
0
299¢
Will Eisner Comic Industry Awards Best Cover Artist 2012
NIGHT SHIFT
A Mystery Novelette by FRANCESCO FRANCAVILLA
FRANCAVILLA F.12
MURDER IN THE MUSEUM!

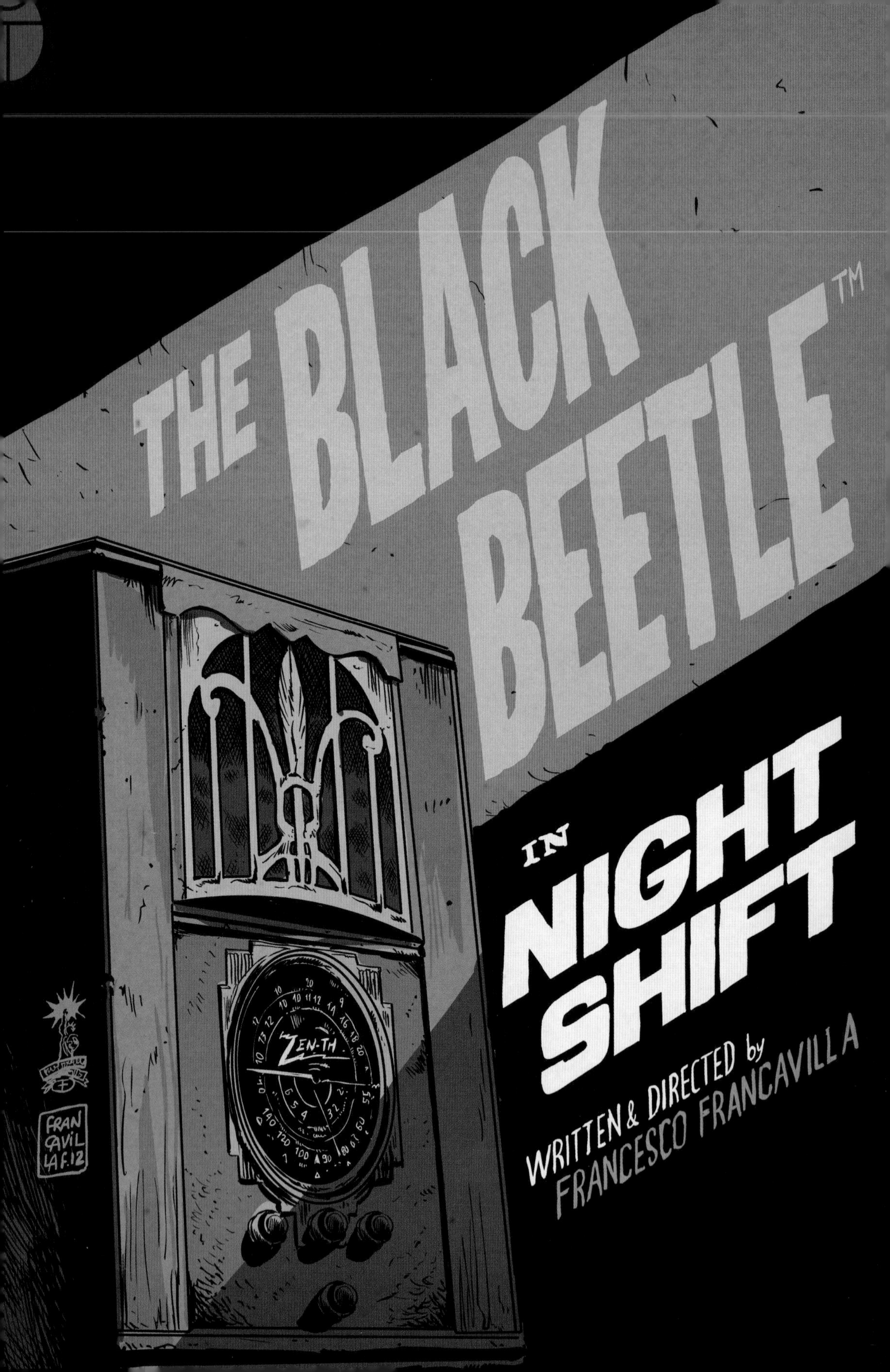
THE BLACK BEETLE™
IN
NIGHT SHIFT
WRITTEN & DIRECTED by
FRANCESCO FRANCAVILLA
ZEN-TH
FRAN CAVIL LA F.12

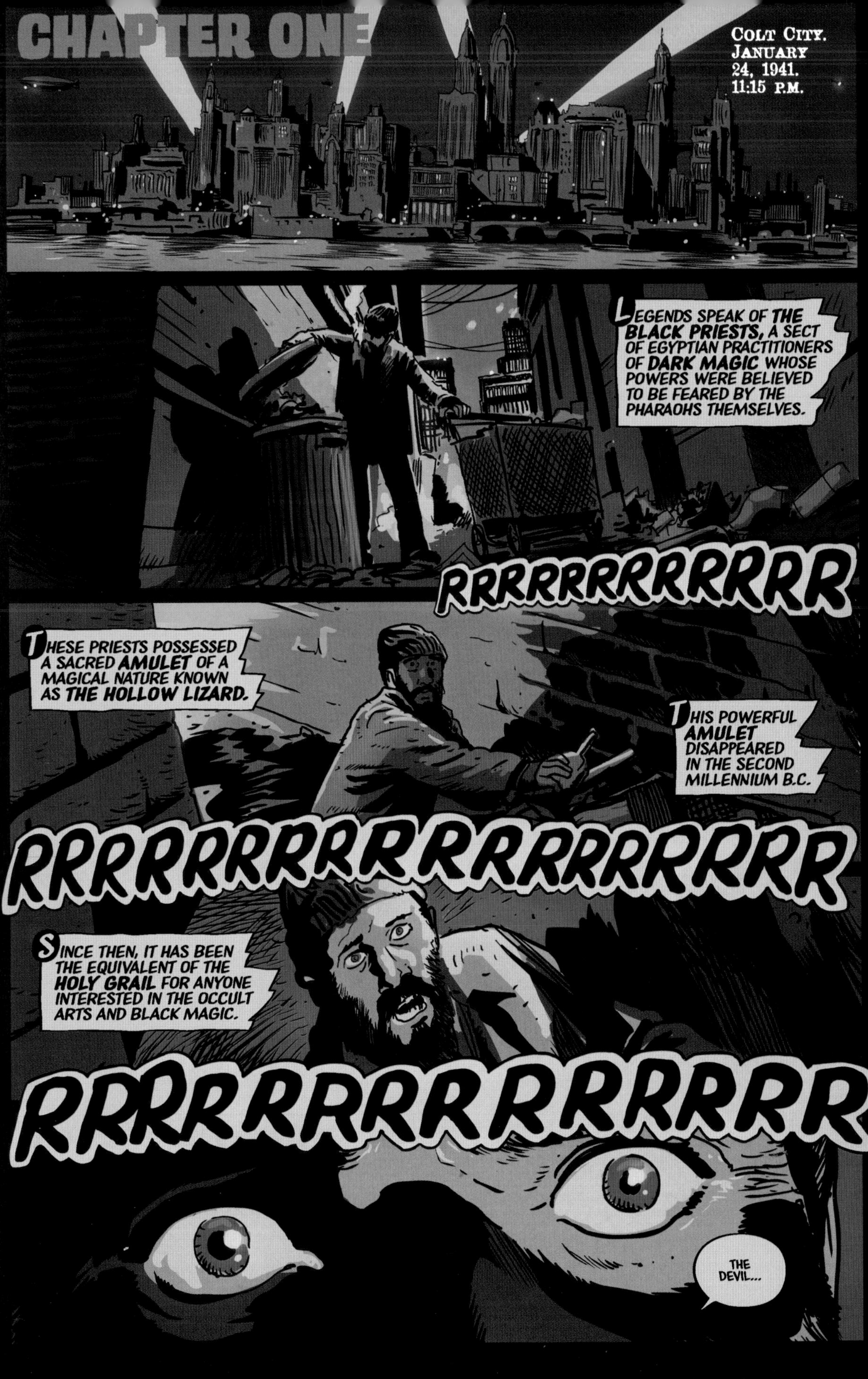
CHAPTER ONE
COLT CITY. JANUARY 24, 1941. 11:15 P.M.
LEGENDS SPEAK OF THE BLACK PRIESTS, A SECT OF EGYPTIAN PRACTITIONERS OF DARK MAGIC WHOSE POWERS WERE BELIEVED TO BE FEARED BY THE PHARAOHS THEMSELVES.
RRRRRRRRRRRR
THESE PRIESTS POSSESSED A SACRED AMULET OF A MAGICAL NATURE KNOWN AS THE HOLLOW LIZARD.
THIS POWERFUL AMULET DISAPPEARED IN THE SECOND MILLENNIUM B.C.
RRRRRRRRRRRRRRRRR
SINCE THEN, IT HAS BEEN THE EQUIVALENT OF THE HOLY GRAIL FOR ANYONE INTERESTED IN THE OCCULT ARTS AND BLACK MAGIC.
RRRRRRRRRRRRRRRR
THE DEVIL...

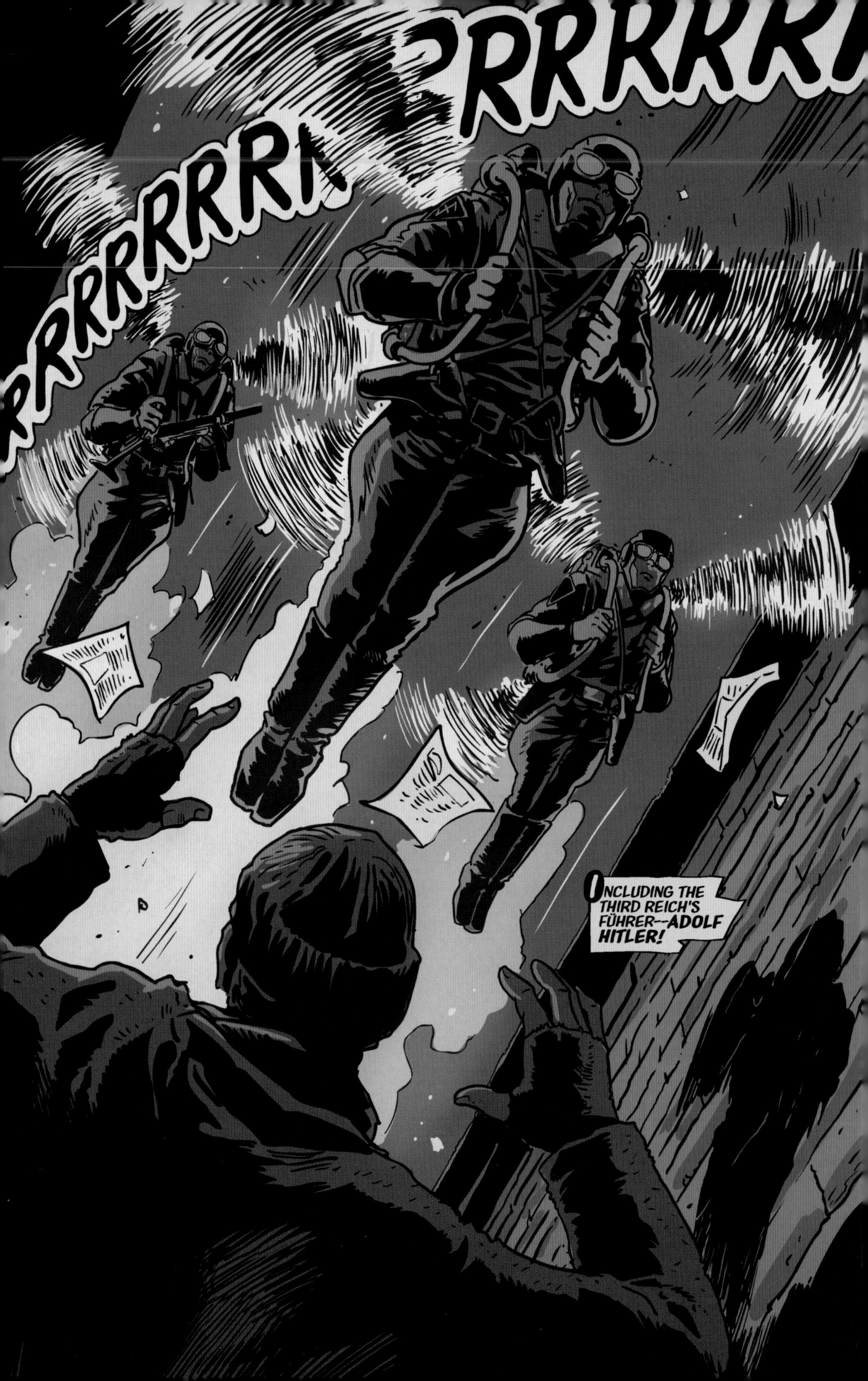
RRRRRRRRRRRRRKKK
INCLUDING THE THIRD REICH'S FÜHRER--ADOLF HITLER!

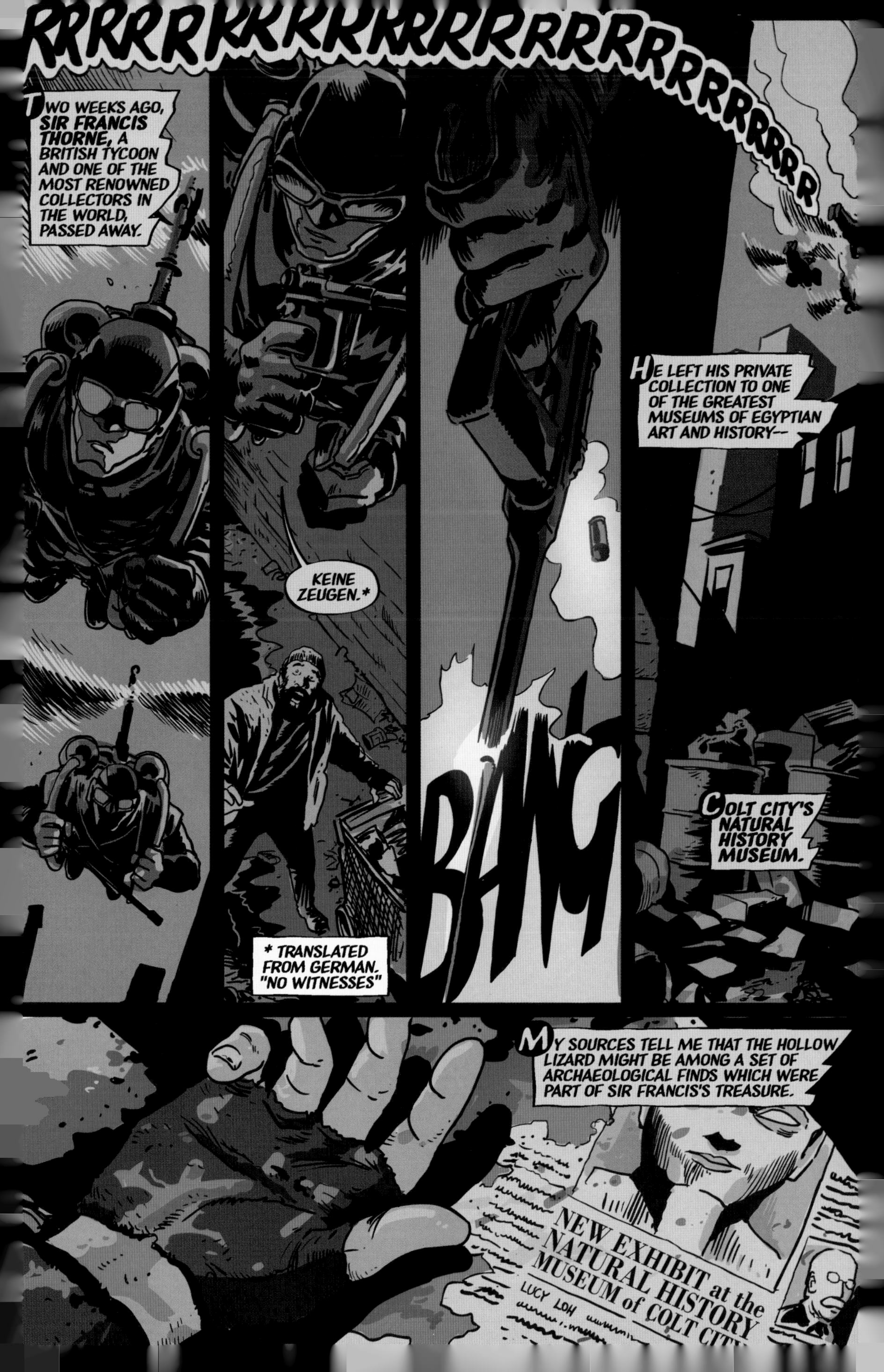
RRRRRKKKKRRRRRRRRRRRRRRRRR
TWO WEEKS AGO, SIR FRANCIS THORNE, A BRITISH TYCOON AND ONE OF THE MOST RENOWNED COLLECTORS IN THE WORLD, PASSED AWAY.
KEINE ZEUGEN.*
* TRANSLATED FROM GERMAN. "NO WITNESSES"
BANG
HE LEFT HIS PRIVATE COLLECTION TO ONE OF THE GREATEST MUSEUMS OF EGYPTIAN ART AND HISTORY--
COLT CITY'S NATURAL HISTORY MUSEUM.
MY SOURCES TELL ME THAT THE HOLLOW LIZARD MIGHT BE AMONG A SET OF ARCHAEOLOGICAL FINDS WHICH WERE PART OF SIR FRANCIS'S TREASURE.
NEW EXHIBIT at the NATURAL HISTORY MUSEUM of COLT CITY
LUCY LOH

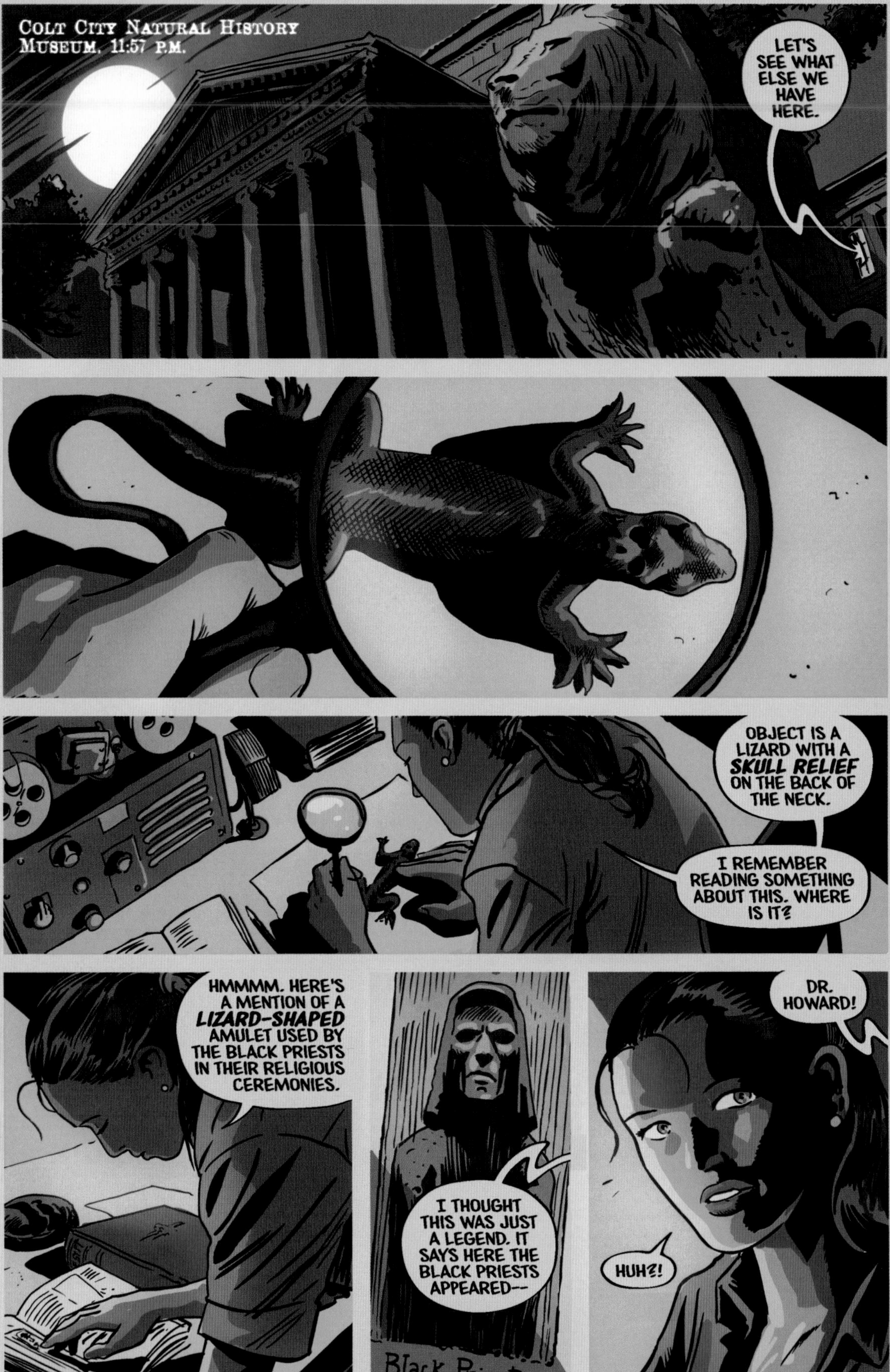
Colt City Natural History Museum, 11:57 p.m.
LET'S SEE WHAT ELSE WE HAVE HERE.
OBJECT IS A LIZARD WITH A SKULL RELIEF ON THE BACK OF THE NECK.
I REMEMBER READING SOMETHING ABOUT THIS. WHERE IS IT?
HMMMM. HERE'S A MENTION OF A LIZARD-SHAPED AMULET USED BY THE BLACK PRIESTS IN THEIR RELIGIOUS CEREMONIES.
I THOUGHT THIS WAS JUST A LEGEND. IT SAYS HERE THE BLACK PRIESTS APPEARED--
Black Priest
DR. HOWARD!
HUH?!

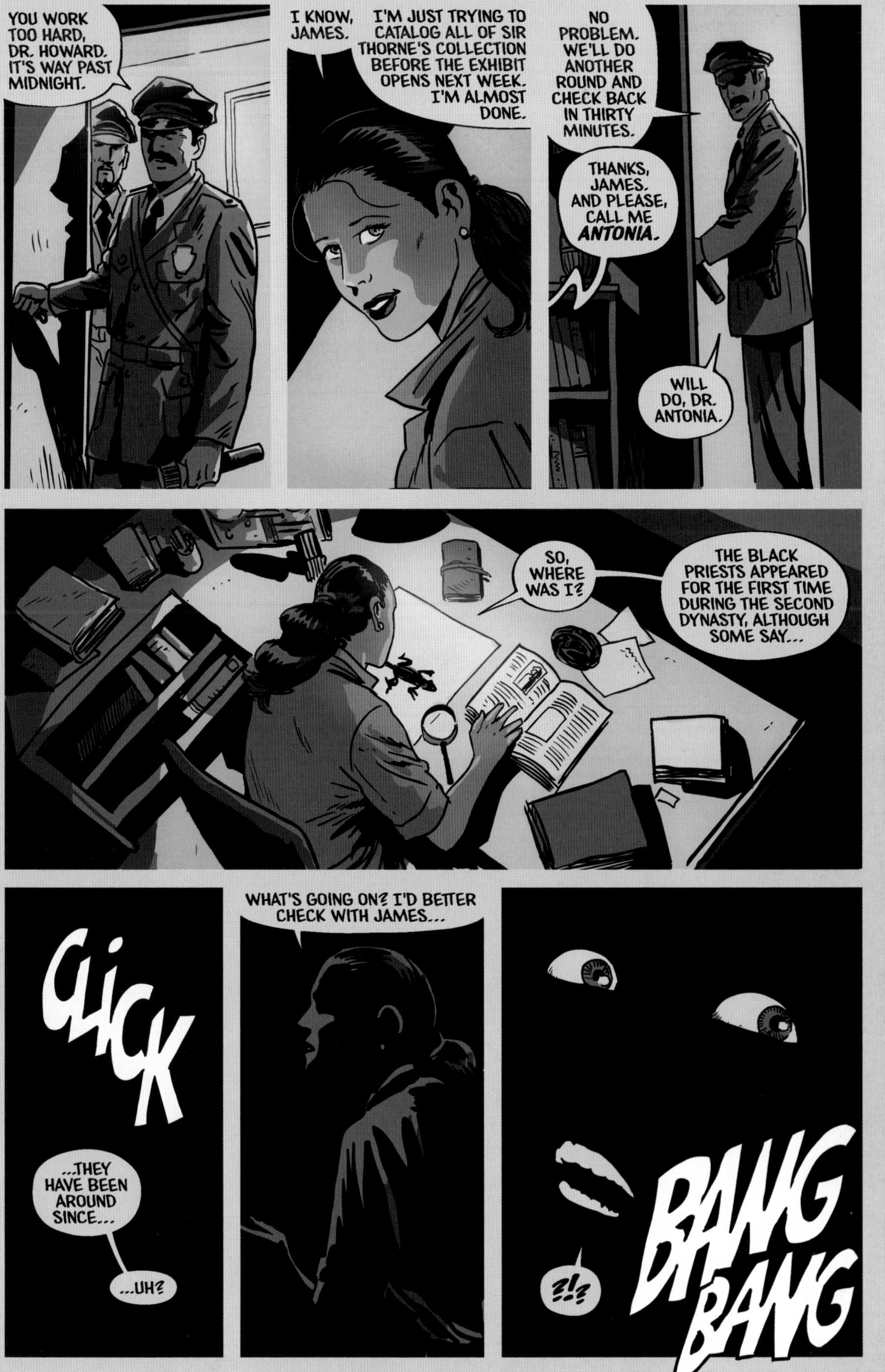
YOU WORK TOO HARD, DR. HOWARD. IT'S WAY PAST MIDNIGHT.
I KNOW, JAMES.
I'M JUST TRYING TO CATALOG ALL OF SIR THORNE'S COLLECTION BEFORE THE EXHIBIT OPENS NEXT WEEK. I'M ALMOST DONE.
NO PROBLEM. WE'LL DO ANOTHER ROUND AND CHECK BACK IN THIRTY MINUTES.
THANKS, JAMES. AND PLEASE, CALL ME *ANTONIA.*
WILL DO, DR. ANTONIA.
SO, WHERE WAS I?
THE BLACK PRIESTS APPEARED FOR THE FIRST TIME DURING THE SECOND DYNASTY, ALTHOUGH SOME SAY...
CLICK
...THEY HAVE BEEN AROUND SINCE...
...UH?
WHAT'S GOING ON? I'D BETTER CHECK WITH JAMES...
?!?
BANG
BANG

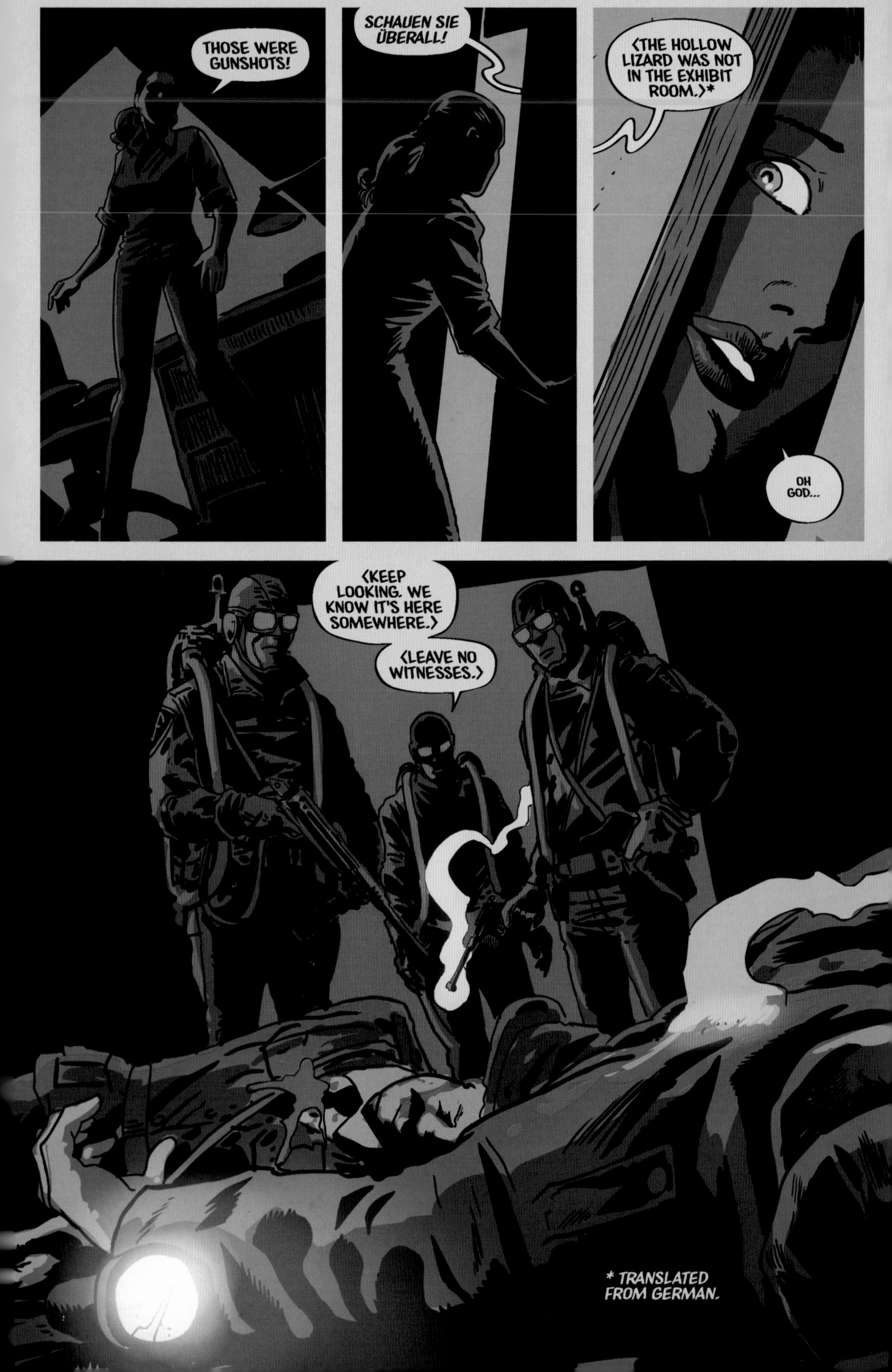
THOSE WERE GUNSHOTS!
SCHAUEN SIE ÜBERALL!
<THE HOLLOW LIZARD WAS NOT IN THE EXHIBIT ROOM.>*
OH GOD...
<KEEP LOOKING. WE KNOW IT'S HERE SOMEWHERE.>
<LEAVE NO WITNESSES.>
* TRANSLATED FROM GERMAN.

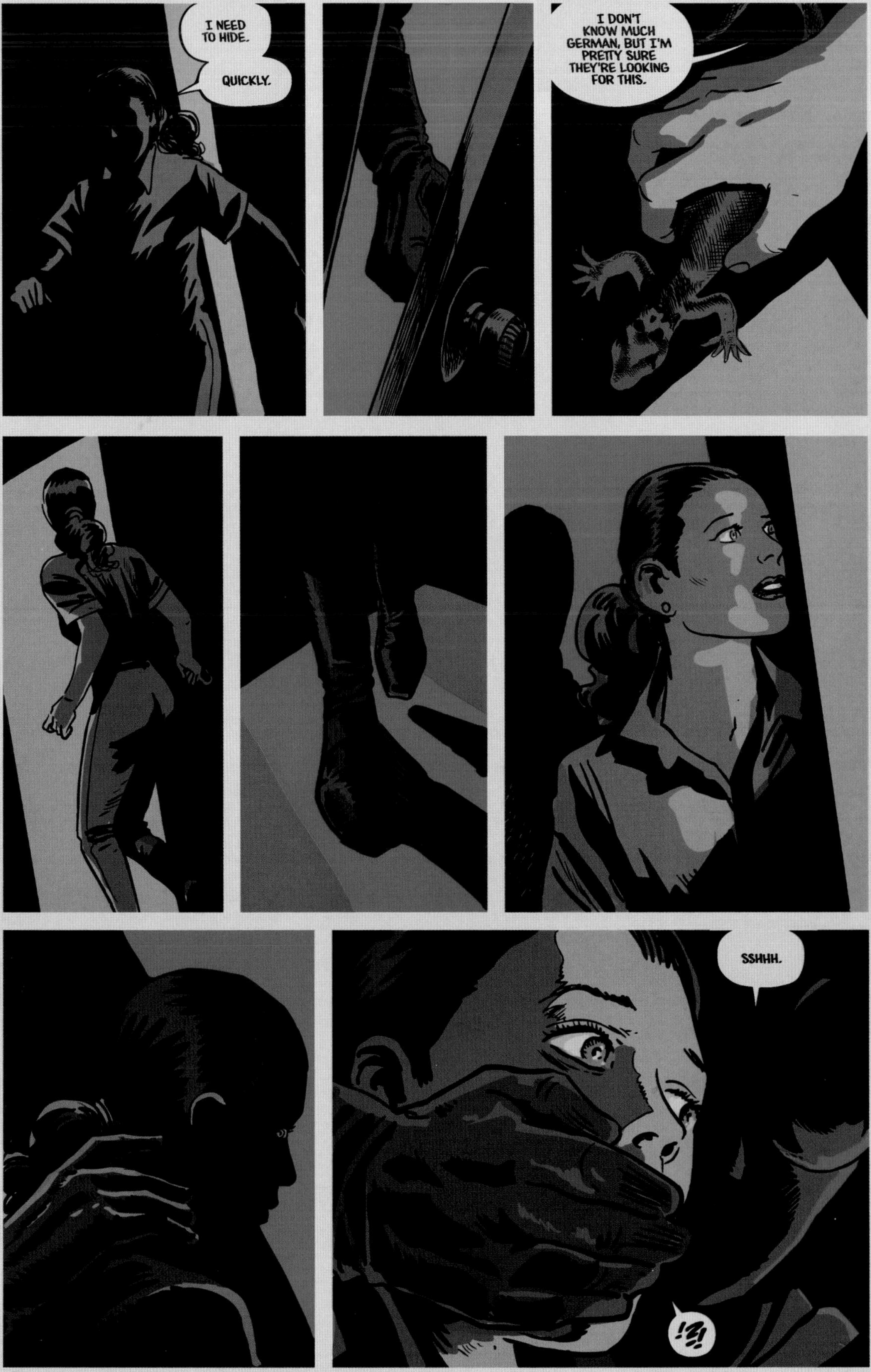
I NEED TO HIDE.
QUICKLY.
I DON'T KNOW MUCH GERMAN, BUT I'M PRETTY SURE THEY'RE LOOKING FOR THIS.
SSHHH.
!?!

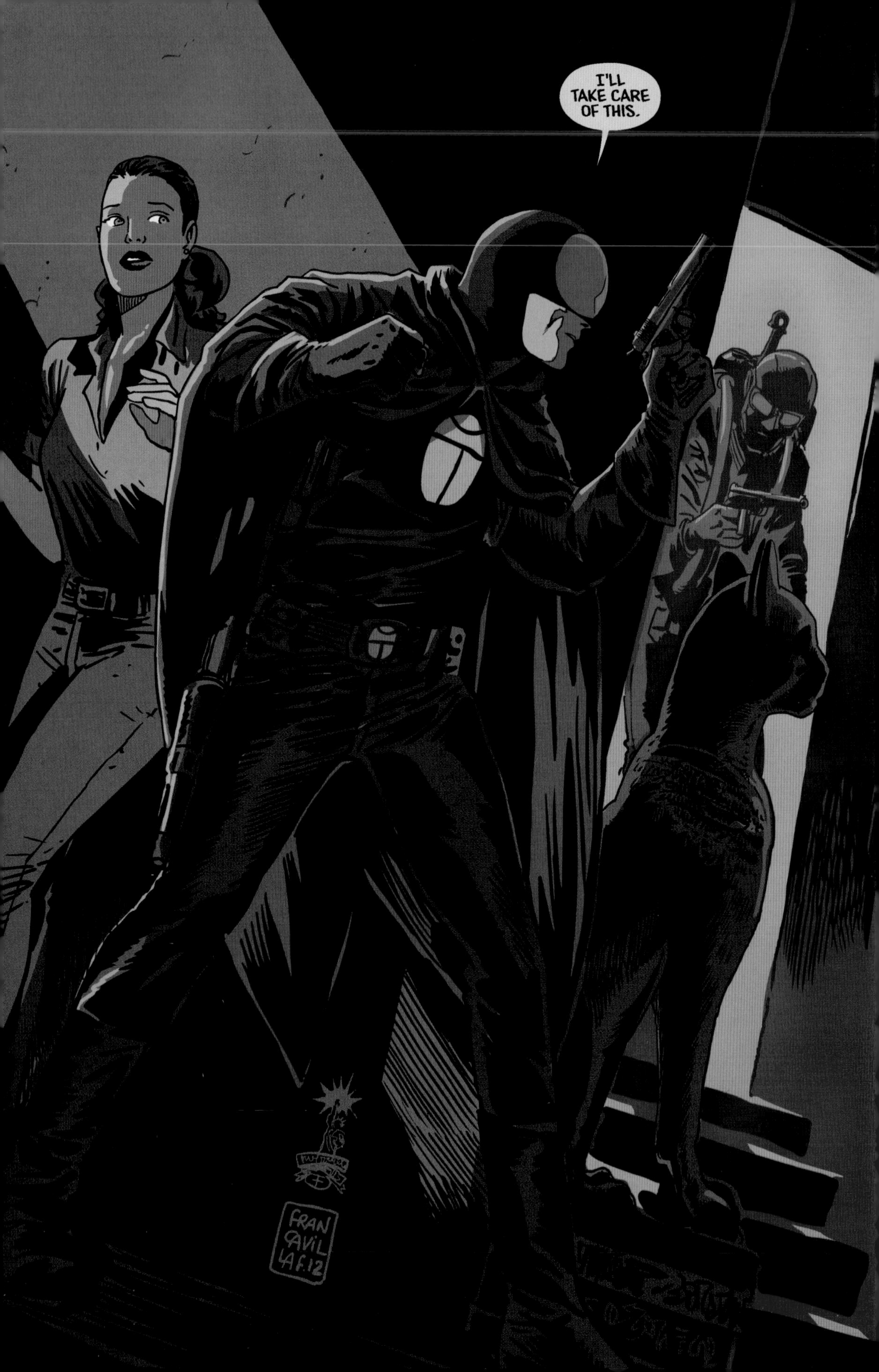
I'LL TAKE CARE OF THIS.

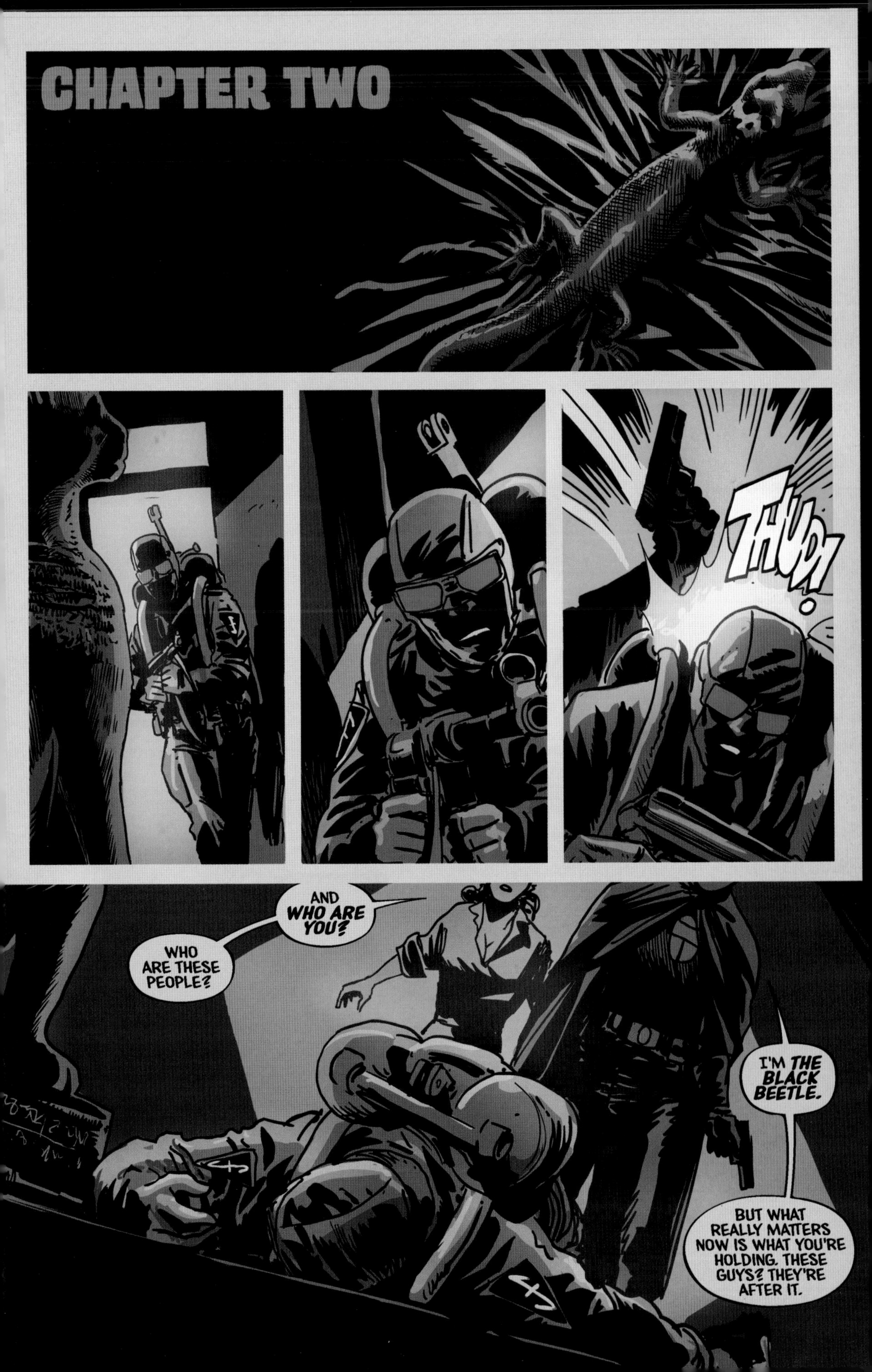
CHAPTER TWO
THUD!
WHO ARE THESE PEOPLE?
AND WHO ARE YOU?
I'M THE BLACK BEETLE.
BUT WHAT REALLY MATTERS NOW IS WHAT YOU'RE HOLDING. THESE GUYS? THEY'RE AFTER IT.

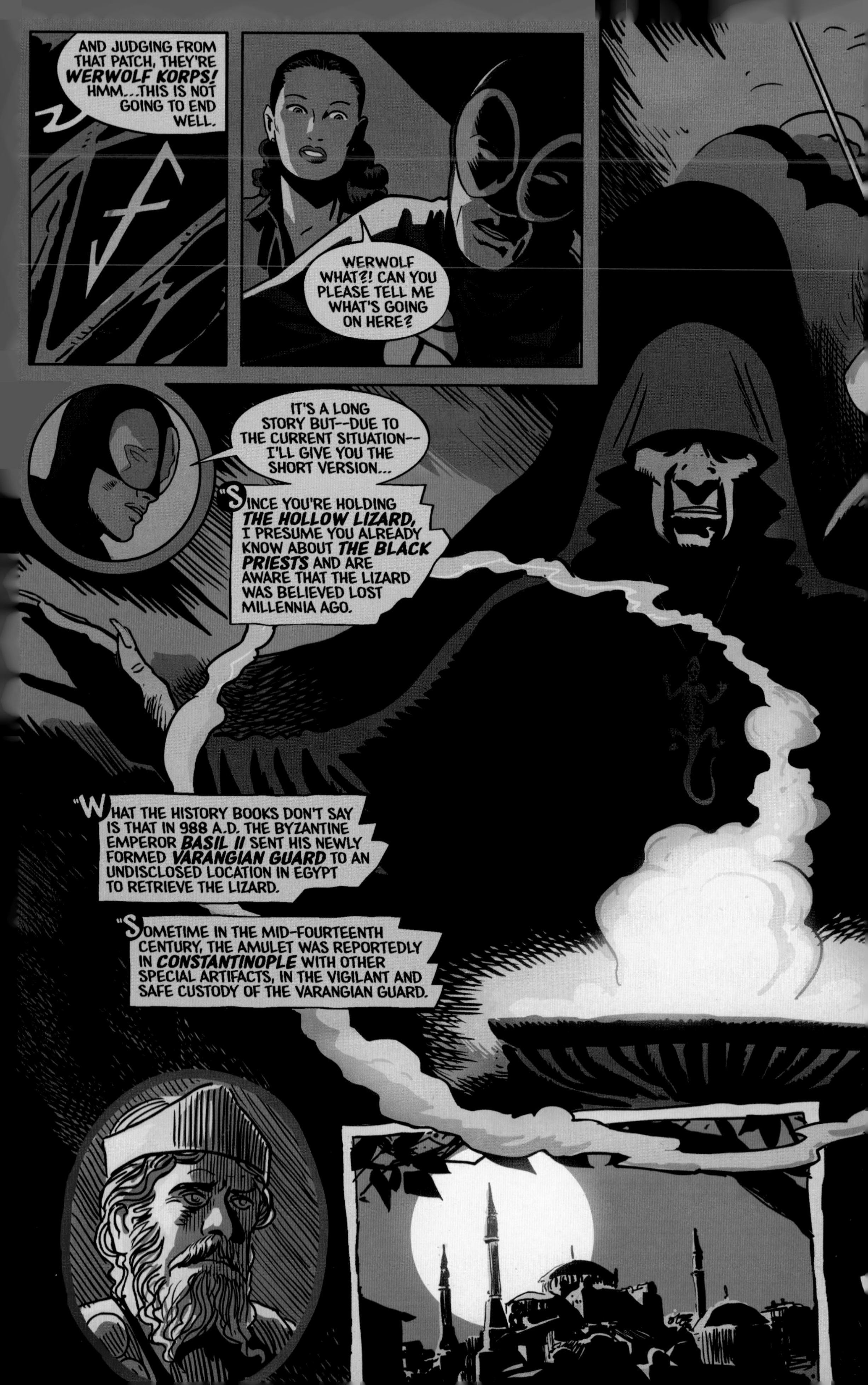

AND JUDGING FROM THAT PATCH, THEY'RE WERWOLF KORPS! HMM... THIS IS NOT GOING TO END WELL.
WERWOLF WHAT?! CAN YOU PLEASE TELL ME WHAT'S GOING ON HERE?
IT'S A LONG STORY BUT--DUE TO THE CURRENT SITUATION--I'LL GIVE YOU THE SHORT VERSION...
"SINCE YOU'RE HOLDING THE HOLLOW LIZARD, I PRESUME YOU ALREADY KNOW ABOUT THE BLACK PRIESTS AND ARE AWARE THAT THE LIZARD WAS BELIEVED LOST MILLENNIA AGO.
"WHAT THE HISTORY BOOKS DON'T SAY IS THAT IN 988 A.D. THE BYZANTINE EMPEROR BASIL II SENT HIS NEWLY FORMED VARANGIAN GUARD TO AN UNDISCLOSED LOCATION IN EGYPT TO RETRIEVE THE LIZARD.
"SOMETIME IN THE MID-FOURTEENTH CENTURY, THE AMULET WAS REPORTEDLY IN CONSTANTINOPLE WITH OTHER SPECIAL ARTIFACTS, IN THE VIGILANT AND SAFE CUSTODY OF THE VARANGIAN GUARD.

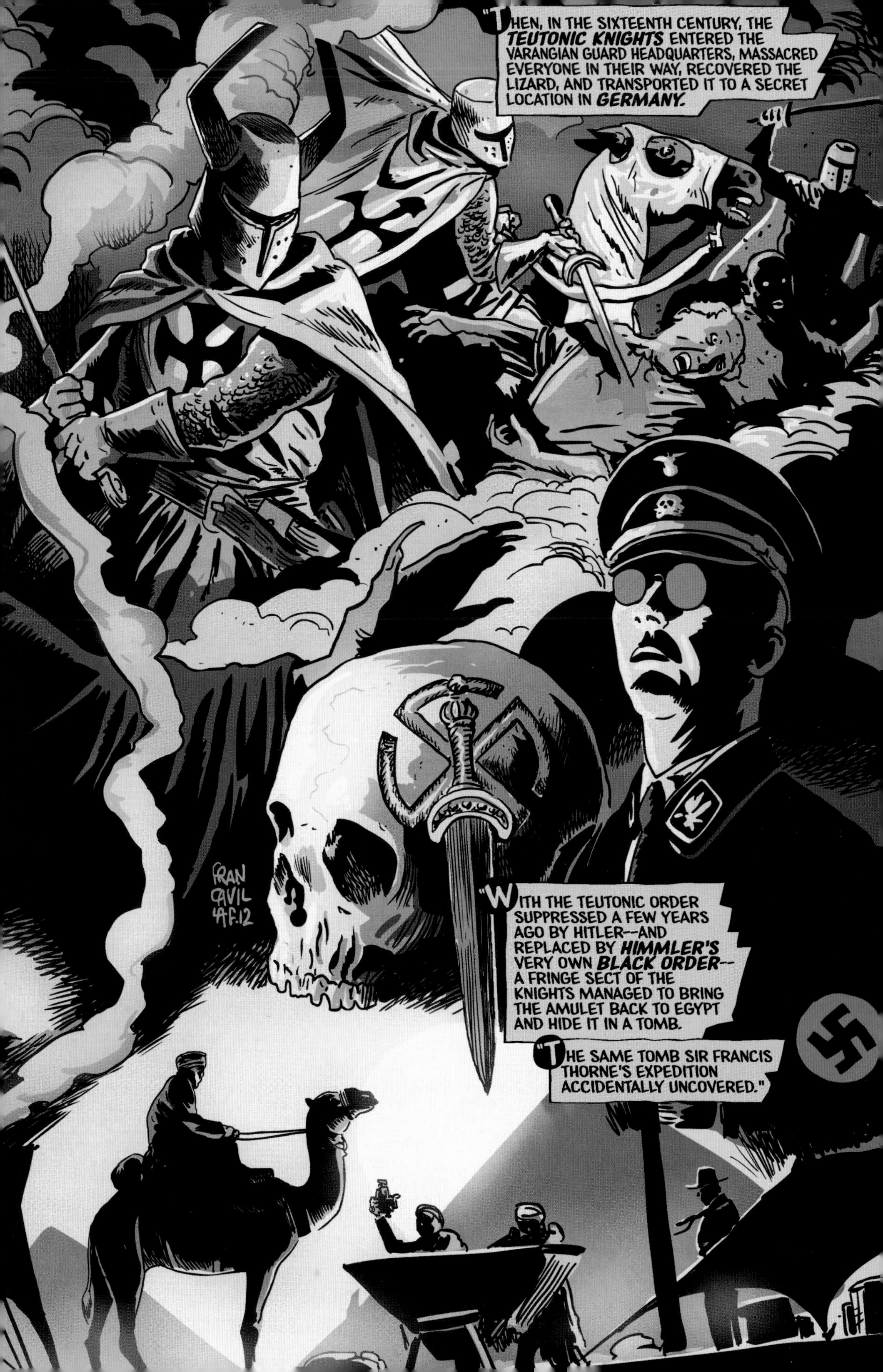
"THEN, IN THE SIXTEENTH CENTURY, THE TEUTONIC KNIGHTS ENTERED THE VARANGIAN GUARD HEADQUARTERS, MASSACRED EVERYONE IN THEIR WAY, RECOVERED THE LIZARD, AND TRANSPORTED IT TO A SECRET LOCATION IN GERMANY.
FRAN GAVIL 4F.12
"WITH THE TEUTONIC ORDER SUPPRESSED A FEW YEARS AGO BY HITLER--AND REPLACED BY HIMMLER'S VERY OWN BLACK ORDER--A FRINGE SECT OF THE KNIGHTS MANAGED TO BRING THE AMULET BACK TO EGYPT AND HIDE IT IN A TOMB.
"THE SAME TOMB SIR FRANCIS THORNE'S EXPEDITION ACCIDENTALLY UNCOVERED."

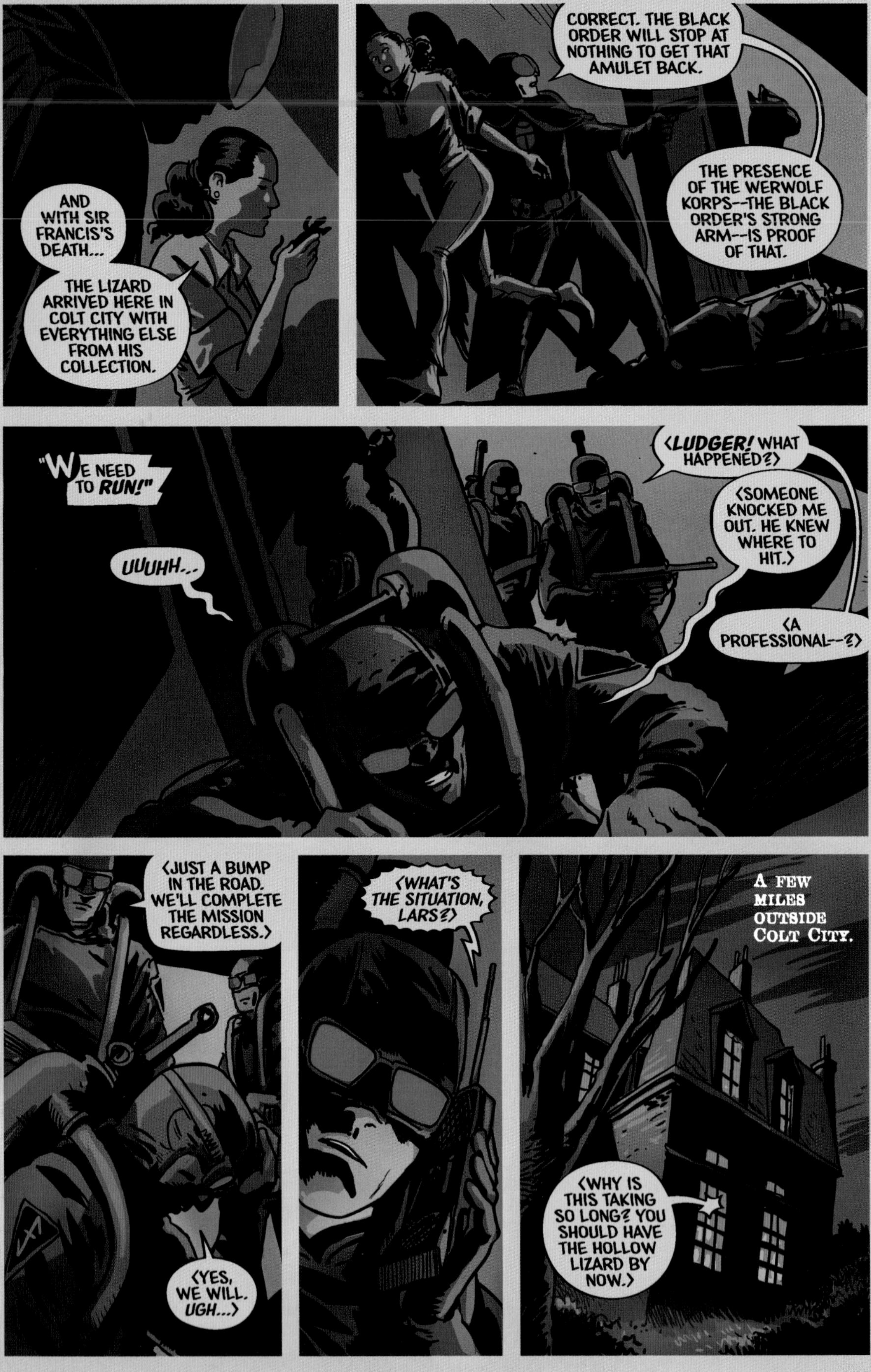
AND WITH SIR FRANCIS'S DEATH...
THE LIZARD ARRIVED HERE IN COLT CITY WITH EVERYTHING ELSE FROM HIS COLLECTION.
CORRECT. THE BLACK ORDER WILL STOP AT NOTHING TO GET THAT AMULET BACK.
THE PRESENCE OF THE WERWOLF KORPS--THE BLACK ORDER'S STRONG ARM--IS PROOF OF THAT.
"WE NEED TO RUN!"
UUUHH...
<LUDGER! WHAT HAPPENED?>
<SOMEONE KNOCKED ME OUT. HE KNEW WHERE TO HIT.>
<A PROFESSIONAL--?>
<JUST A BUMP IN THE ROAD. WE'LL COMPLETE THE MISSION REGARDLESS.>
<YES, WE WILL. UGH...>
<WHAT'S THE SITUATION, LARS?>
A FEW MILES OUTSIDE COLT CITY.
<WHY IS THIS TAKING SO LONG? YOU SHOULD HAVE THE HOLLOW LIZARD BY NOW.>

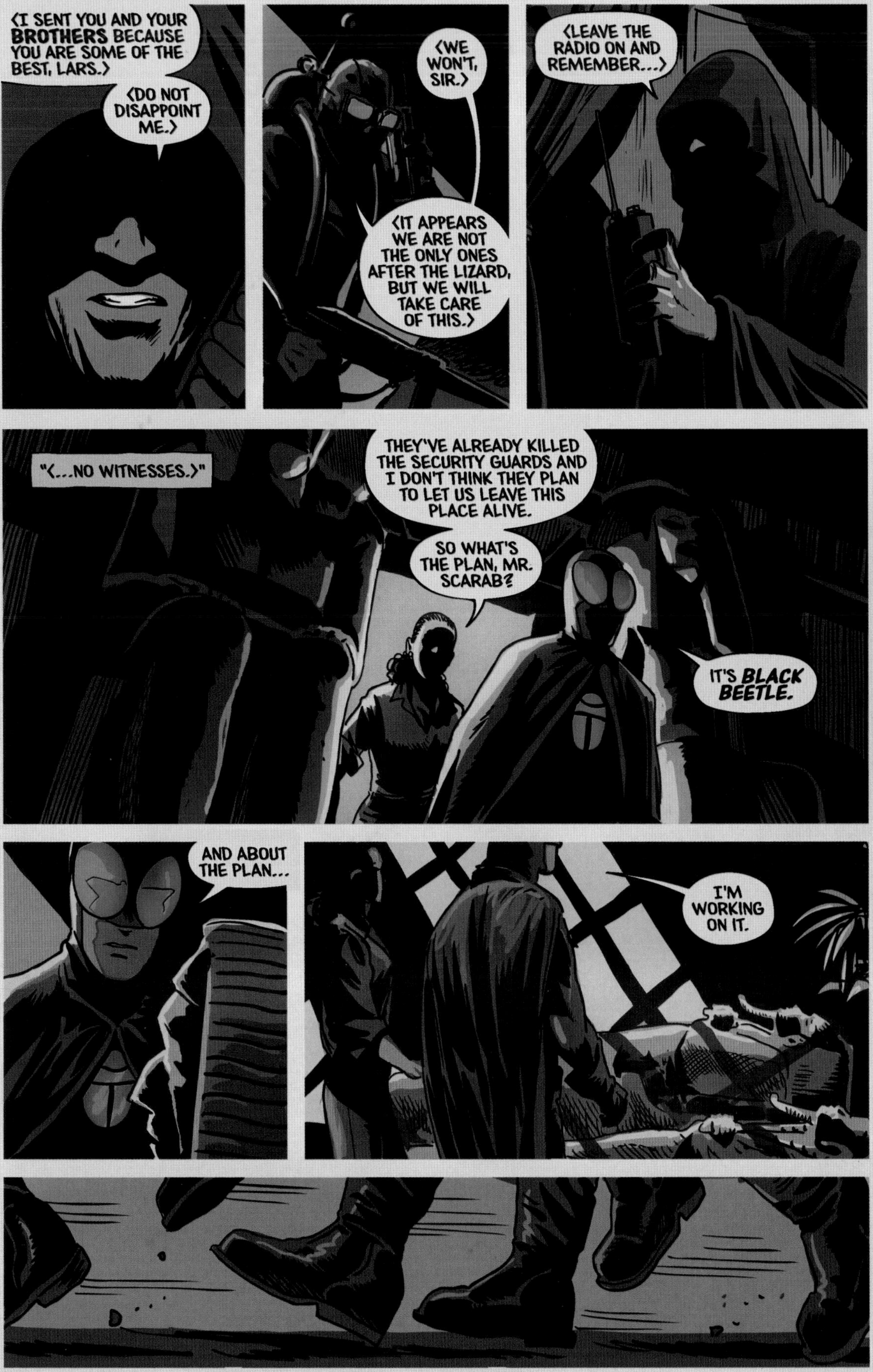

<I SENT YOU AND YOUR **BROTHERS** BECAUSE YOU ARE SOME OF THE BEST, LARS.>
<DO NOT DISAPPOINT ME.>
<WE WON'T, SIR.>
<IT APPEARS WE ARE NOT THE ONLY ONES AFTER THE LIZARD, BUT WE WILL TAKE CARE OF THIS.>
<LEAVE THE RADIO ON AND REMEMBER...>
"<...NO WITNESSES.>"
THEY'VE ALREADY KILLED THE SECURITY GUARDS AND I DON'T THINK THEY PLAN TO LET US LEAVE THIS PLACE ALIVE.
SO WHAT'S THE PLAN, MR. SCARAB?
IT'S ***BLACK BEETLE.***
AND ABOUT THE PLAN...
I'M WORKING ON IT.

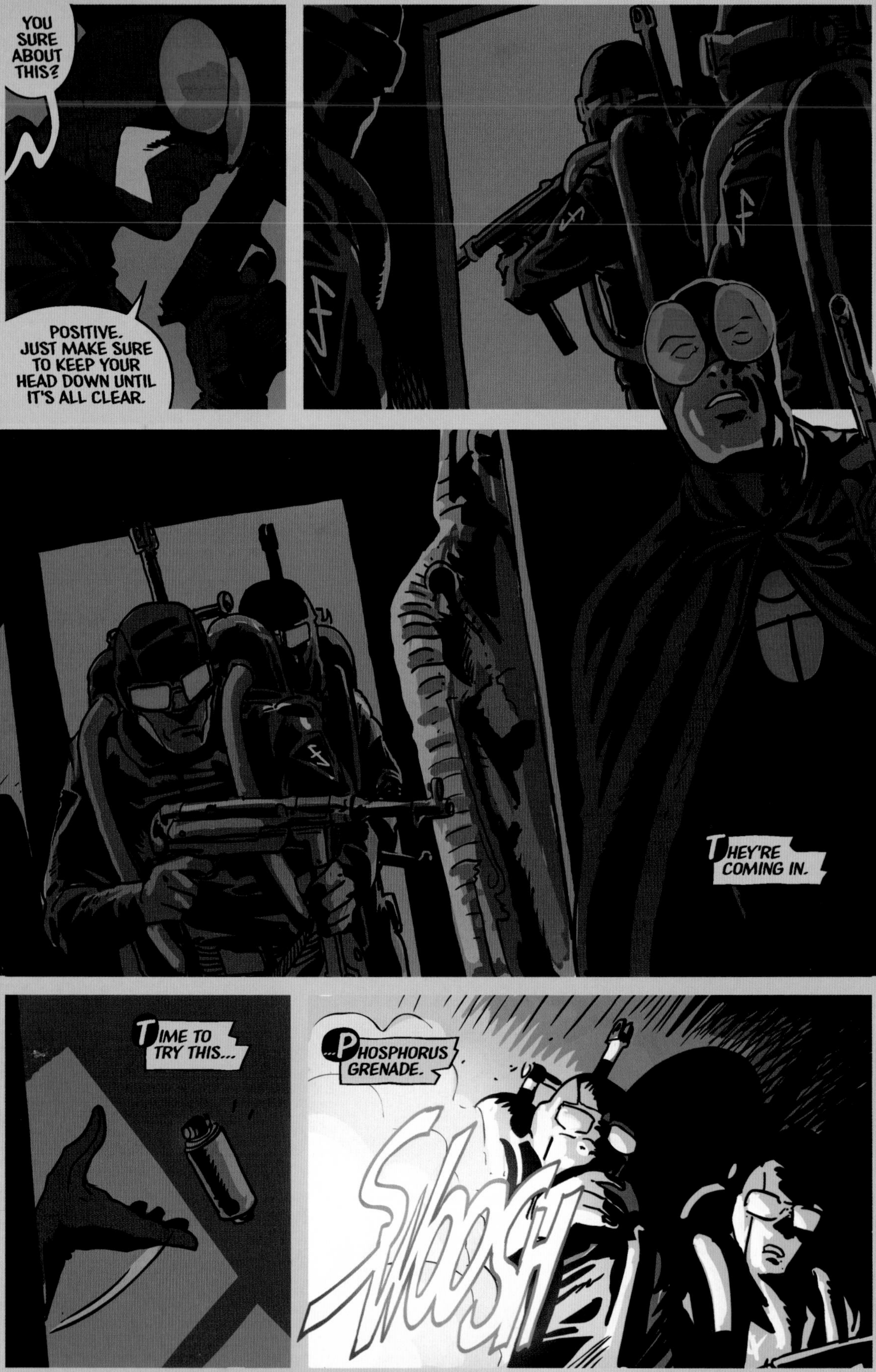
YOU SURE ABOUT THIS?
POSITIVE. JUST MAKE SURE TO KEEP YOUR HEAD DOWN UNTIL IT'S ALL CLEAR.
THEY'RE COMING IN.
TIME TO TRY THIS...
...PHOSPHORUS GRENADE.
SHOOSH

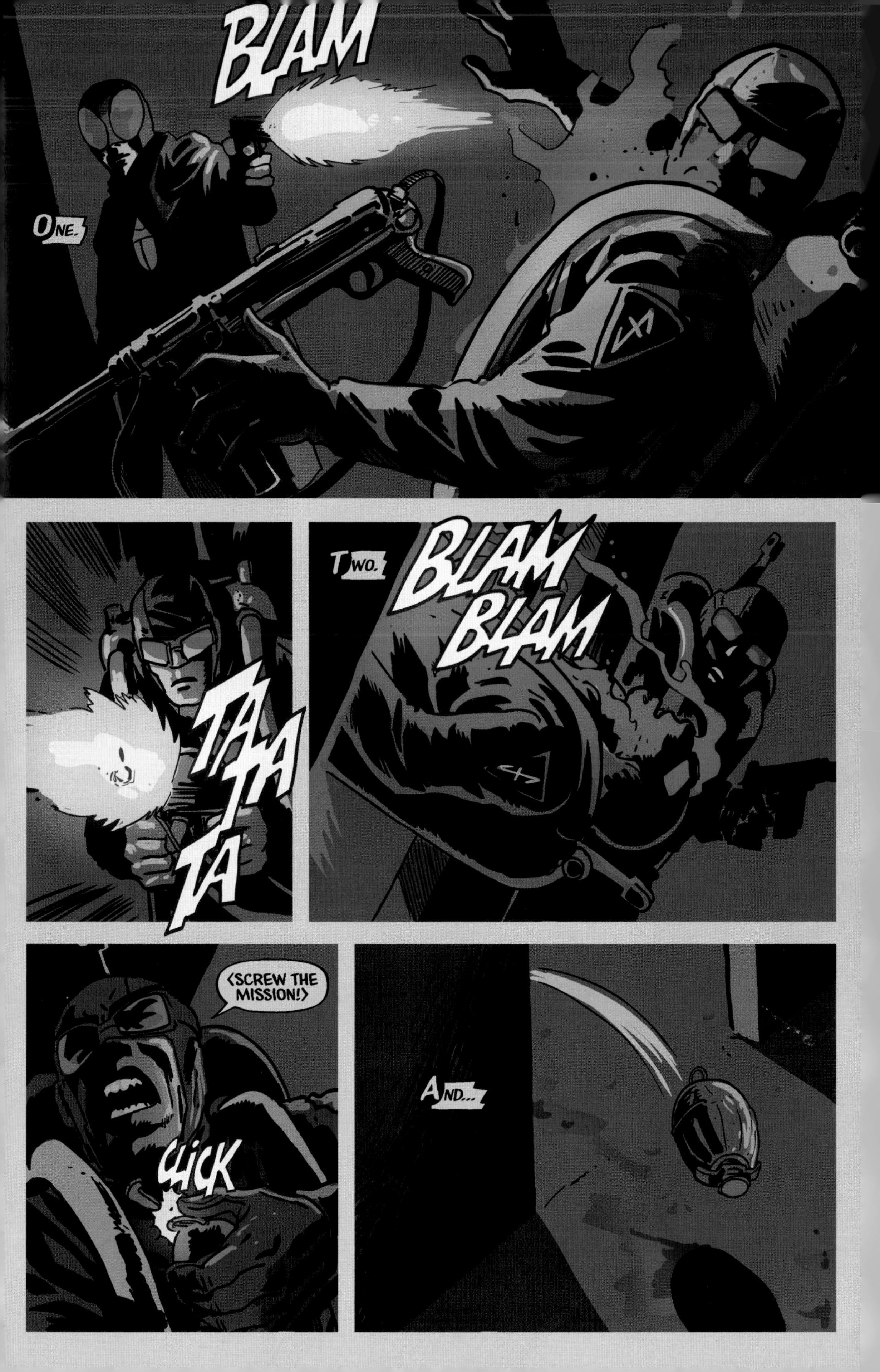
BLAM
ONE.
TA TA TA TA
TWO.
BLAM BLAM
‹SCREW THE MISSION!›
CLICK
AND...

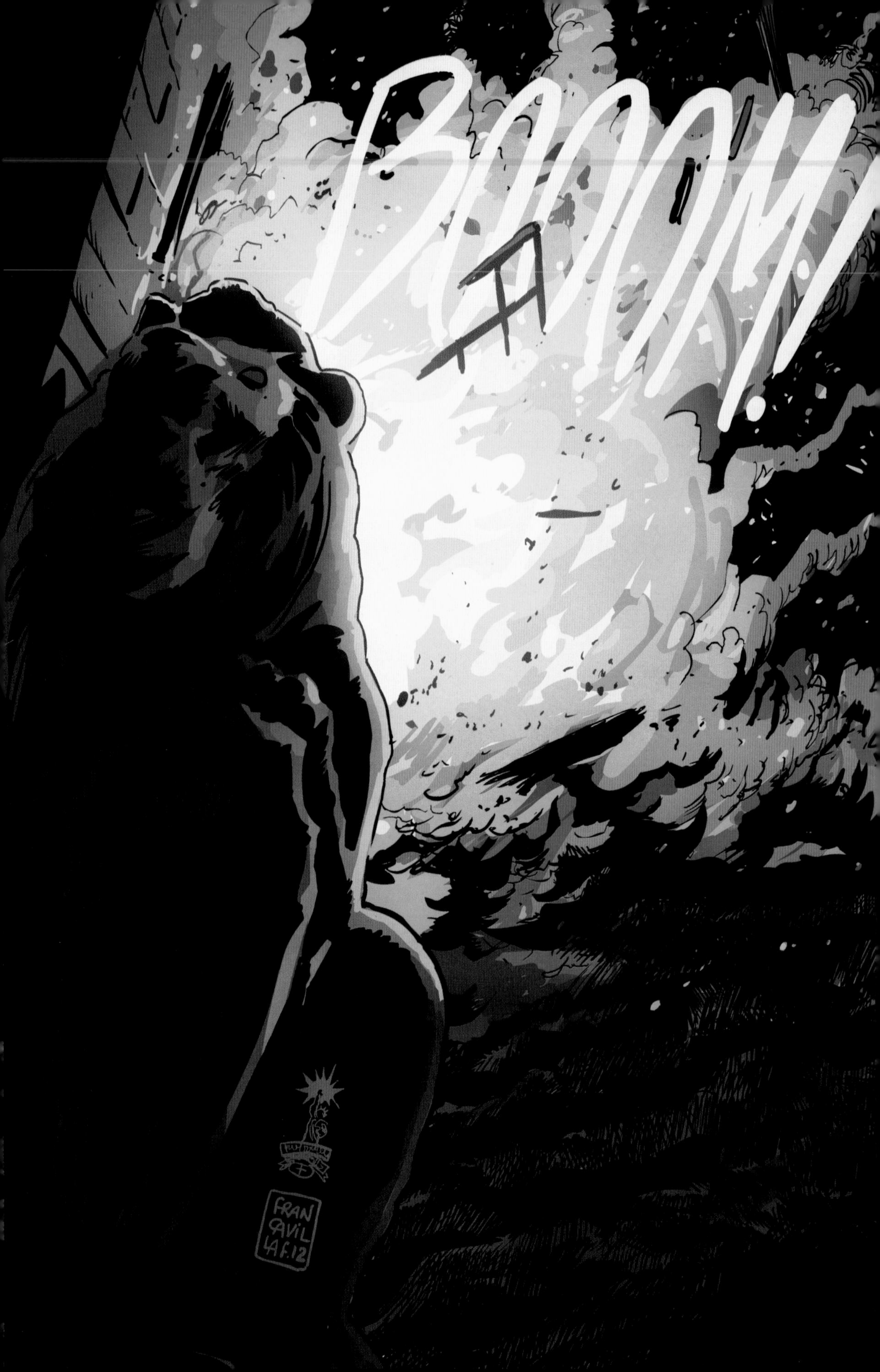
BOOOM!!
FRAN
CAVIL
LA F.12

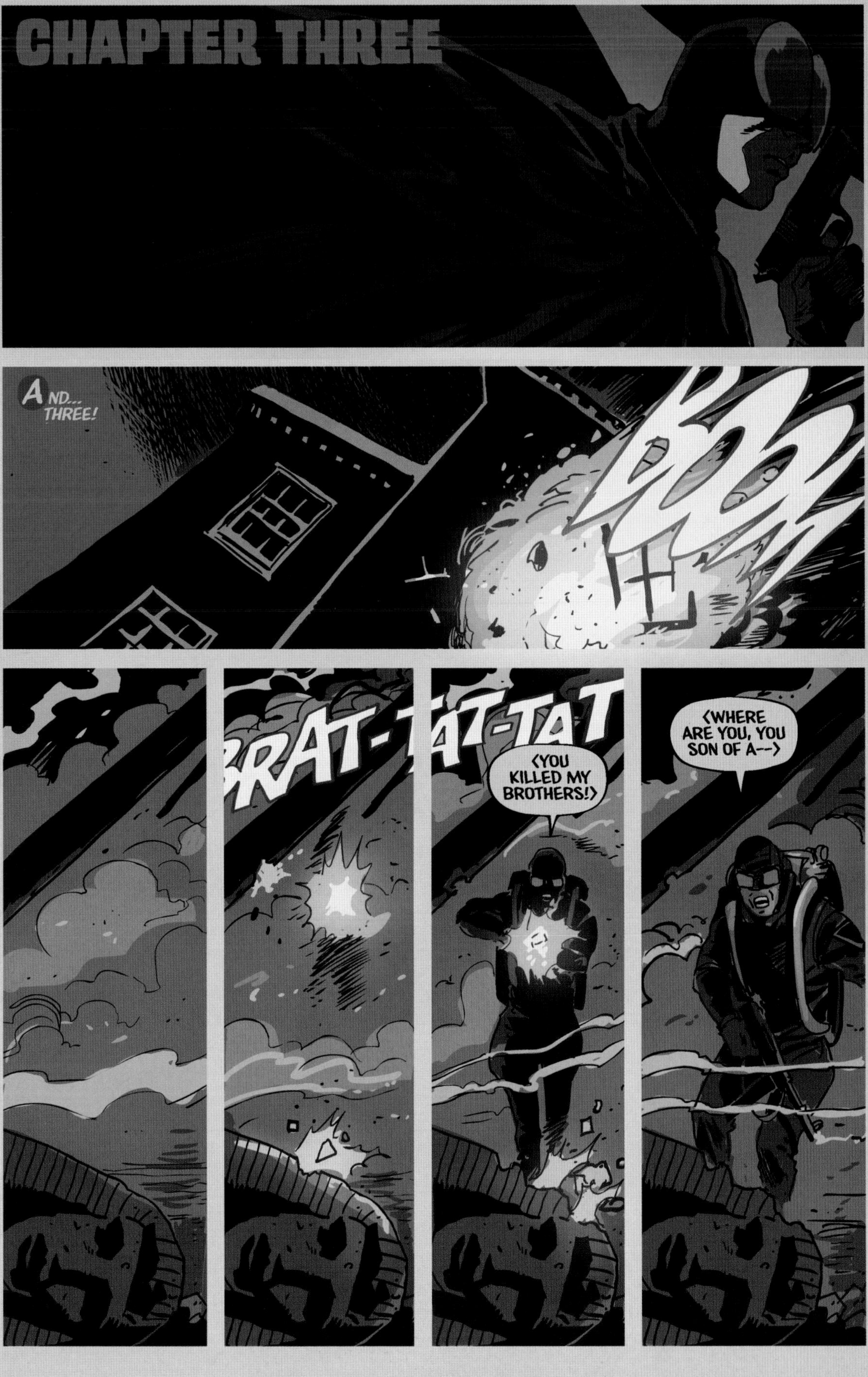
CHAPTER THREE
AND... THREE!
BRAT-TAT-TAT
<YOU KILLED MY BROTHERS!>
<WHERE ARE YOU, YOU SON OF A-->

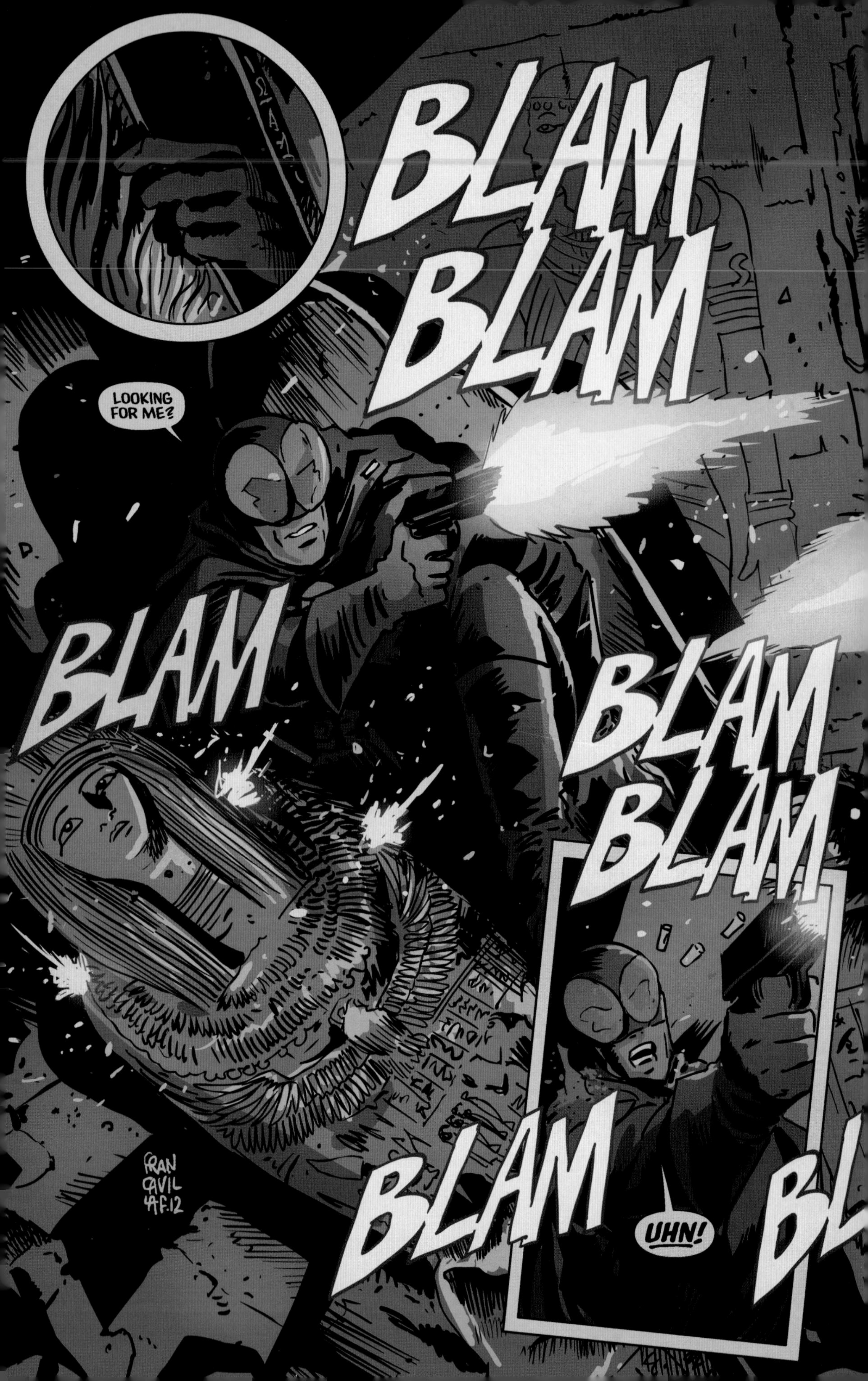
BLAM
BLAM
LOOKING FOR ME?
BLAM
BLAM
BLAM
FRAN CAVIL
BLAM
UHN!
BL

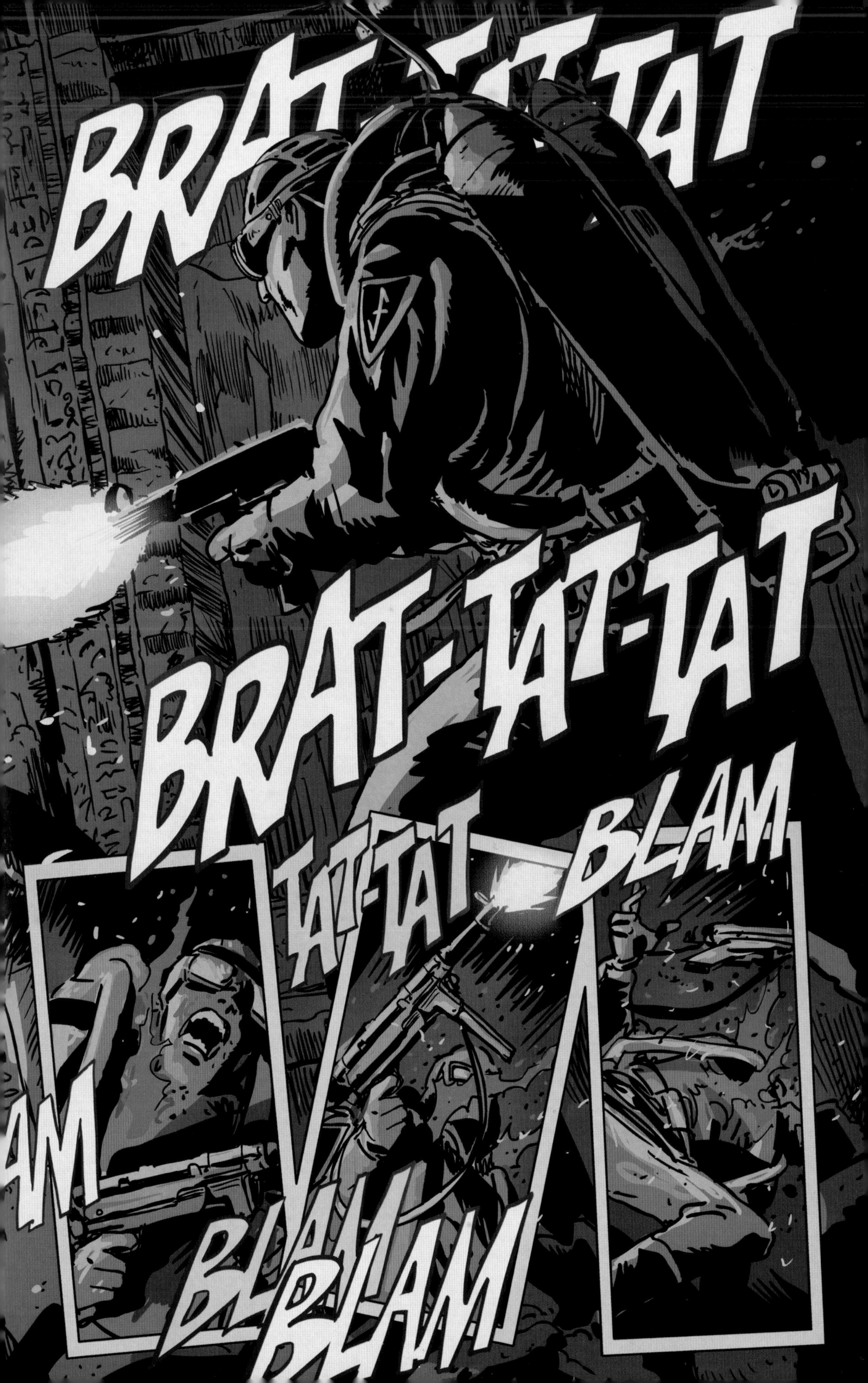
BRAT TAT
BRAT-TAT-TAT
TAT-TAT
BLAM
AM
BLAM
BLAM

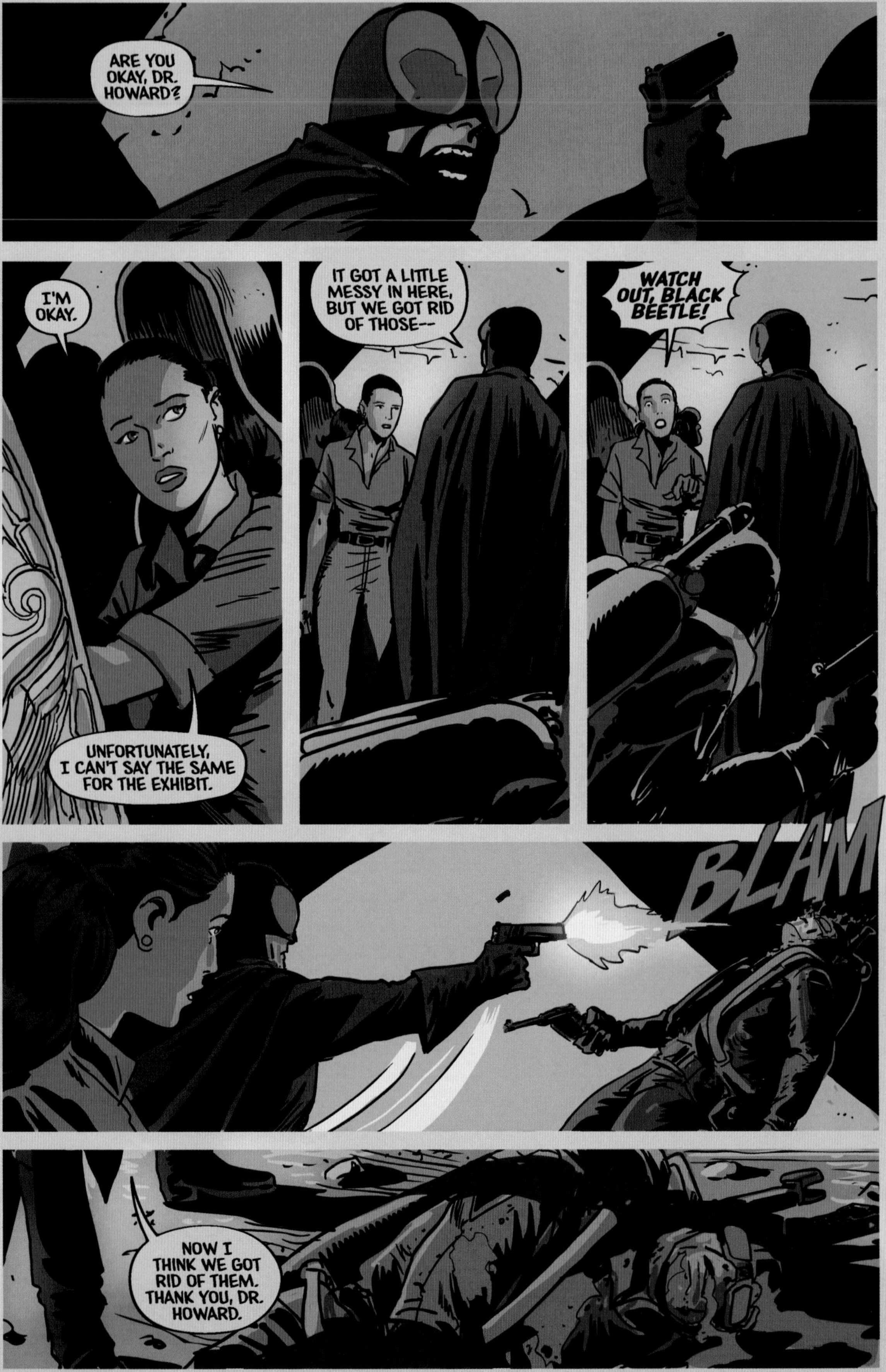
ARE YOU OKAY, DR. HOWARD?
I'M OKAY.
UNFORTUNATELY, I CAN'T SAY THE SAME FOR THE EXHIBIT.
IT GOT A LITTLE MESSY IN HERE, BUT WE GOT RID OF THOSE--
WATCH OUT, BLACK BEETLE!
BLAM
NOW I THINK WE GOT RID OF THEM. THANK YOU, DR. HOWARD.

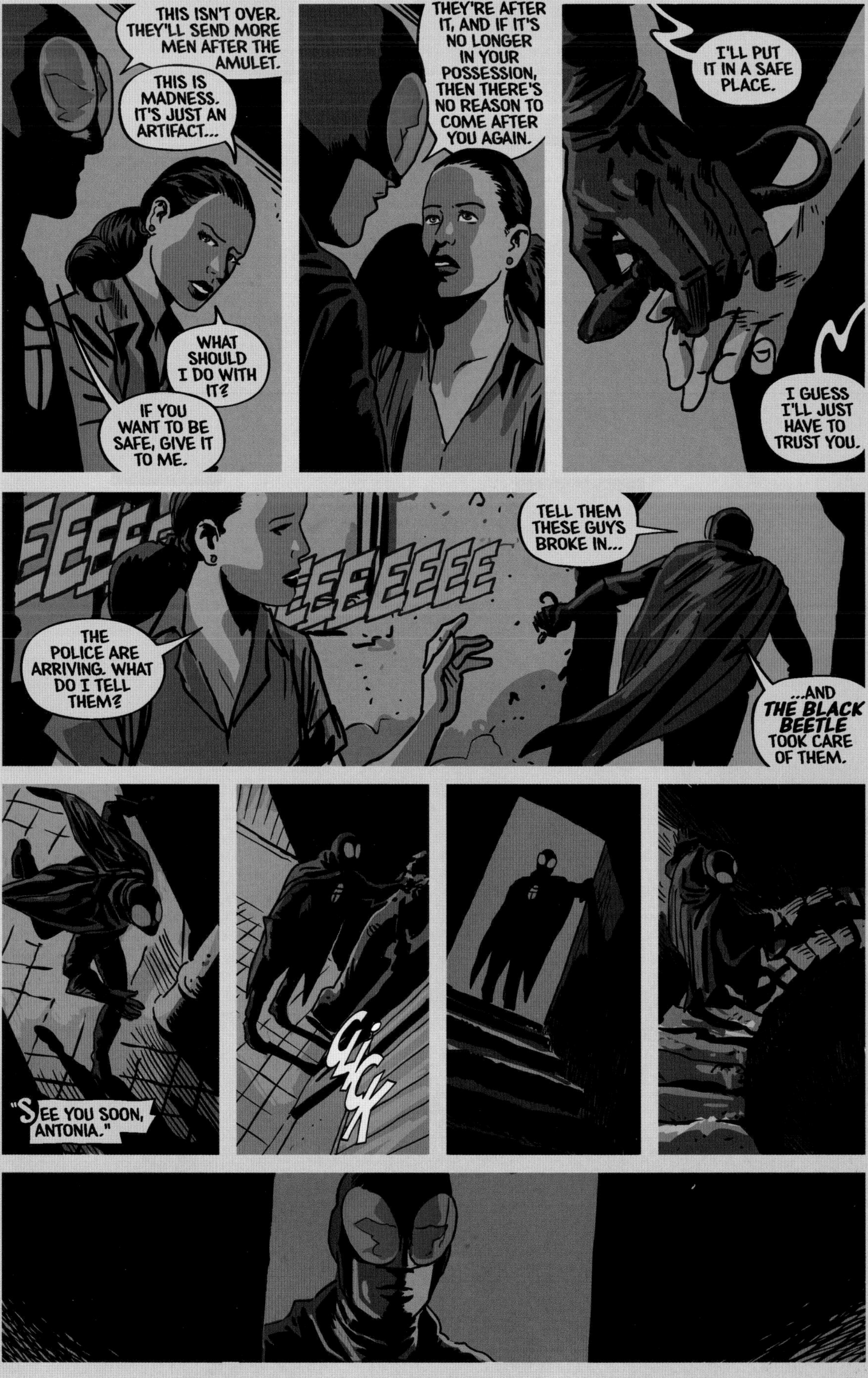
THIS ISN'T OVER. THEY'LL SEND MORE MEN AFTER THE AMULET.
THIS IS MADNESS. IT'S JUST AN ARTIFACT...
WHAT SHOULD I DO WITH IT?
IF YOU WANT TO BE SAFE, GIVE IT TO ME.
THEY'RE AFTER IT, AND IF IT'S NO LONGER IN YOUR POSSESSION, THEN THERE'S NO REASON TO COME AFTER YOU AGAIN.
I'LL PUT IT IN A SAFE PLACE.
I GUESS I'LL JUST HAVE TO TRUST YOU.
EEEEE
EEEEEEE
THE POLICE ARE ARRIVING. WHAT DO I TELL THEM?
TELL THEM THESE GUYS BROKE IN...
...AND *THE BLACK BEETLE* TOOK CARE OF THEM.
"SEE YOU SOON, ANTONIA."
GICK

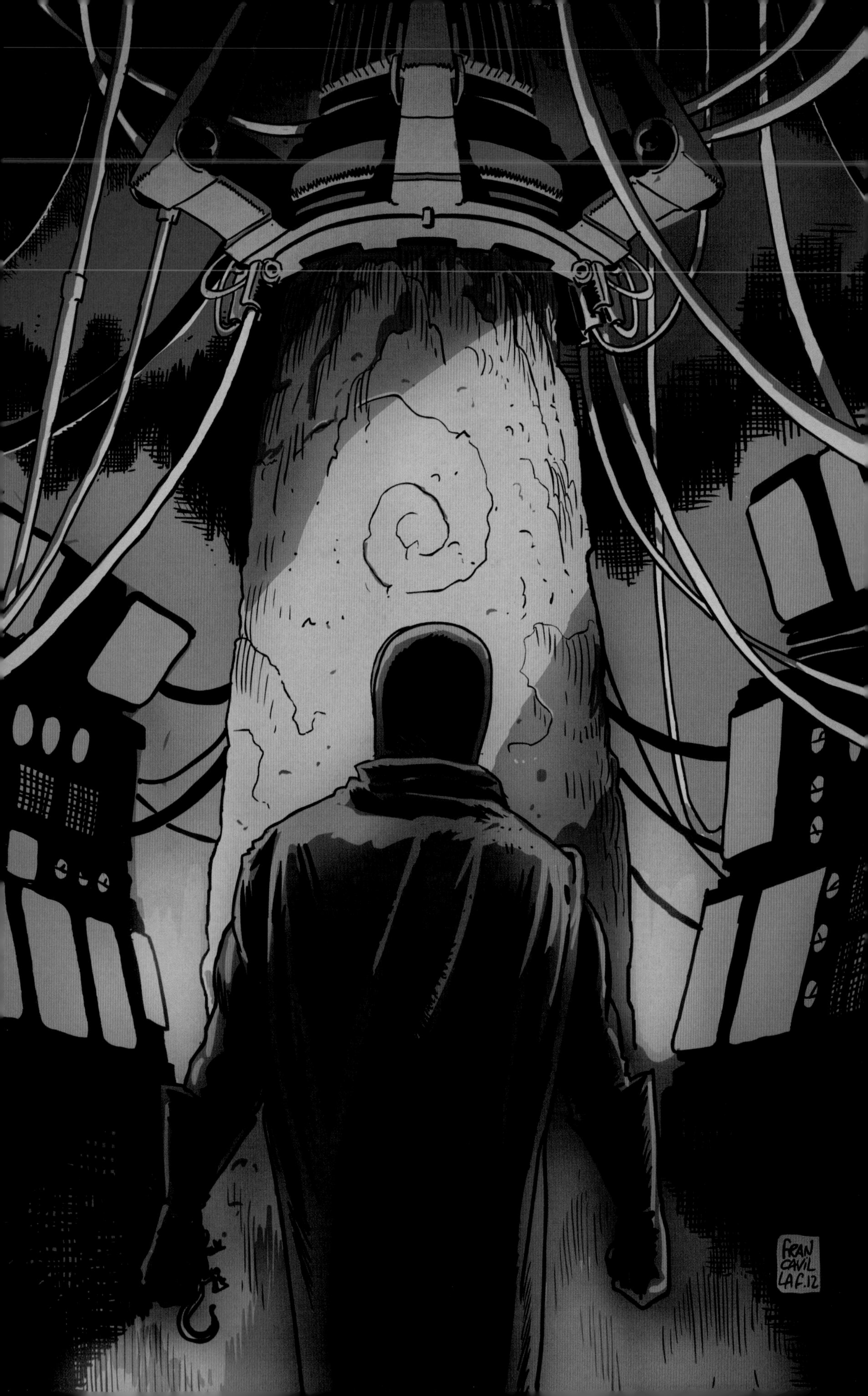
FRAN
CAVIL
LA F.12

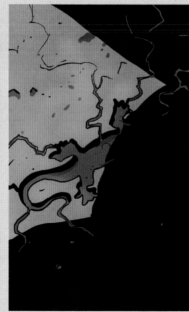

WWWWRRRRRRRRR

IT BEGINS.

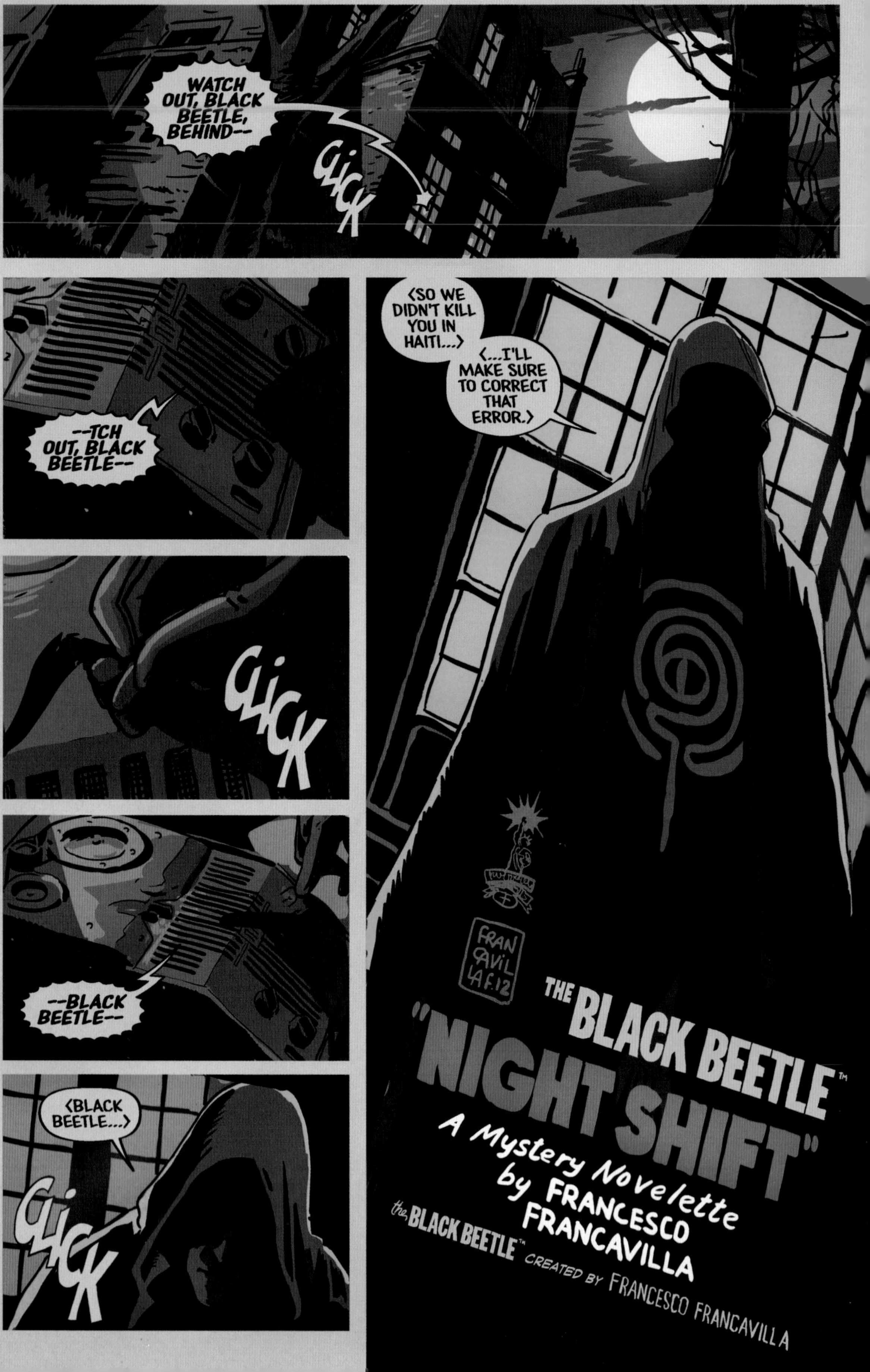
WATCH OUT, BLACK BEETLE, BEHIND--
CLICK
--TCH OUT, BLACK BEETLE--
CLICK
--BLACK BEETLE--
<BLACK BEETLE...>
CLICK
<SO WE DIDN'T KILL YOU IN HAITI...>
<...I'LL MAKE SURE TO CORRECT THAT ERROR.>
FRANCAVILLA F.12
THE BLACK BEETLE™
"NIGHT SHIFT"
A Mystery Novelette by FRANCESCO FRANCAVILLA
THE BLACK BEETLE™ CREATED BY FRANCESCO FRANCAVILLA

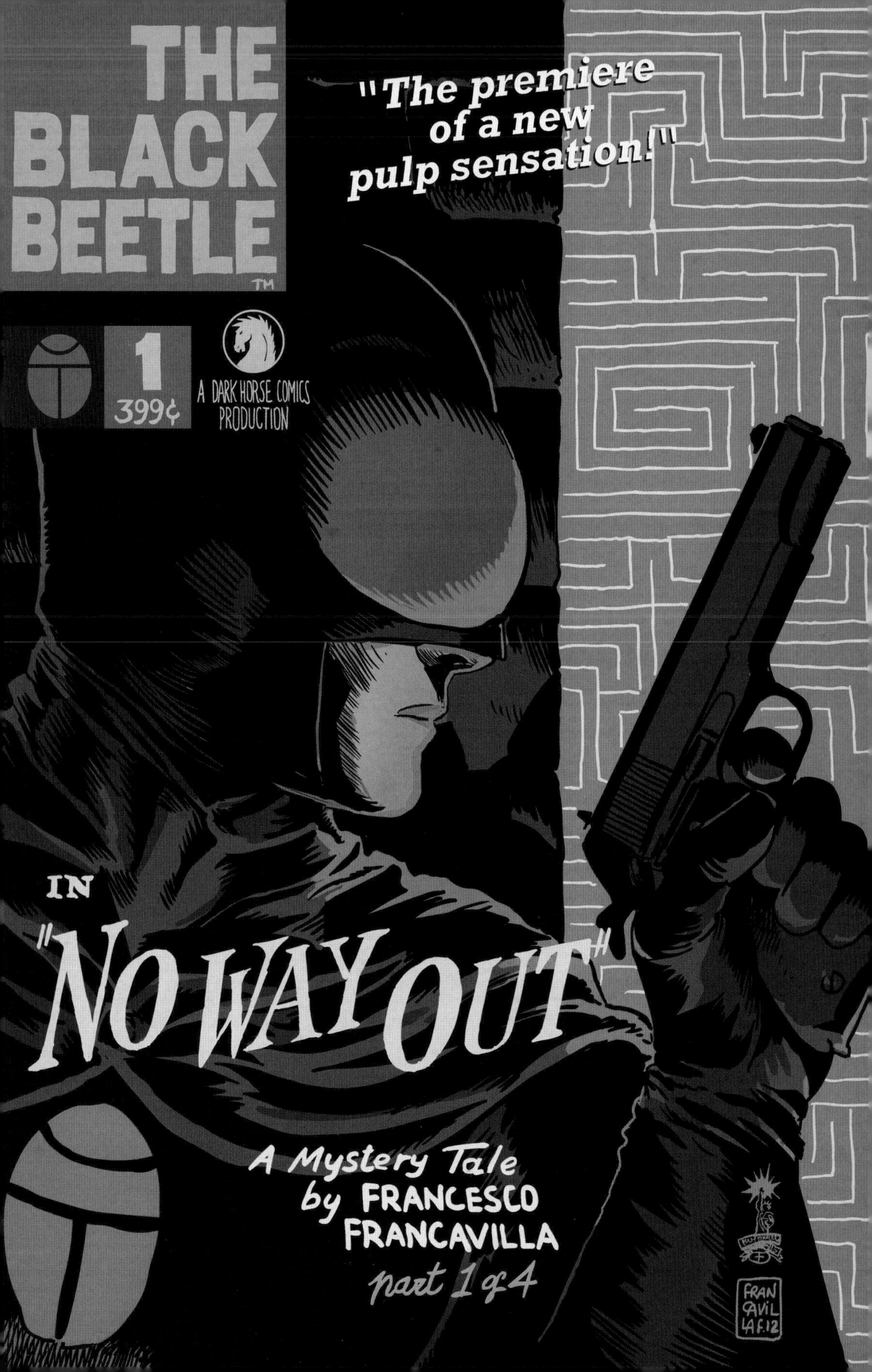
THE BLACK BEETLE™
"The premiere of a new pulp sensation!"
1
399¢
A DARK HORSE COMICS PRODUCTION
IN
"NO WAY OUT"
A Mystery Tale by FRANCESCO FRANCAVILLA
part 1 of 4
FRAN CAVIL LA F.12

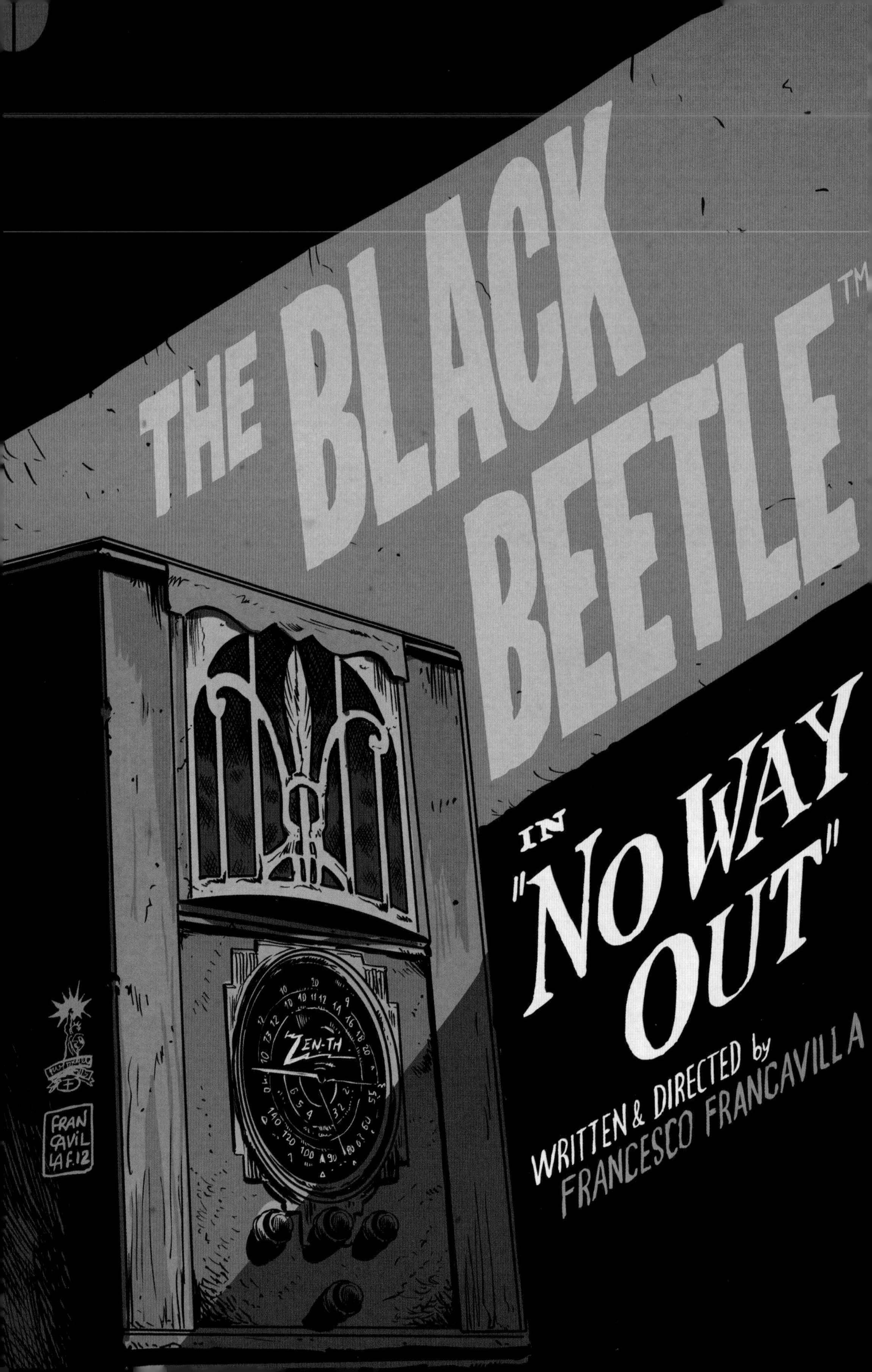
THE BLACK BEETLE™
IN "NO WAY OUT"
WRITTEN & DIRECTED by
FRANCESCO FRANCAVILLA
ZEN-TH
FRAN CAVIL LA F.12

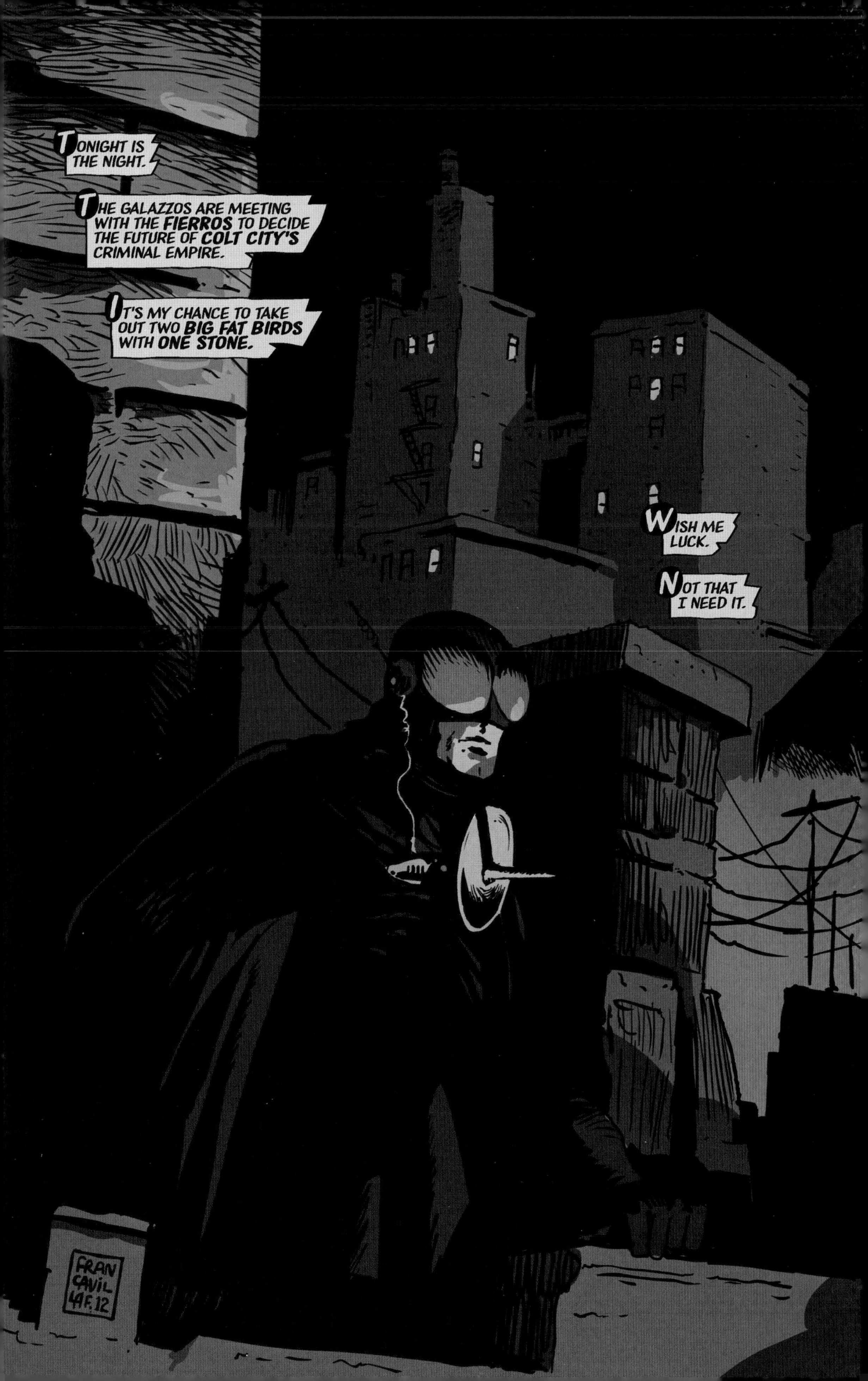
TONIGHT IS THE NIGHT.
THE GALAZZOS ARE MEETING WITH THE FIERROS TO DECIDE THE FUTURE OF COLT CITY'S CRIMINAL EMPIRE.
IT'S MY CHANCE TO TAKE OUT TWO BIG FAT BIRDS WITH ONE STONE.
WISH ME LUCK.
NOT THAT I NEED IT.
FRAN CAVIL 4F.12

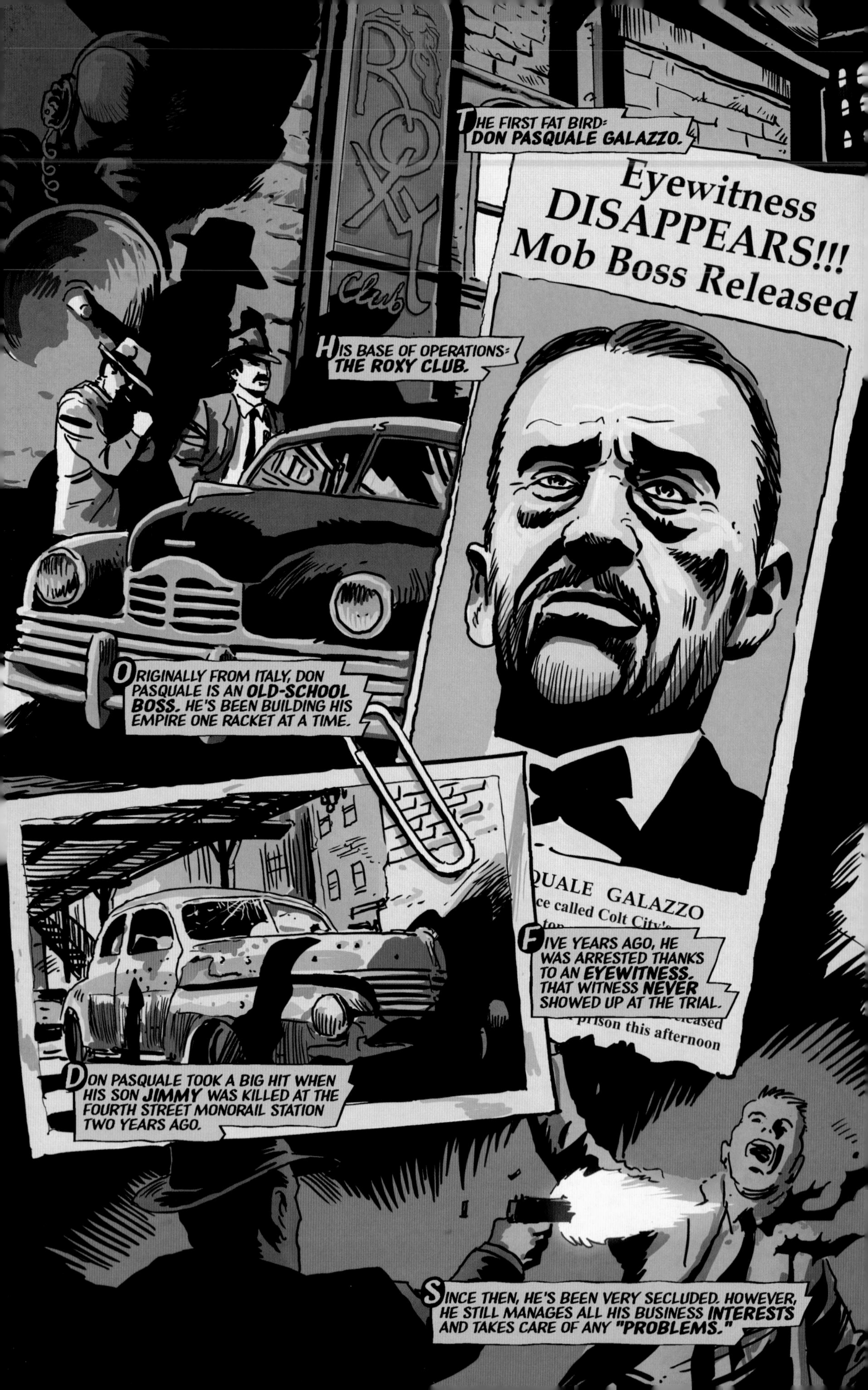
THE FIRST FAT BIRD: DON PASQUALE GALAZZO.
Eyewitness DISAPPEARS!!! Mob Boss Released
HIS BASE OF OPERATIONS: THE ROXY CLUB.
ORIGINALLY FROM ITALY, DON PASQUALE IS AN OLD-SCHOOL BOSS. HE'S BEEN BUILDING HIS EMPIRE ONE RACKET AT A TIME.
QUALE GALAZZO
ce called Colt City's
prison this afternoon
FIVE YEARS AGO, HE WAS ARRESTED THANKS TO AN EYEWITNESS. THAT WITNESS NEVER SHOWED UP AT THE TRIAL.
DON PASQUALE TOOK A BIG HIT WHEN HIS SON JIMMY WAS KILLED AT THE FOURTH STREET MONORAIL STATION TWO YEARS AGO.
SINCE THEN, HE'S BEEN VERY SECLUDED. HOWEVER, HE STILL MANAGES ALL HIS BUSINESS INTERESTS AND TAKES CARE OF ANY "PROBLEMS."

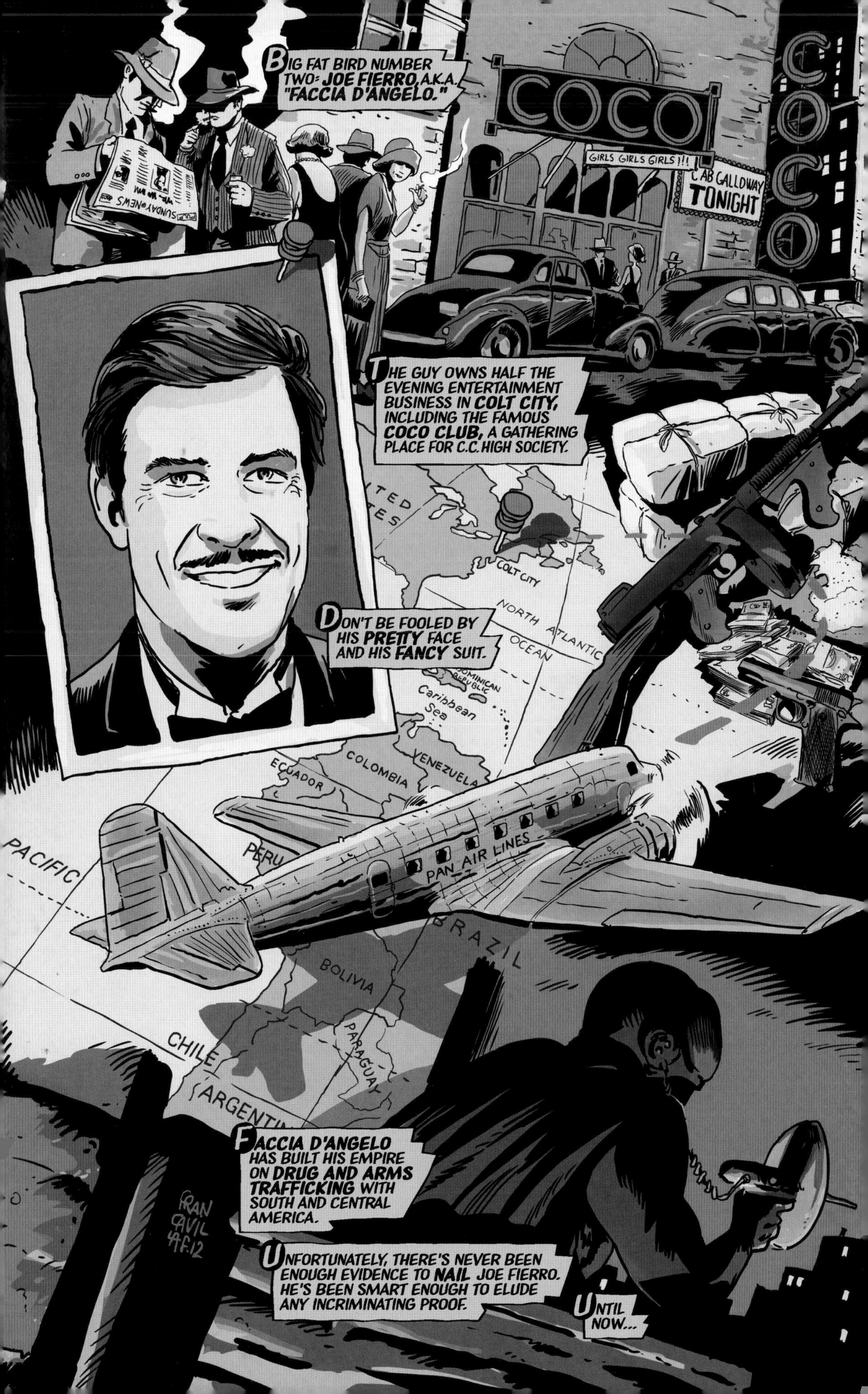
BIG FAT BIRD NUMBER TWO: JOE FIERRO, A.K.A. "FACCIA D'ANGELO."
COCO
SUNDAY NEWS
GIRLS GIRLS GIRLS!!!
CAB GALLOWAY TONIGHT
THE GUY OWNS HALF THE EVENING ENTERTAINMENT BUSINESS IN COLT CITY, INCLUDING THE FAMOUS COCO CLUB, A GATHERING PLACE FOR C.C. HIGH SOCIETY.
COLT CITY
NORTH ATLANTIC
OCEAN
DOMINICAN REPUBLIC
Caribbean Sea
DON'T BE FOOLED BY HIS PRETTY FACE AND HIS FANCY SUIT.
ECUADOR
COLOMBIA
VENEZUELA
PACIFIC
PERU
PAN AIR LINES
BRAZIL
BOLIVIA
CHILE
PARAGUAY
ARGENTI
FACCIA D'ANGELO HAS BUILT HIS EMPIRE ON DRUG AND ARMS TRAFFICKING WITH SOUTH AND CENTRAL AMERICA.
FRAN CAVIL
UNFORTUNATELY, THERE'S NEVER BEEN ENOUGH EVIDENCE TO NAIL JOE FIERRO. HE'S BEEN SMART ENOUGH TO ELUDE ANY INCRIMINATING PROOF.
UNTIL NOW...

THEY'RE MEETING AT SPENCER'S-- NEUTRAL TERRITORY.
SPENCER
TWO ITALIANS MEET AT AN IRISH PUB. ALMOST SOUNDS LIKE THE BEGINNING OF A JOKE...
THIS IS NO JOKE, THOUGH. THE PLACE HAS MORE SECURITY THAN FORT KNOX!
THIS WILL REQUIRE SOME EXTRA WORK, I RECKON.
PUB
BUT ENOUGH WITH TALKIN' FOR NOW...

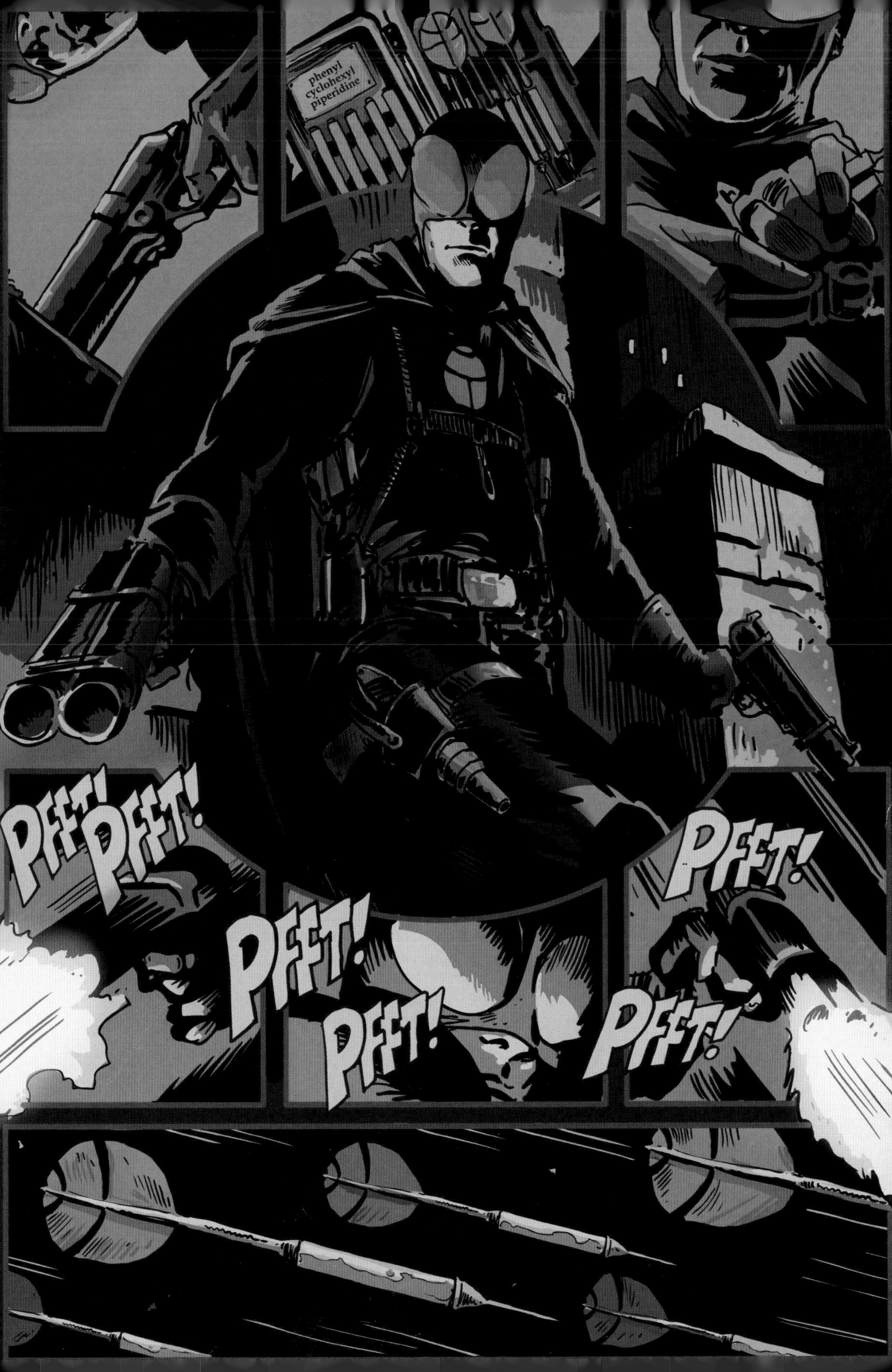
phenyl
cyclohexyl
piperidine
PFFT! PFFT!
PFFT!
PFFT!
PFFT!
PFFT!

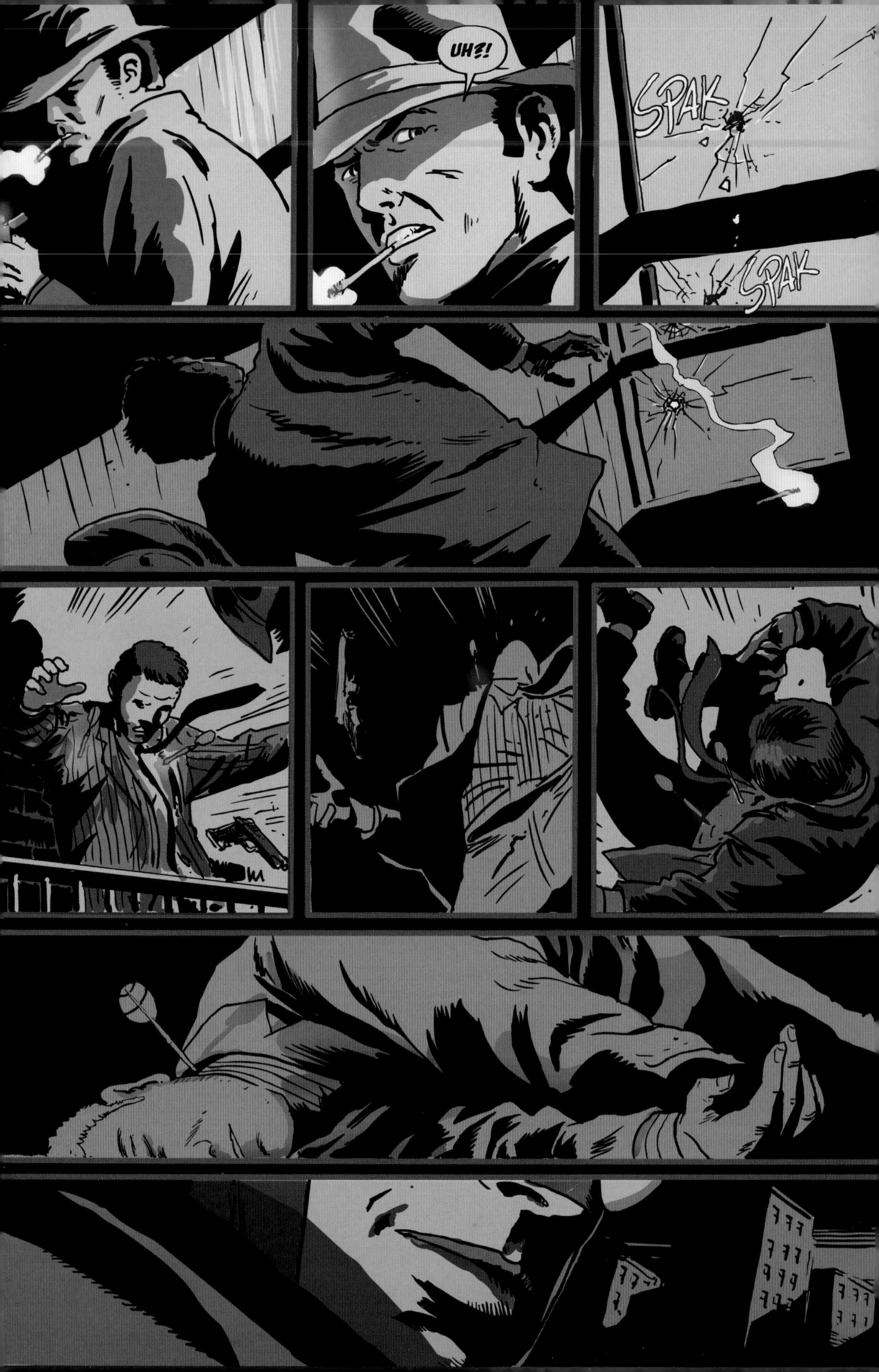
UH?!
SPAK
SPAK

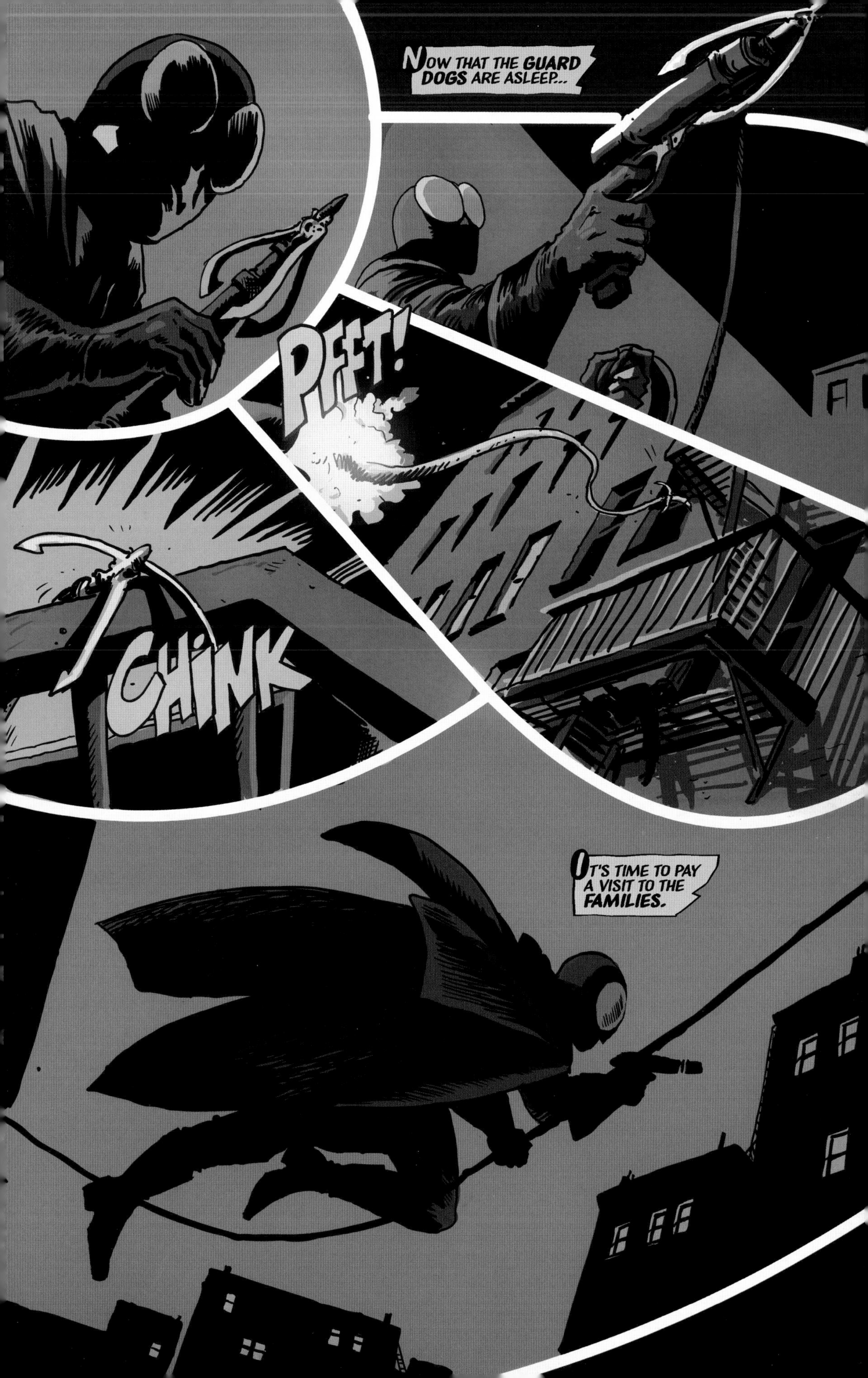
NOW THAT THE GUARD DOGS ARE ASLEEP...
PFFT!
CHINK
IT'S TIME TO PAY A VISIT TO THE FAMILIES.

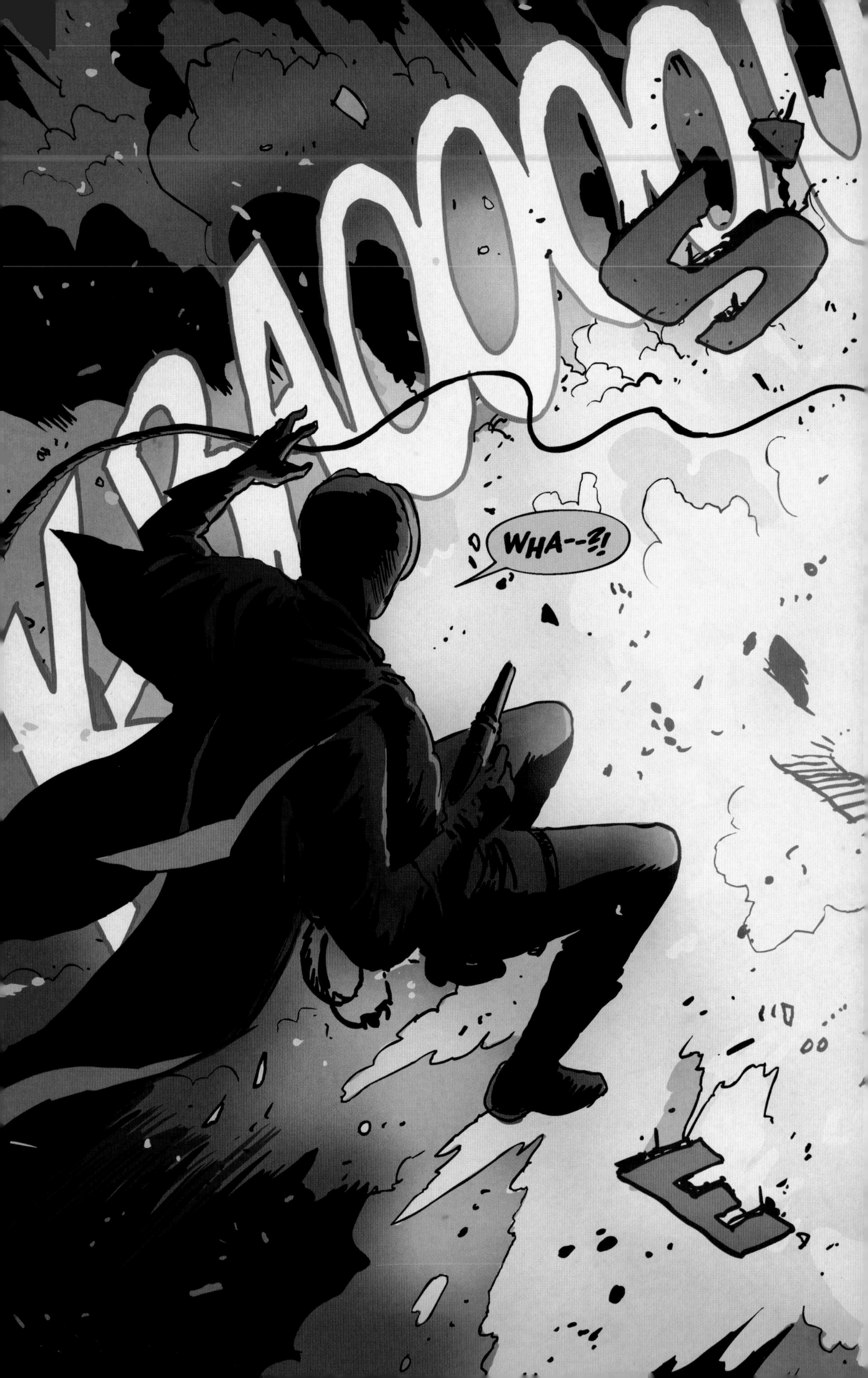
WHA--?!

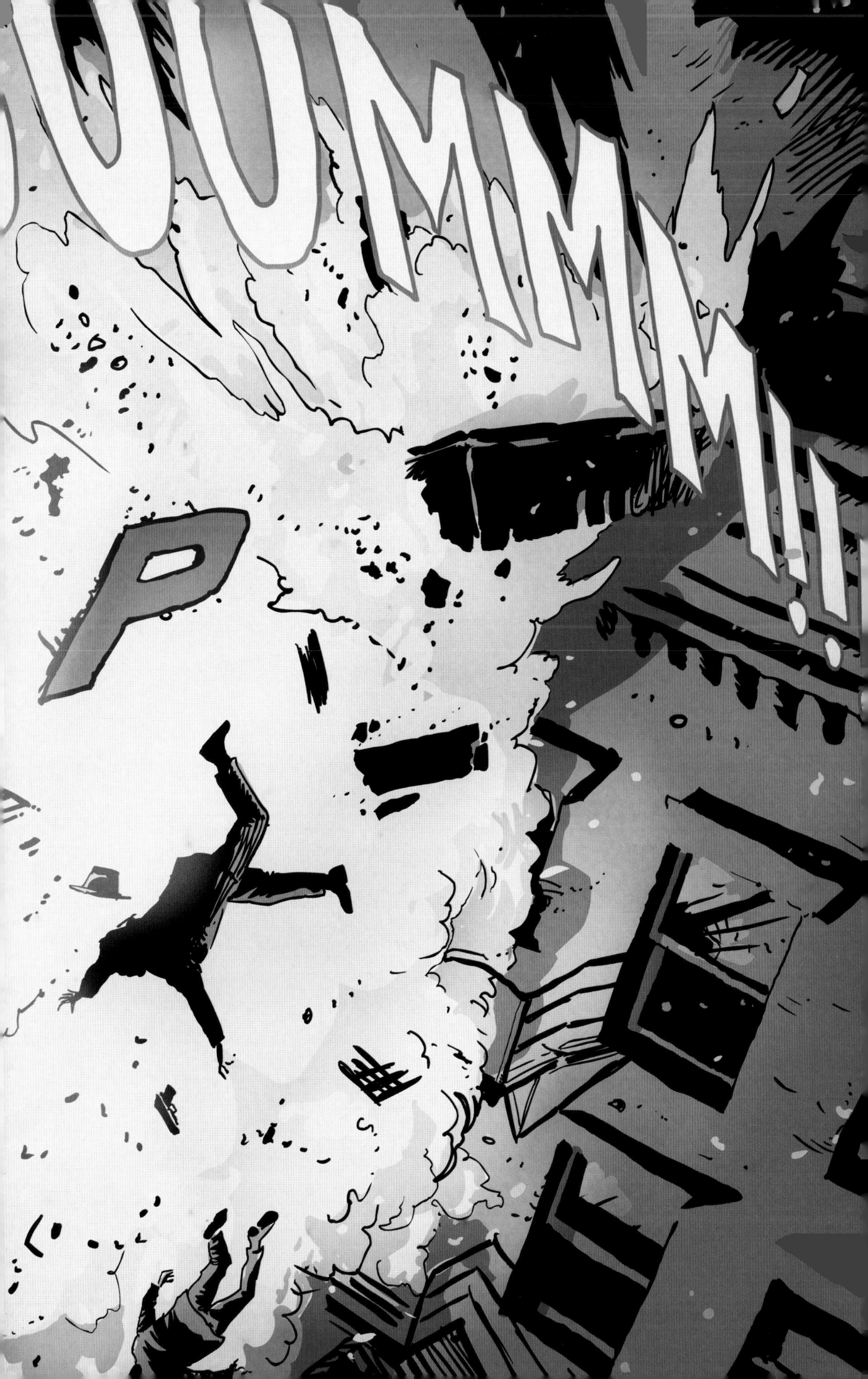
OOMMMM!!!

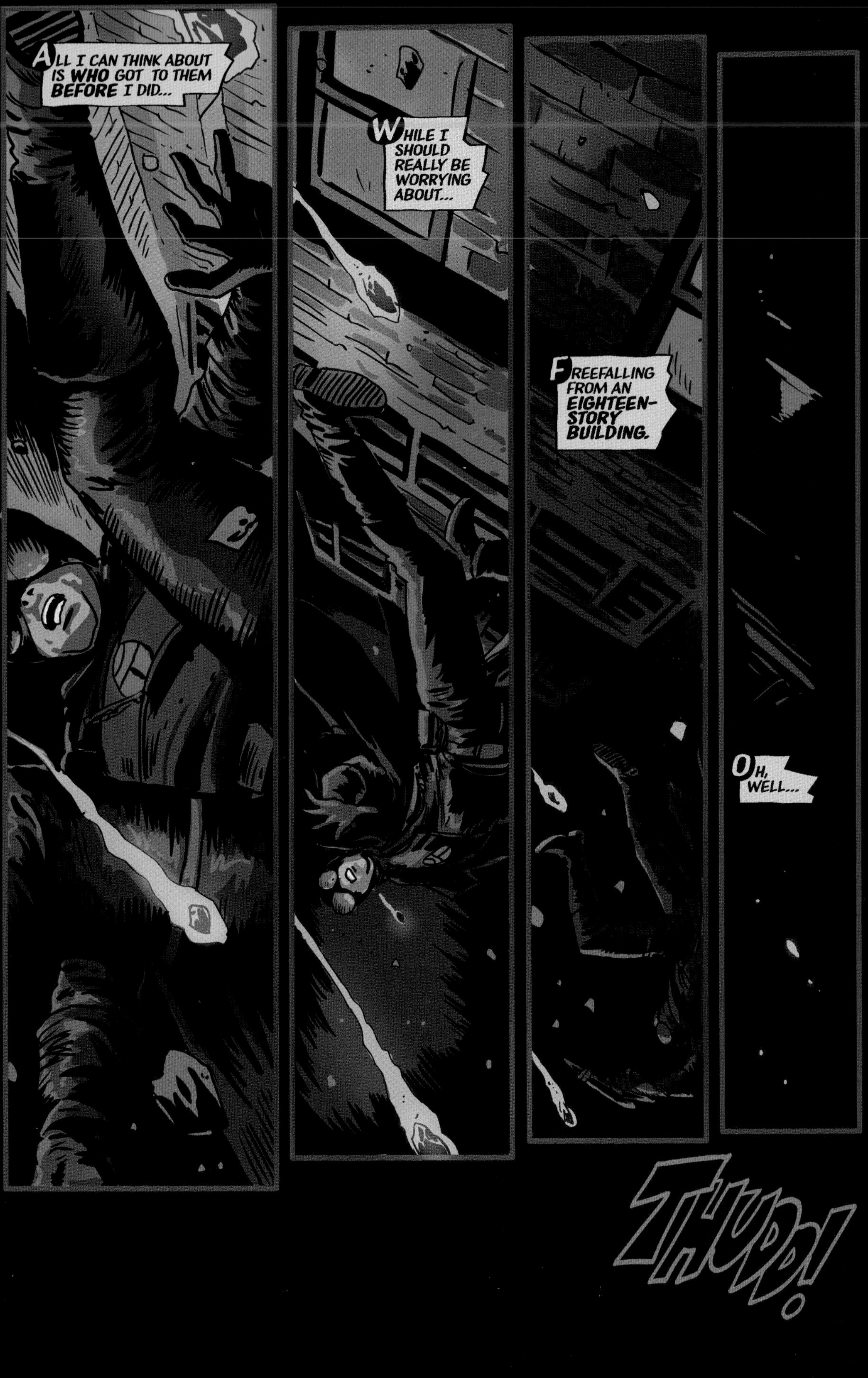

ALL I CAN THINK ABOUT IS WHO GOT TO THEM BEFORE I DID...
WHILE I SHOULD REALLY BE WORRYING ABOUT...
FREEFALLING FROM AN EIGHTEEN-STORY BUILDING.
OH, WELL...
THUDD!

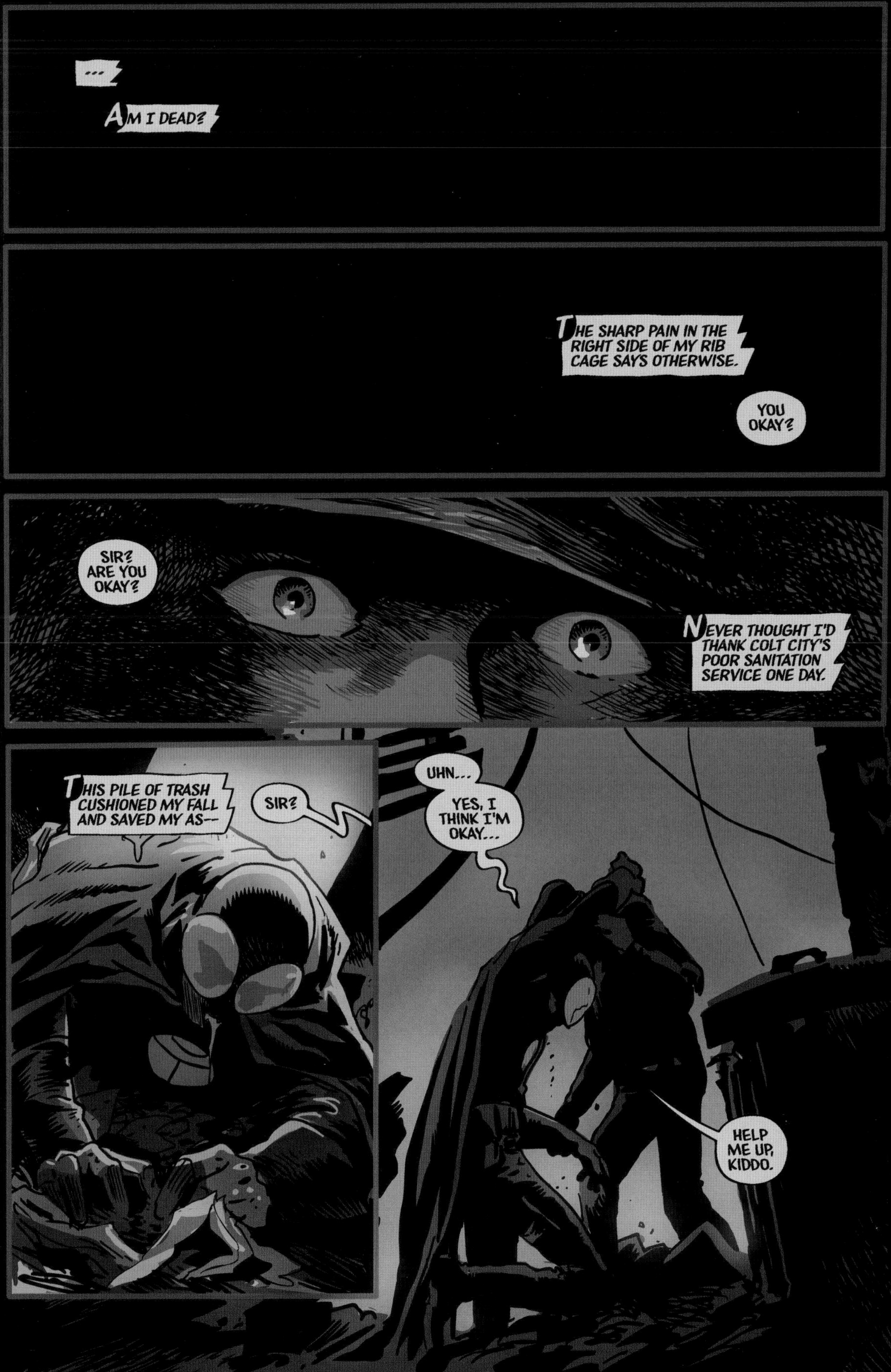
...
AM I DEAD?
THE SHARP PAIN IN THE RIGHT SIDE OF MY RIB CAGE SAYS OTHERWISE.
YOU OKAY?
SIR? ARE YOU OKAY?
NEVER THOUGHT I'D THANK COLT CITY'S POOR SANITATION SERVICE ONE DAY.
THIS PILE OF TRASH CUSHIONED MY FALL AND SAVED MY AS--
SIR?
UHN...
YES, I THINK I'M OKAY...
HELP ME UP, KIDDO.

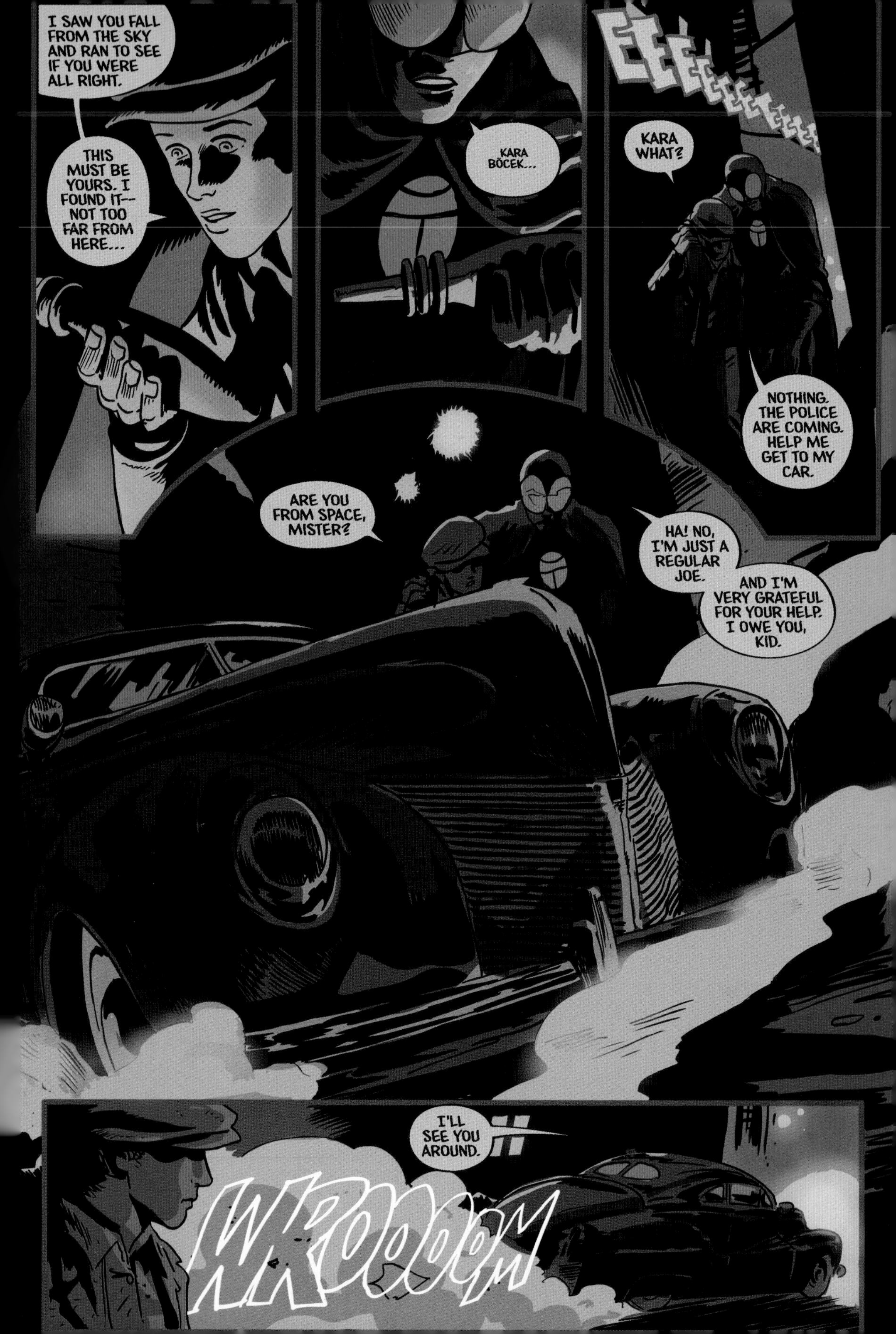
I SAW YOU FALL FROM THE SKY AND RAN TO SEE IF YOU WERE ALL RIGHT.
THIS MUST BE YOURS. I FOUND IT-- NOT TOO FAR FROM HERE...
KARA BÖCEK...
EEEEEEEEEEEE
KARA WHAT?
NOTHING. THE POLICE ARE COMING. HELP ME GET TO MY CAR.
ARE YOU FROM SPACE, MISTER?
HA! NO, I'M JUST A REGULAR JOE.
AND I'M VERY GRATEFUL FOR YOUR HELP. I OWE YOU, KID.
I'LL SEE YOU AROUND.
WROOOOOM

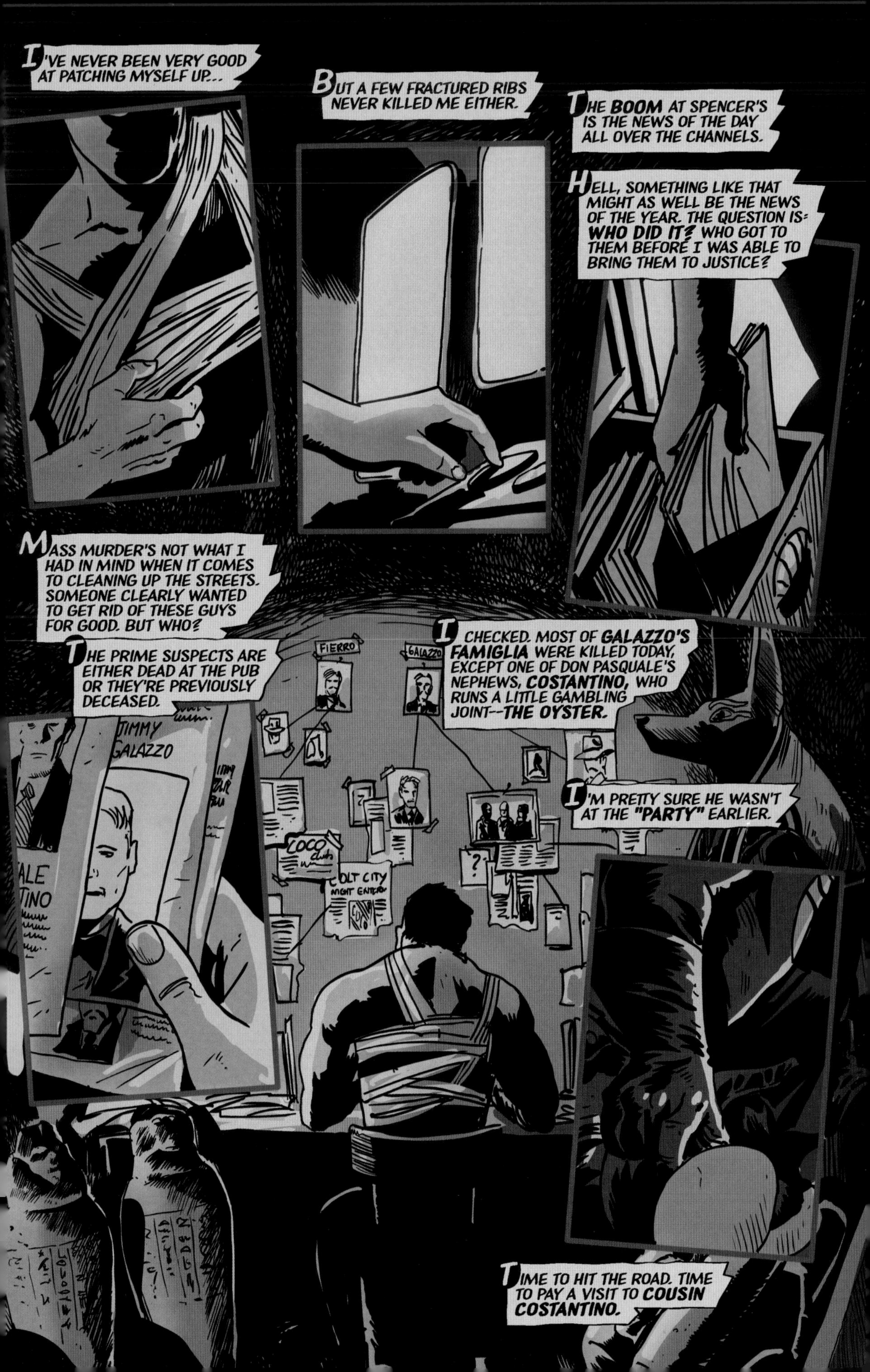
I'VE NEVER BEEN VERY GOOD AT PATCHING MYSELF UP...
BUT A FEW FRACTURED RIBS NEVER KILLED ME EITHER.
THE BOOM AT SPENCER'S IS THE NEWS OF THE DAY ALL OVER THE CHANNELS.
HELL, SOMETHING LIKE THAT MIGHT AS WELL BE THE NEWS OF THE YEAR. THE QUESTION IS: WHO DID IT? WHO GOT TO THEM BEFORE I WAS ABLE TO BRING THEM TO JUSTICE?
MASS MURDER'S NOT WHAT I HAD IN MIND WHEN IT COMES TO CLEANING UP THE STREETS. SOMEONE CLEARLY WANTED TO GET RID OF THESE GUYS FOR GOOD. BUT WHO?
THE PRIME SUSPECTS ARE EITHER DEAD AT THE PUB OR THEY'RE PREVIOUSLY DECEASED.
FIERRO
GALAZZO
I CHECKED. MOST OF GALAZZO'S FAMIGLIA WERE KILLED TODAY, EXCEPT ONE OF DON PASQUALE'S NEPHEWS, COSTANTINO, WHO RUNS A LITTLE GAMBLING JOINT--THE OYSTER.
JIMMY GALAZZO
COCO
COLT CITY
I'M PRETTY SURE HE WASN'T AT THE "PARTY" EARLIER.
TIME TO HIT THE ROAD. TIME TO PAY A VISIT TO COUSIN COSTANTINO.

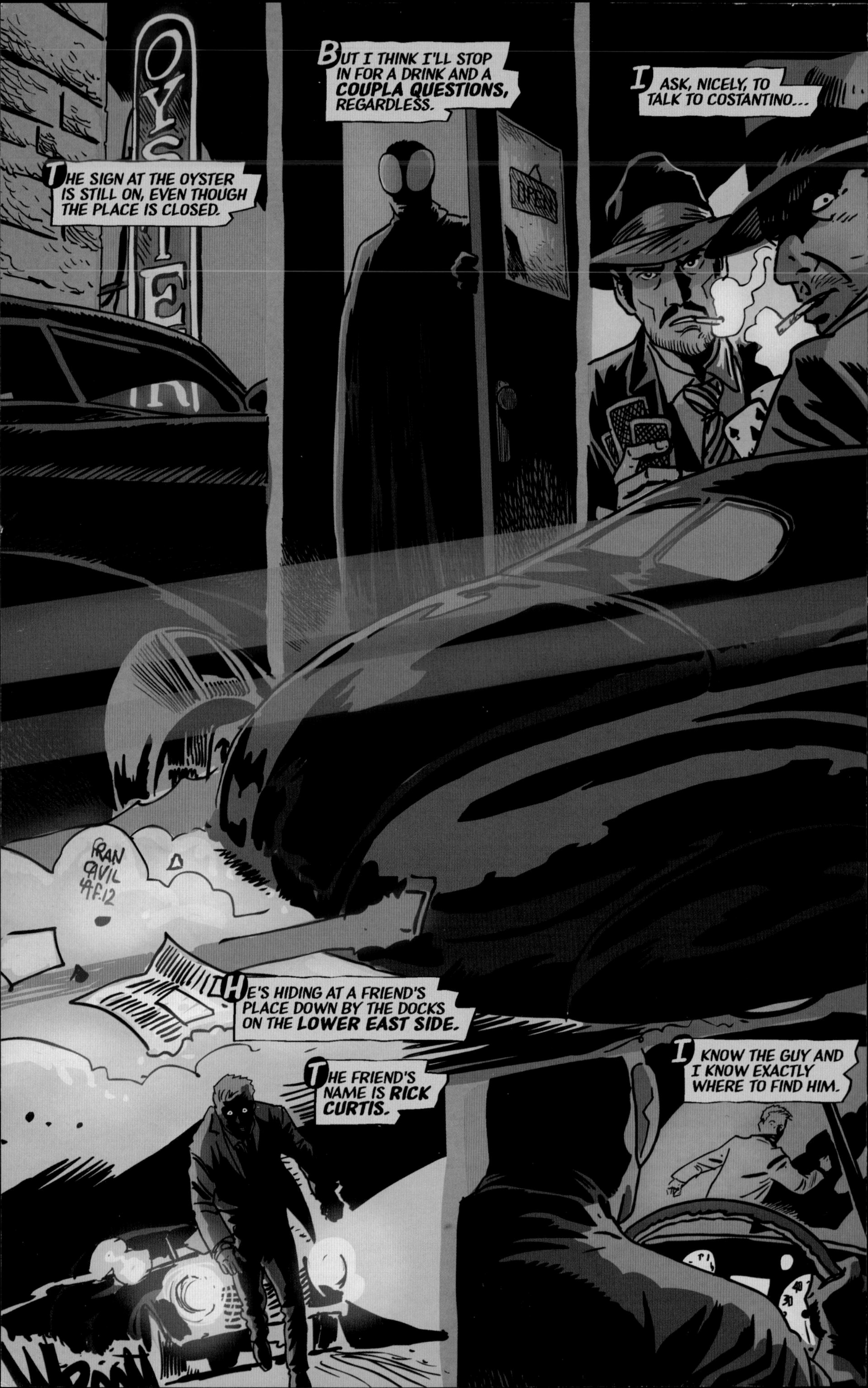
OYSTER
THE SIGN AT THE OYSTER IS STILL ON, EVEN THOUGH THE PLACE IS CLOSED.
BUT I THINK I'LL STOP IN FOR A DRINK AND A COUPLA QUESTIONS, REGARDLESS.
OPEN
I ASK, NICELY, TO TALK TO COSTANTINO...
HE'S HIDING AT A FRIEND'S PLACE DOWN BY THE DOCKS ON THE LOWER EAST SIDE.
THE FRIEND'S NAME IS RICK CURTIS.
I KNOW THE GUY AND I KNOW EXACTLY WHERE TO FIND HIM.

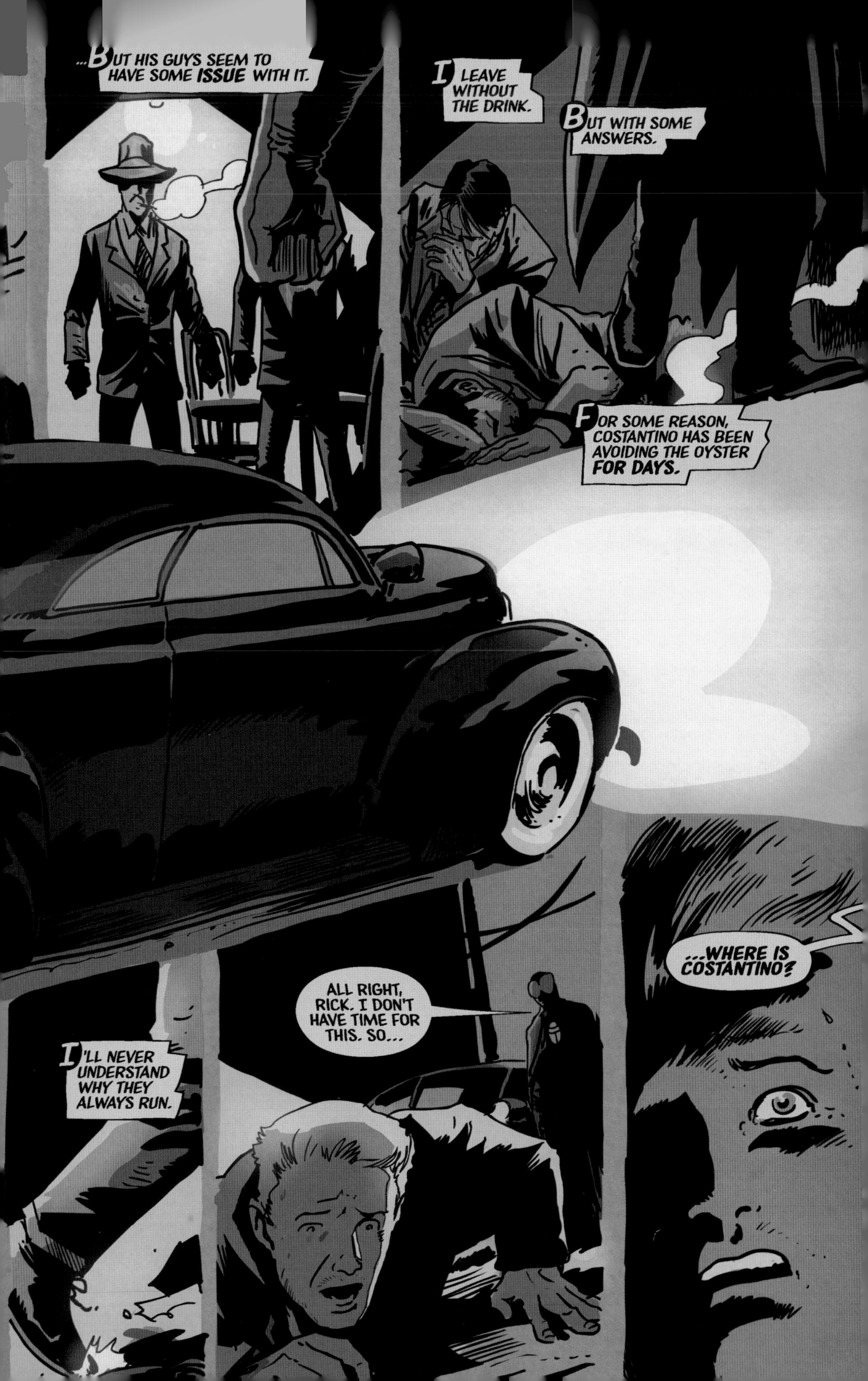
...BUT HIS GUYS SEEM TO HAVE SOME ISSUE WITH IT.
I LEAVE WITHOUT THE DRINK.
BUT WITH SOME ANSWERS.
FOR SOME REASON, COSTANTINO HAS BEEN AVOIDING THE OYSTER FOR DAYS.
I'LL NEVER UNDERSTAND WHY THEY ALWAYS RUN.
ALL RIGHT, RICK. I DON'T HAVE TIME FOR THIS. SO...
...WHERE IS COSTANTINO?

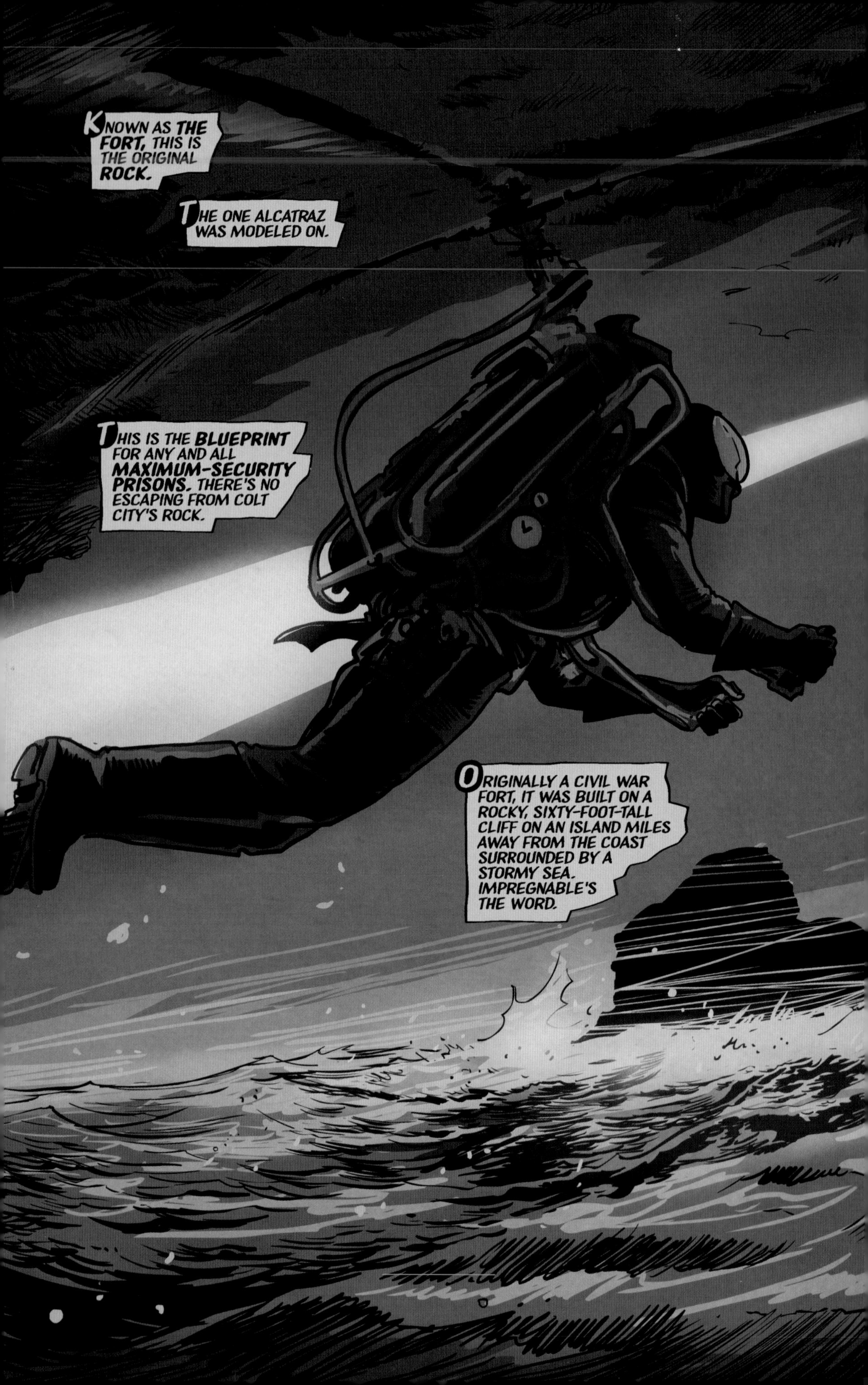
KNOWN AS THE FORT, THIS IS THE ORIGINAL ROCK.
THE ONE ALCATRAZ WAS MODELED ON.
THIS IS THE BLUEPRINT FOR ANY AND ALL MAXIMUM-SECURITY PRISONS. THERE'S NO ESCAPING FROM COLT CITY'S ROCK.
ORIGINALLY A CIVIL WAR FORT, IT WAS BUILT ON A ROCKY, SIXTY-FOOT-TALL CLIFF ON AN ISLAND MILES AWAY FROM THE COAST SURROUNDED BY A STORMY SEA. IMPREGNABLE'S THE WORD.

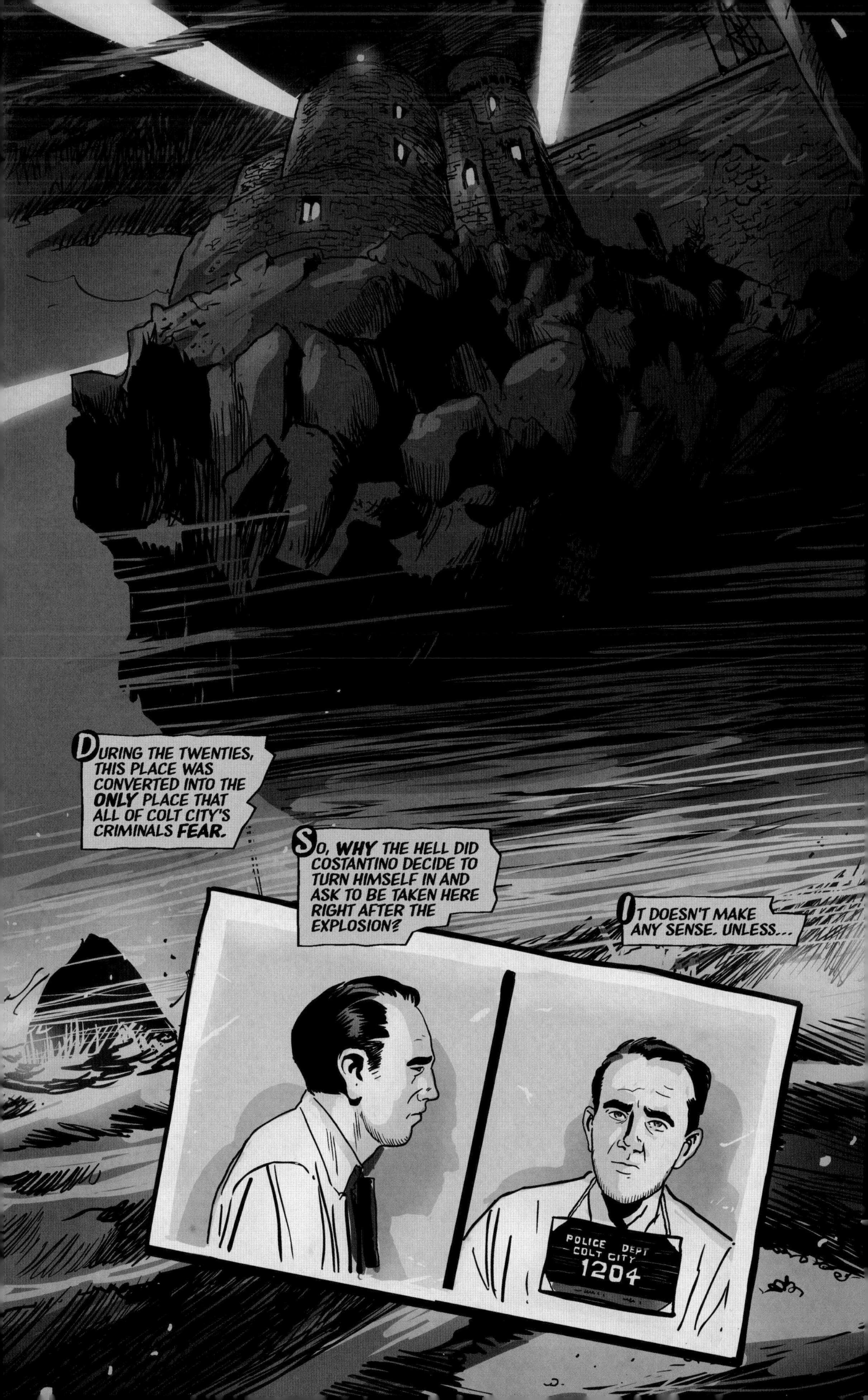
DURING THE TWENTIES, THIS PLACE WAS CONVERTED INTO THE ONLY PLACE THAT ALL OF COLT CITY'S CRIMINALS FEAR.
SO, WHY THE HELL DID COSTANTINO DECIDE TO TURN HIMSELF IN AND ASK TO BE TAKEN HERE RIGHT AFTER THE EXPLOSION?
IT DOESN'T MAKE ANY SENSE. UNLESS...
POLICE DEPT
COLT CITY
1204

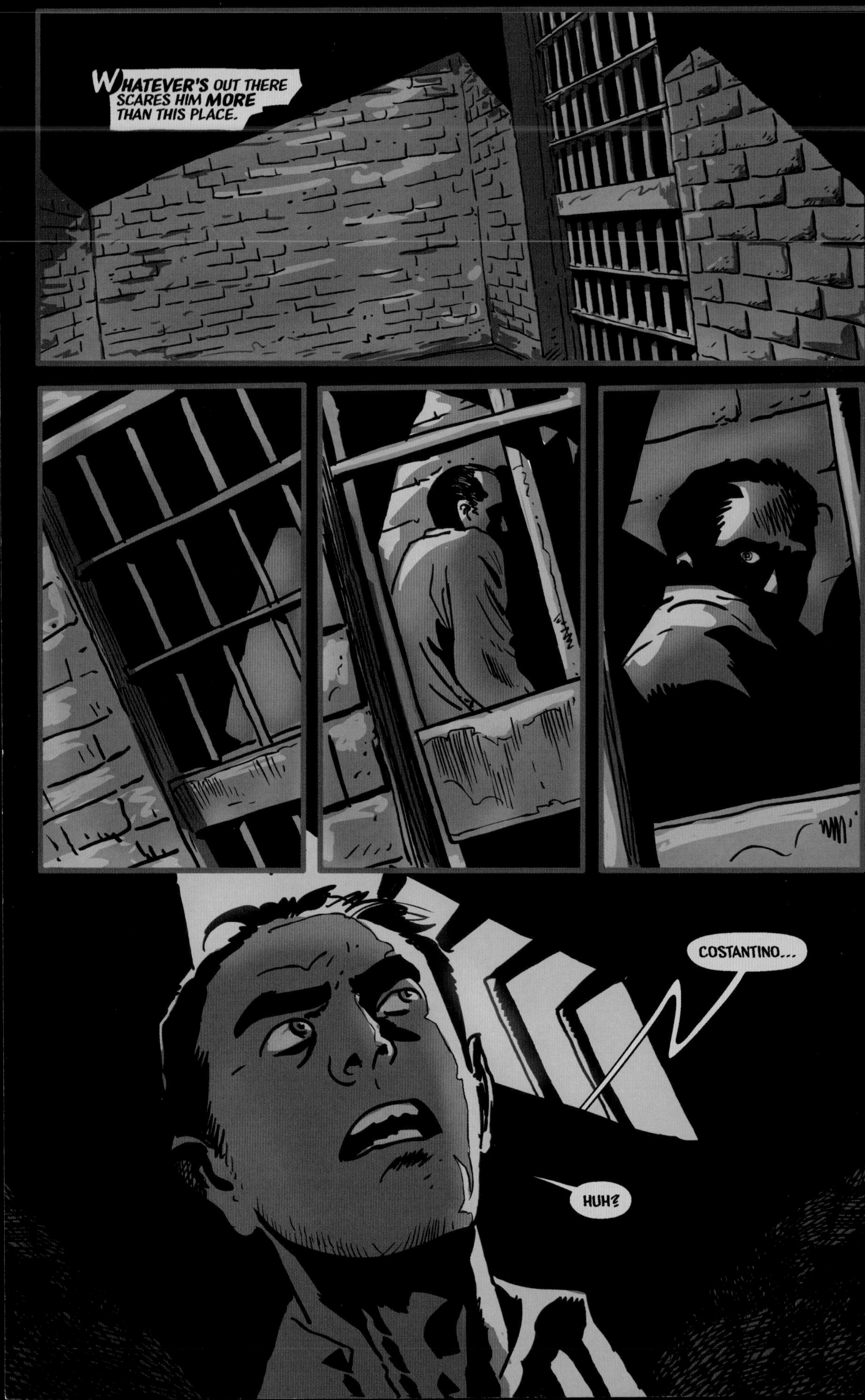
WHATEVER'S OUT THERE SCARES HIM MORE THAN THIS PLACE.
COSTANTINO...
HUH?

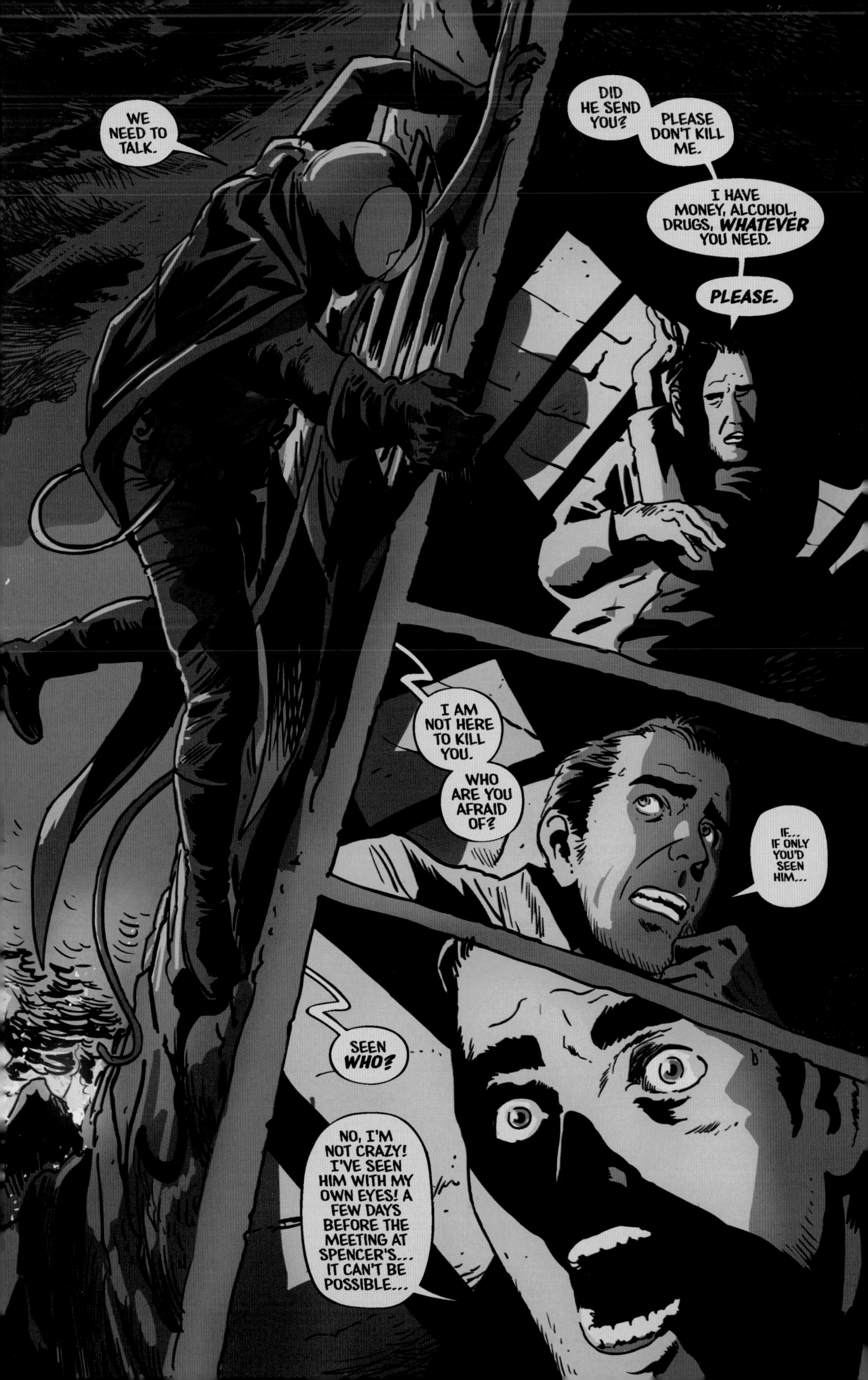
WE NEED TO TALK.
DID HE SEND YOU?
PLEASE DON'T KILL ME.
I HAVE MONEY, ALCOHOL, DRUGS, WHATEVER YOU NEED.
PLEASE.
I AM NOT HERE TO KILL YOU.
WHO ARE YOU AFRAID OF?
IF... IF ONLY YOU'D SEEN HIM...
SEEN WHO?
NO, I'M NOT CRAZY! I'VE SEEN HIM WITH MY OWN EYES! A FEW DAYS BEFORE THE MEETING AT SPENCER'S... IT CAN'T BE POSSIBLE...

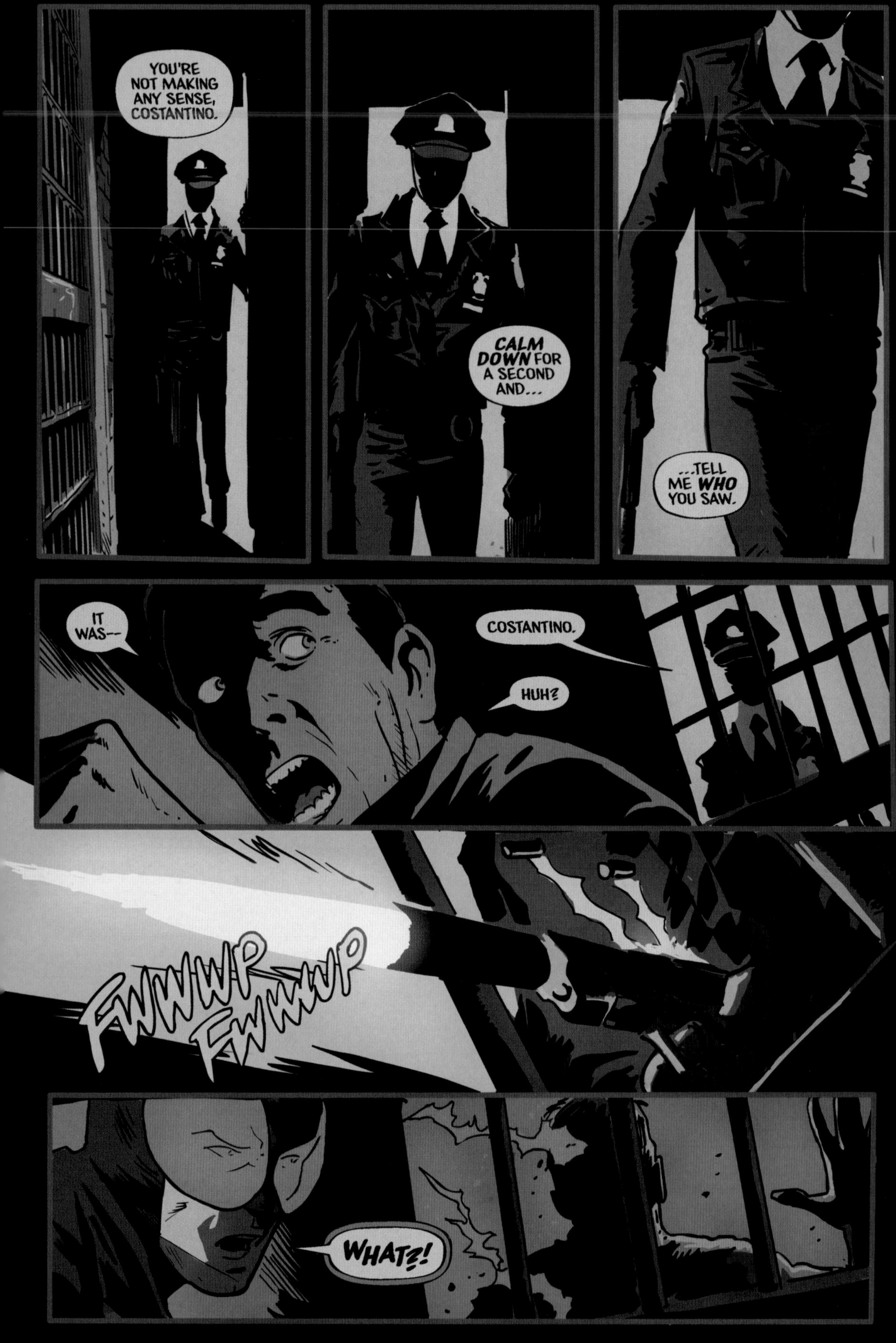
YOU'RE NOT MAKING ANY SENSE, COSTANTINO.
CALM DOWN FOR A SECOND AND...
...TELL ME WHO YOU SAW.
IT WAS--
COSTANTINO.
HUH?
FWWWP FWWWP
WHAT?!

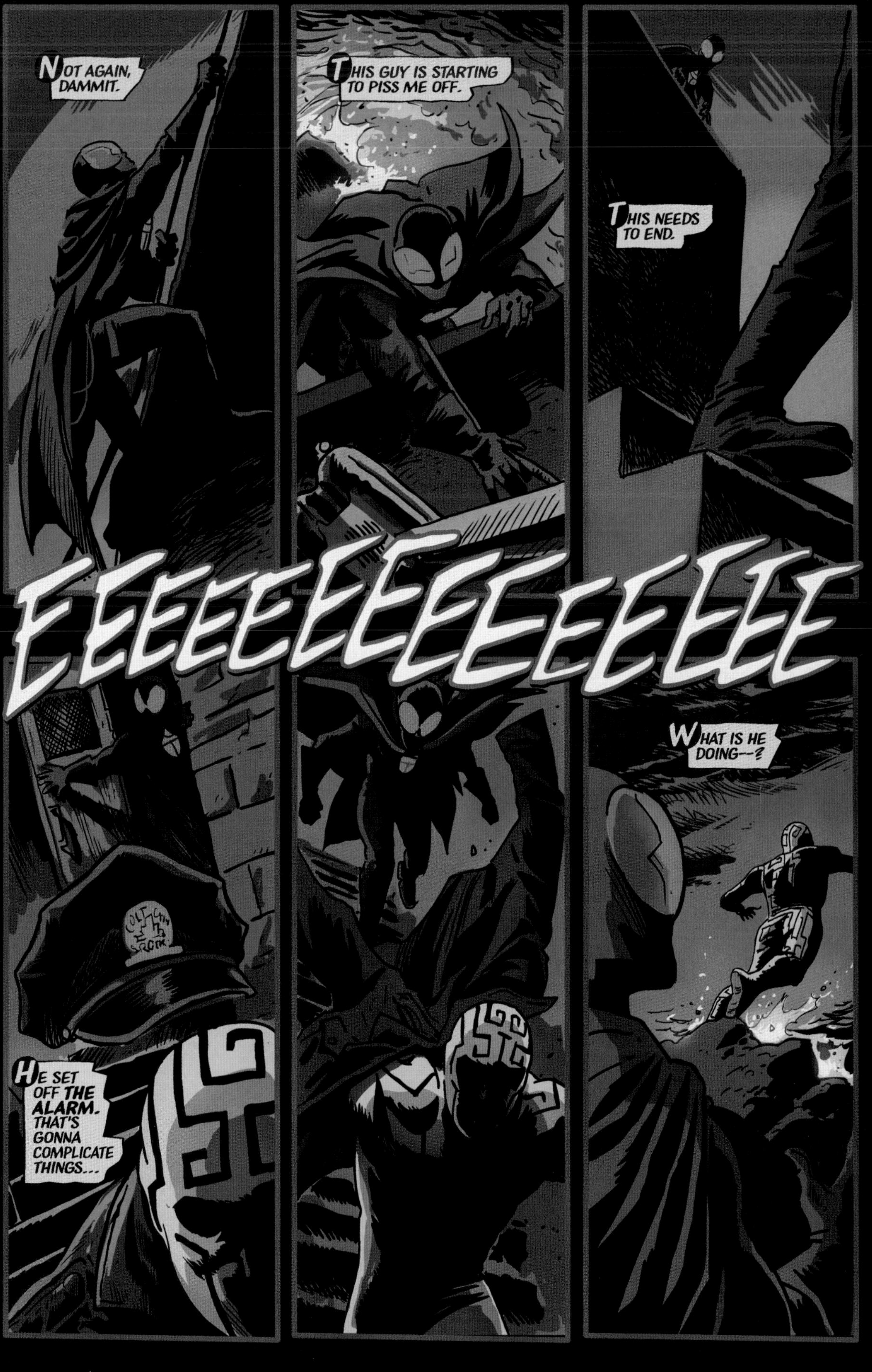

NOT AGAIN, DAMMIT.
THIS GUY IS STARTING TO PISS ME OFF.
THIS NEEDS TO END.
EEEEEEEEEEEEEEE
HE SET OFF THE ALARM. THAT'S GONNA COMPLICATE THINGS...
WHAT IS HE DOING--?

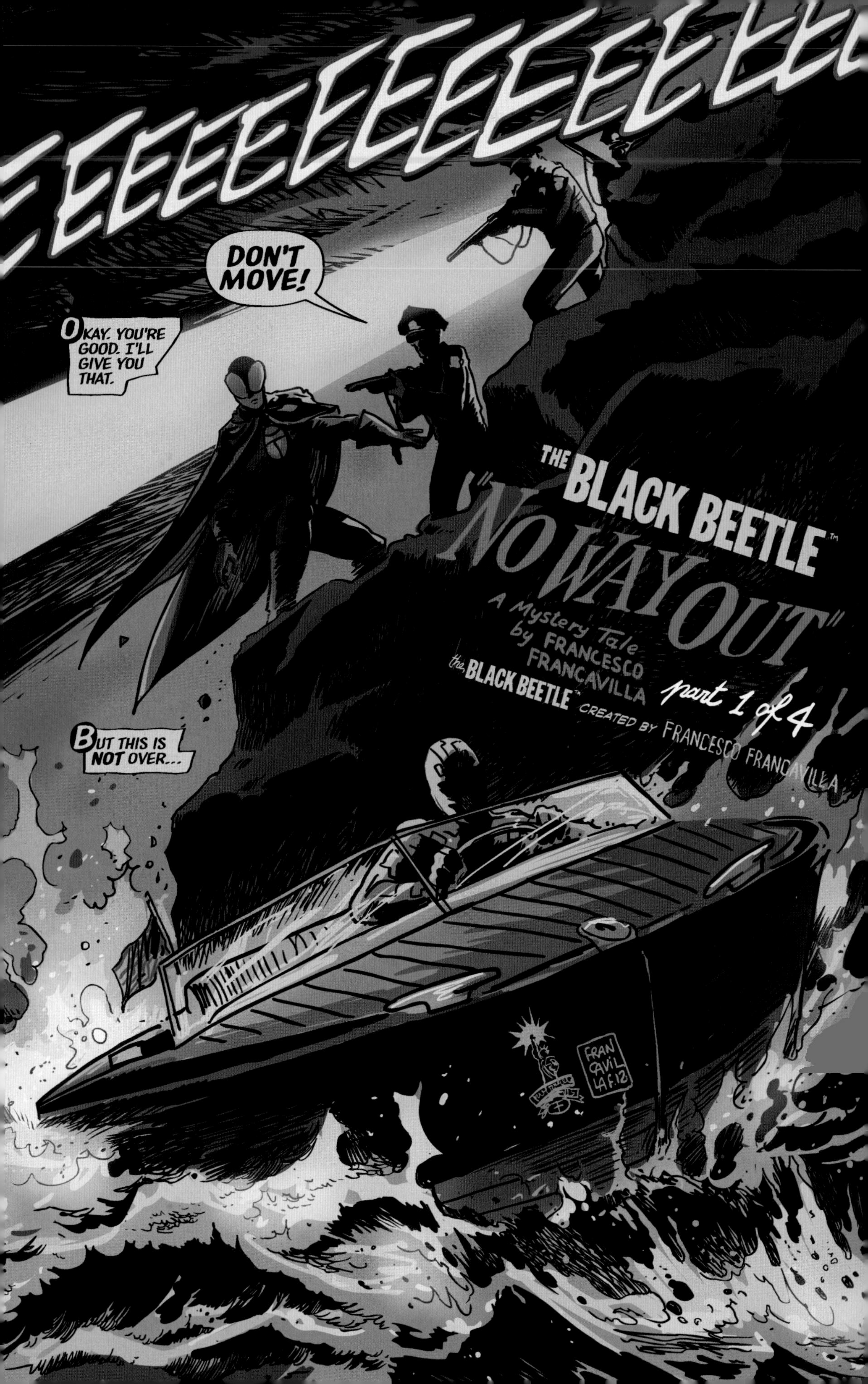
EEEEEEEEEEEEEEE
DON'T MOVE!
OKAY. YOU'RE GOOD. I'LL GIVE YOU THAT.
THE BLACK BEETLE™
"NO WAY OUT"
A Mystery Tale by FRANCESCO FRANCAVILLA
part 1 of 4
the BLACK BEETLE™ CREATED BY FRANCESCO FRANCAVILLA
BUT THIS IS NOT OVER...
FRANCAVILLA F.12

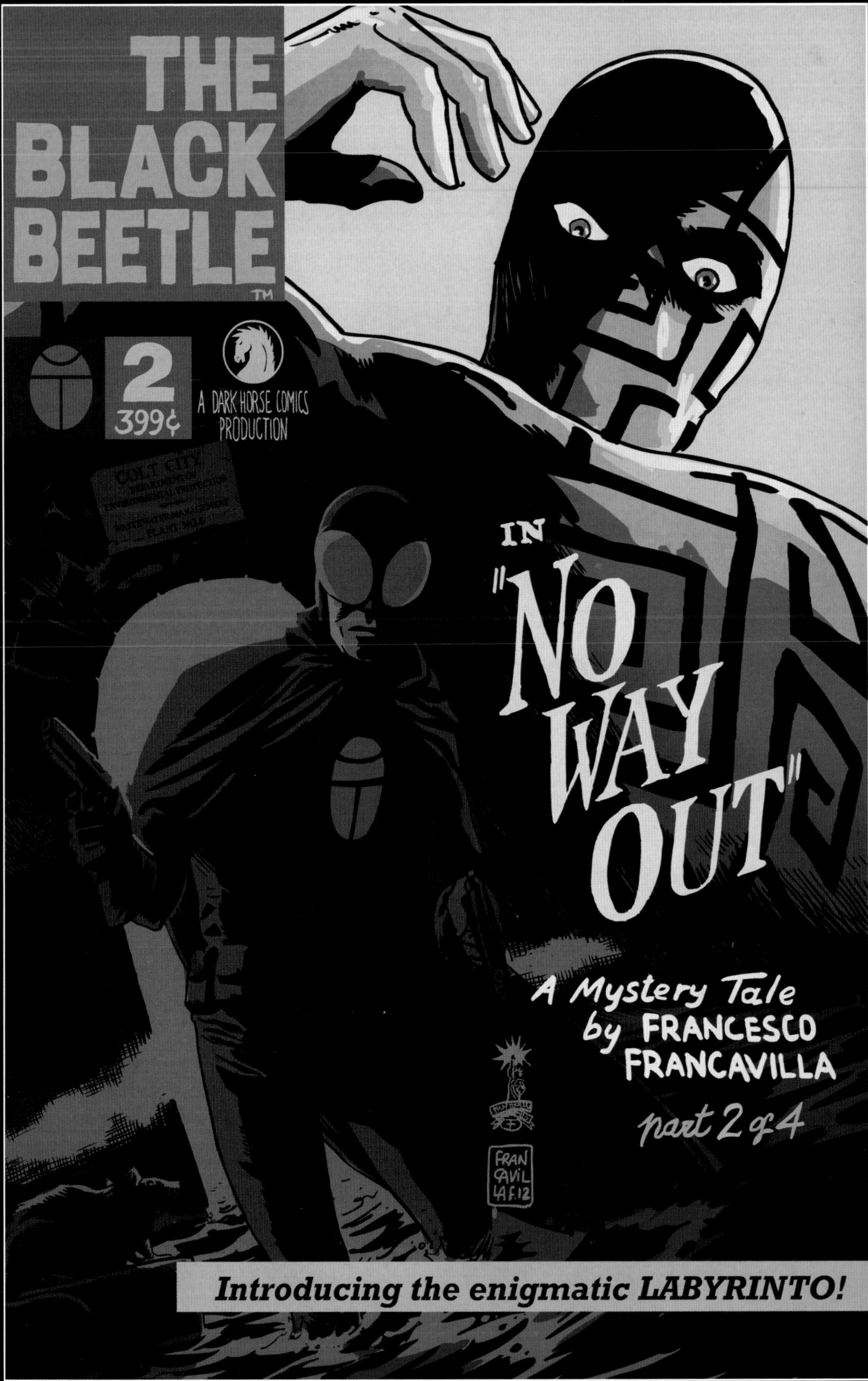
THE BLACK BEETLE™
2
399¢
A DARK HORSE COMICS PRODUCTION
COLT CITY
IN "NO WAY OUT"
A Mystery Tale by FRANCESCO FRANCAVILLA
part 2 of 4
FRAN CAVIL LA F.12
Introducing the enigmatic LABYRINTO!

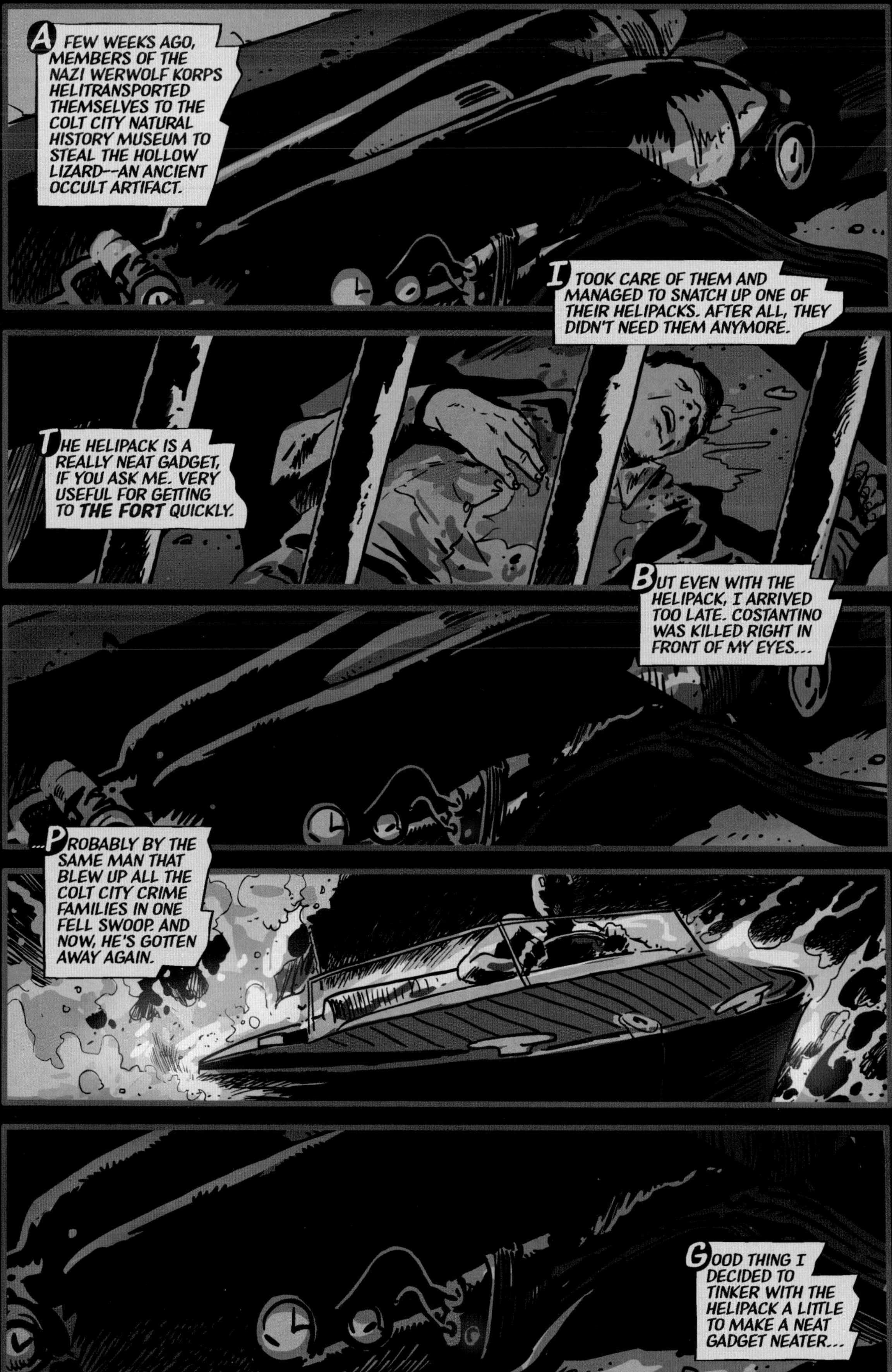
A FEW WEEKS AGO, MEMBERS OF THE NAZI WERWOLF KORPS HELITRANSPORTED THEMSELVES TO THE COLT CITY NATURAL HISTORY MUSEUM TO STEAL THE HOLLOW LIZARD--AN ANCIENT OCCULT ARTIFACT.
I TOOK CARE OF THEM AND MANAGED TO SNATCH UP ONE OF THEIR HELIPACKS. AFTER ALL, THEY DIDN'T NEED THEM ANYMORE.
THE HELIPACK IS A REALLY NEAT GADGET, IF YOU ASK ME. VERY USEFUL FOR GETTING TO THE FORT QUICKLY.
BUT EVEN WITH THE HELIPACK, I ARRIVED TOO LATE. COSTANTINO WAS KILLED RIGHT IN FRONT OF MY EYES...
...PROBABLY BY THE SAME MAN THAT BLEW UP ALL THE COLT CITY CRIME FAMILIES IN ONE FELL SWOOP. AND NOW, HE'S GOTTEN AWAY AGAIN.
GOOD THING I DECIDED TO TINKER WITH THE HELIPACK A LITTLE TO MAKE A NEAT GADGET NEATER...

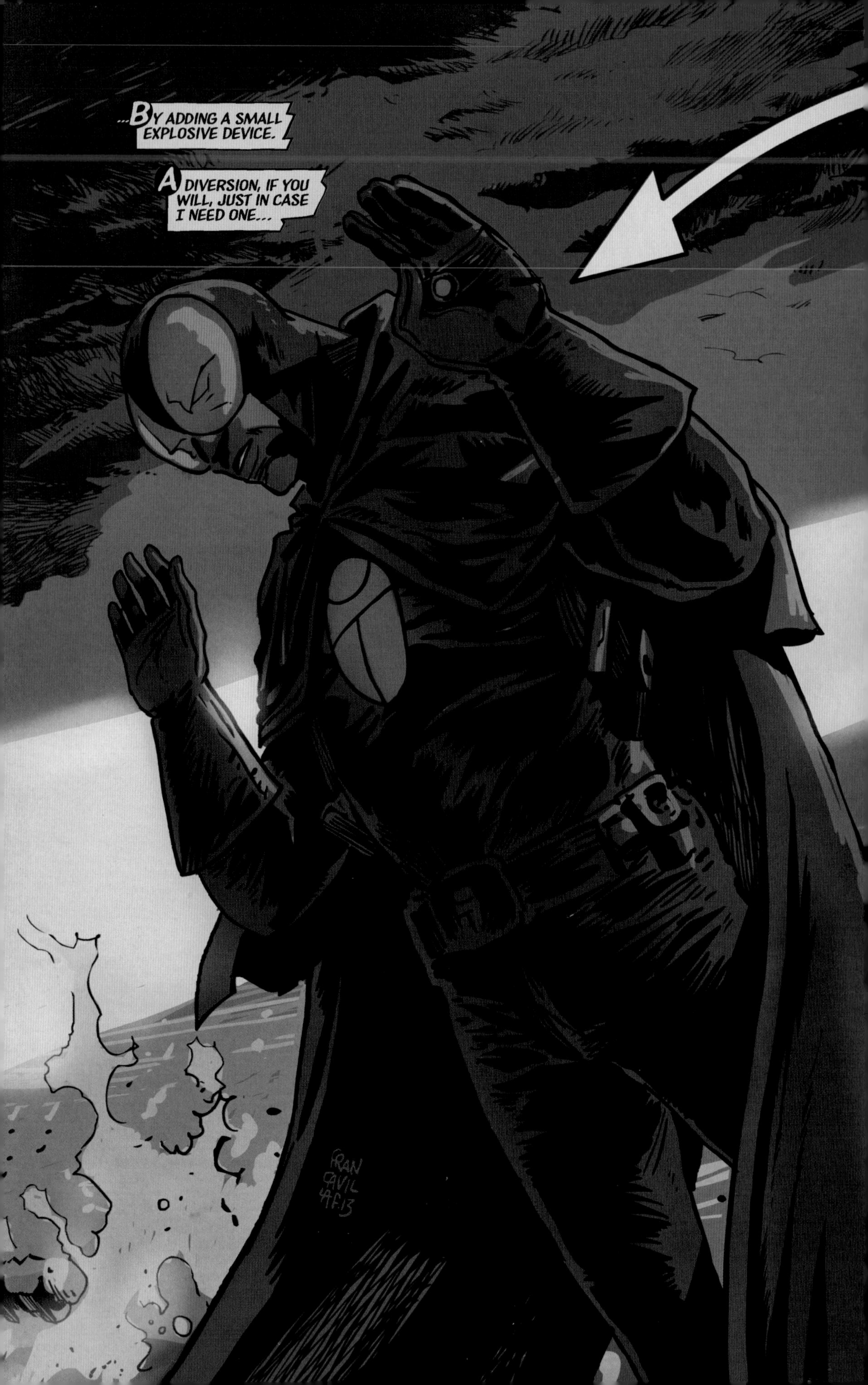
...BY ADDING A SMALL EXPLOSIVE DEVICE.
A DIVERSION, IF YOU WILL, JUST IN CASE I NEED ONE...
FRAN CAVIL

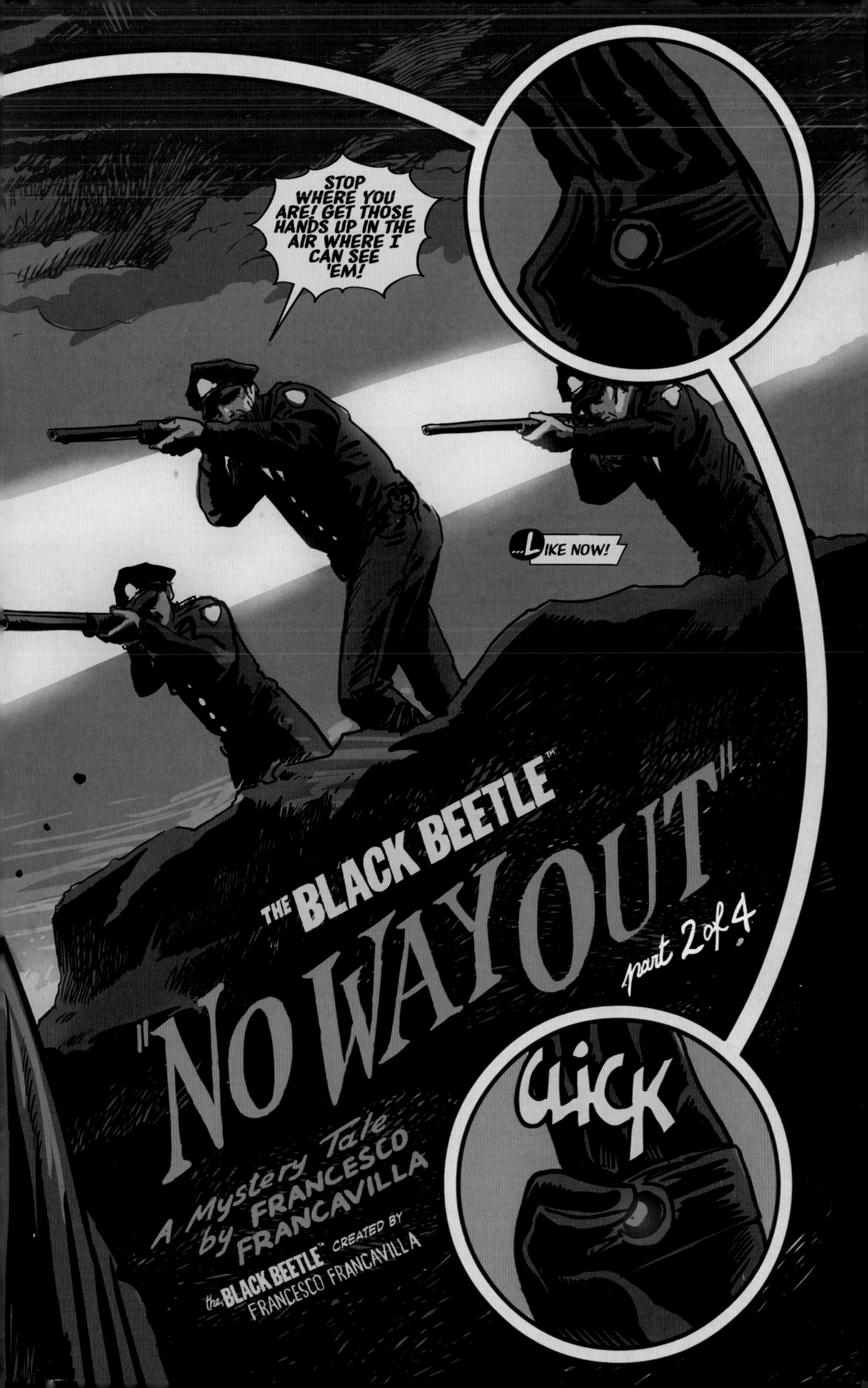
STOP WHERE YOU ARE! GET THOSE HANDS UP IN THE AIR WHERE I CAN SEE 'EM!
...LIKE NOW!
THE BLACK BEETLE™
"NO WAY OUT"
part 2 of 4
A Mystery Tale by FRANCESCO FRANCAVILLA
the BLACK BEETLE™ CREATED BY FRANCESCO FRANCAVILLA
CLICK

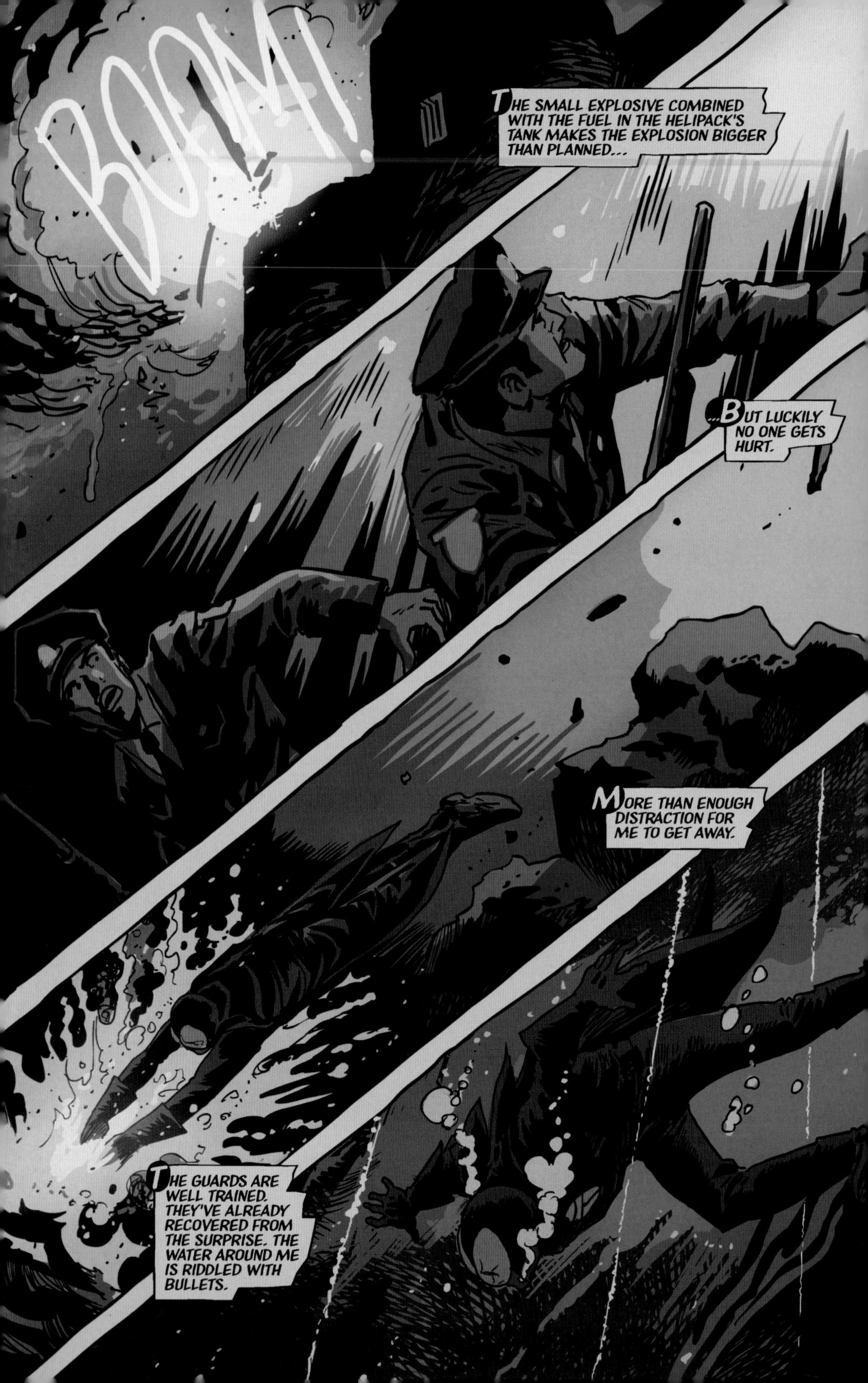
BOOM!
THE SMALL EXPLOSIVE COMBINED WITH THE FUEL IN THE HELIPACK'S TANK MAKES THE EXPLOSION BIGGER THAN PLANNED...
...BUT LUCKILY NO ONE GETS HURT.
MORE THAN ENOUGH DISTRACTION FOR ME TO GET AWAY.
THE GUARDS ARE WELL TRAINED. THEY'VE ALREADY RECOVERED FROM THE SURPRISE. THE WATER AROUND ME IS RIDDLED WITH BULLETS.

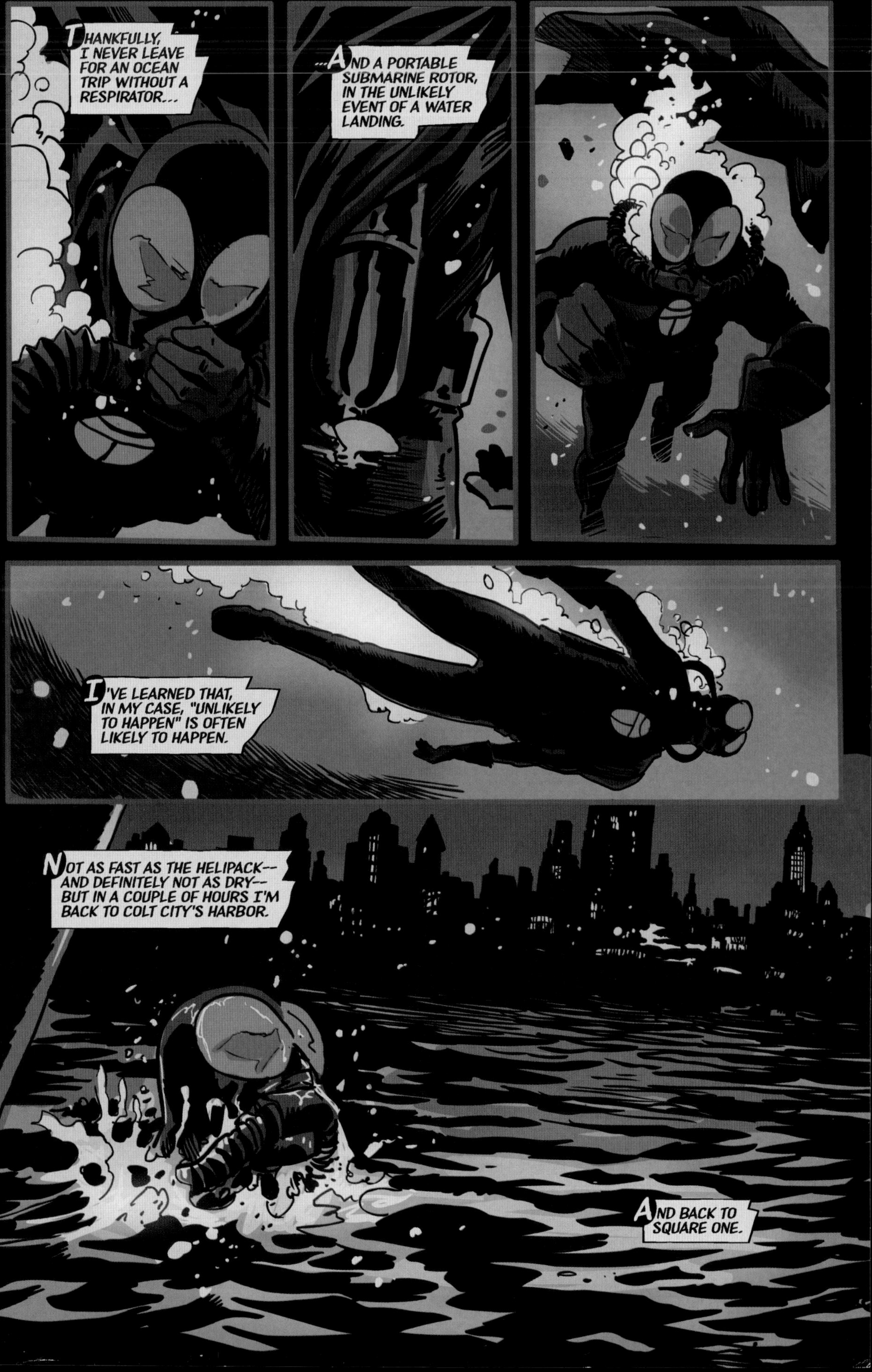
THANKFULLY, I NEVER LEAVE FOR AN OCEAN TRIP WITHOUT A RESPIRATOR...
...AND A PORTABLE SUBMARINE ROTOR, IN THE UNLIKELY EVENT OF A WATER LANDING.
I'VE LEARNED THAT, IN MY CASE, "UNLIKELY TO HAPPEN" IS OFTEN LIKELY TO HAPPEN.
NOT AS FAST AS THE HELIPACK-- AND DEFINITELY NOT AS DRY-- BUT IN A COUPLE OF HOURS I'M BACK TO COLT CITY'S HARBOR.
AND BACK TO SQUARE ONE.

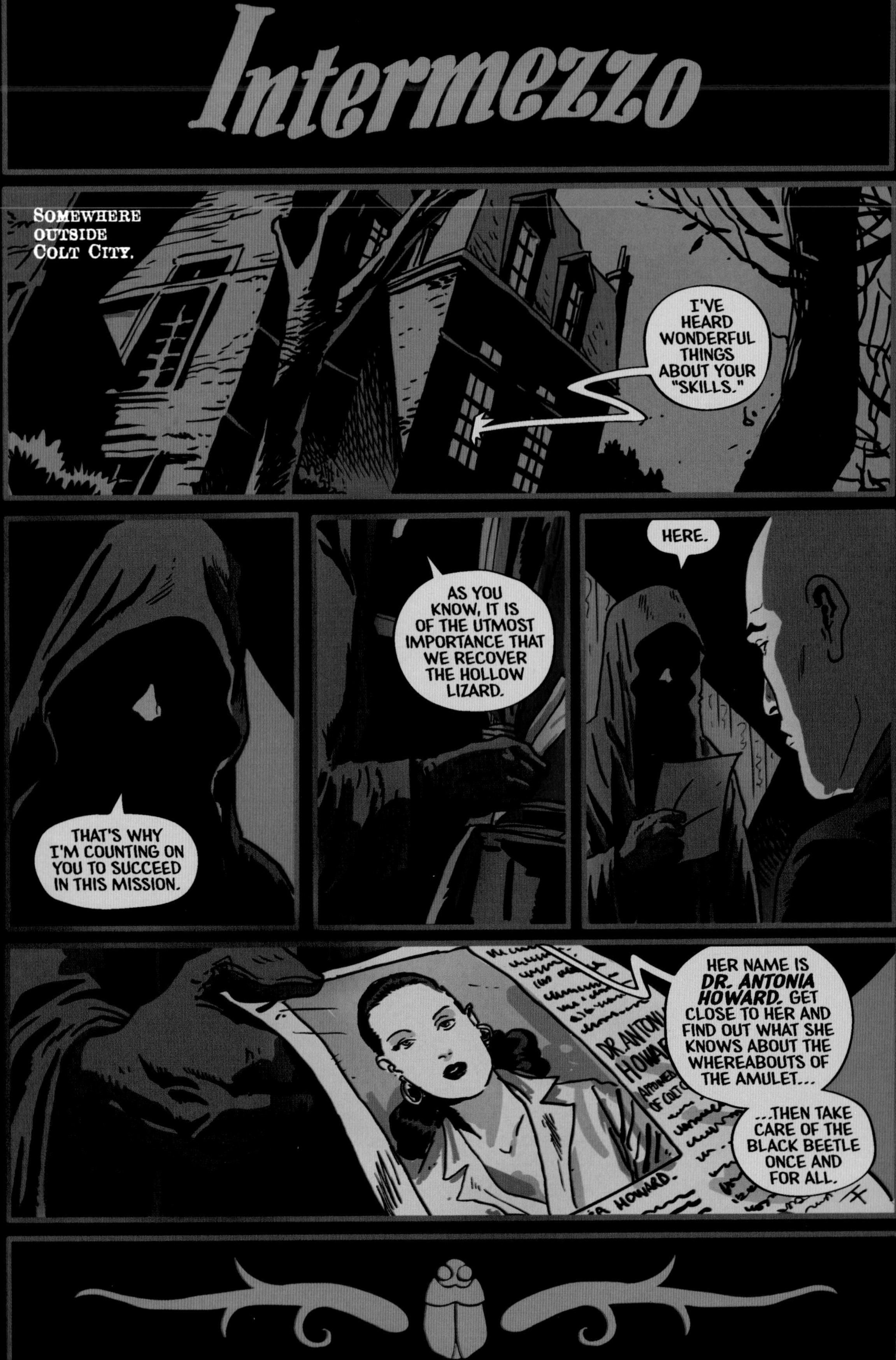
Intermezzo
SOMEWHERE OUTSIDE COLT CITY.
I'VE HEARD WONDERFUL THINGS ABOUT YOUR "SKILLS."
THAT'S WHY I'M COUNTING ON YOU TO SUCCEED IN THIS MISSION.
AS YOU KNOW, IT IS OF THE UTMOST IMPORTANCE THAT WE RECOVER THE HOLLOW LIZARD.
HERE.
HER NAME IS DR. ANTONIA HOWARD. GET CLOSE TO HER AND FIND OUT WHAT SHE KNOWS ABOUT THE WHEREABOUTS OF THE AMULET...
...THEN TAKE CARE OF THE BLACK BEETLE ONCE AND FOR ALL.

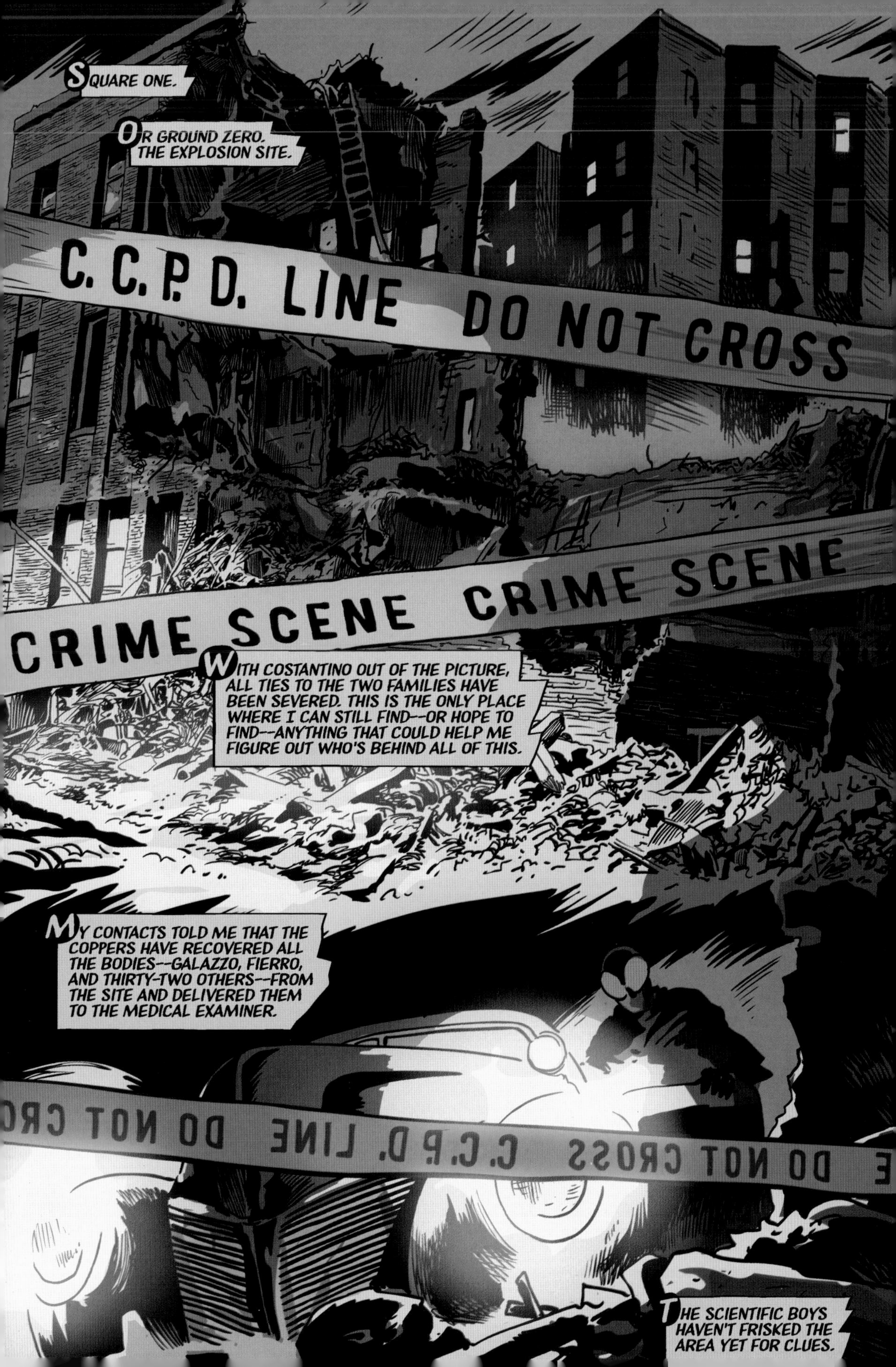
SQUARE ONE.
OR GROUND ZERO. THE EXPLOSION SITE.
C.C.P.D. LINE DO NOT CROSS
CRIME SCENE CRIME SCENE
WITH COSTANTINO OUT OF THE PICTURE, ALL TIES TO THE TWO FAMILIES HAVE BEEN SEVERED. THIS IS THE ONLY PLACE WHERE I CAN STILL FIND--OR HOPE TO FIND--ANYTHING THAT COULD HELP ME FIGURE OUT WHO'S BEHIND ALL OF THIS.
MY CONTACTS TOLD ME THAT THE COPPERS HAVE RECOVERED ALL THE BODIES--GALAZZO, FIERRO, AND THIRTY-TWO OTHERS--FROM THE SITE AND DELIVERED THEM TO THE MEDICAL EXAMINER.
THE SCIENTIFIC BOYS HAVEN'T FRISKED THE AREA YET FOR CLUES.

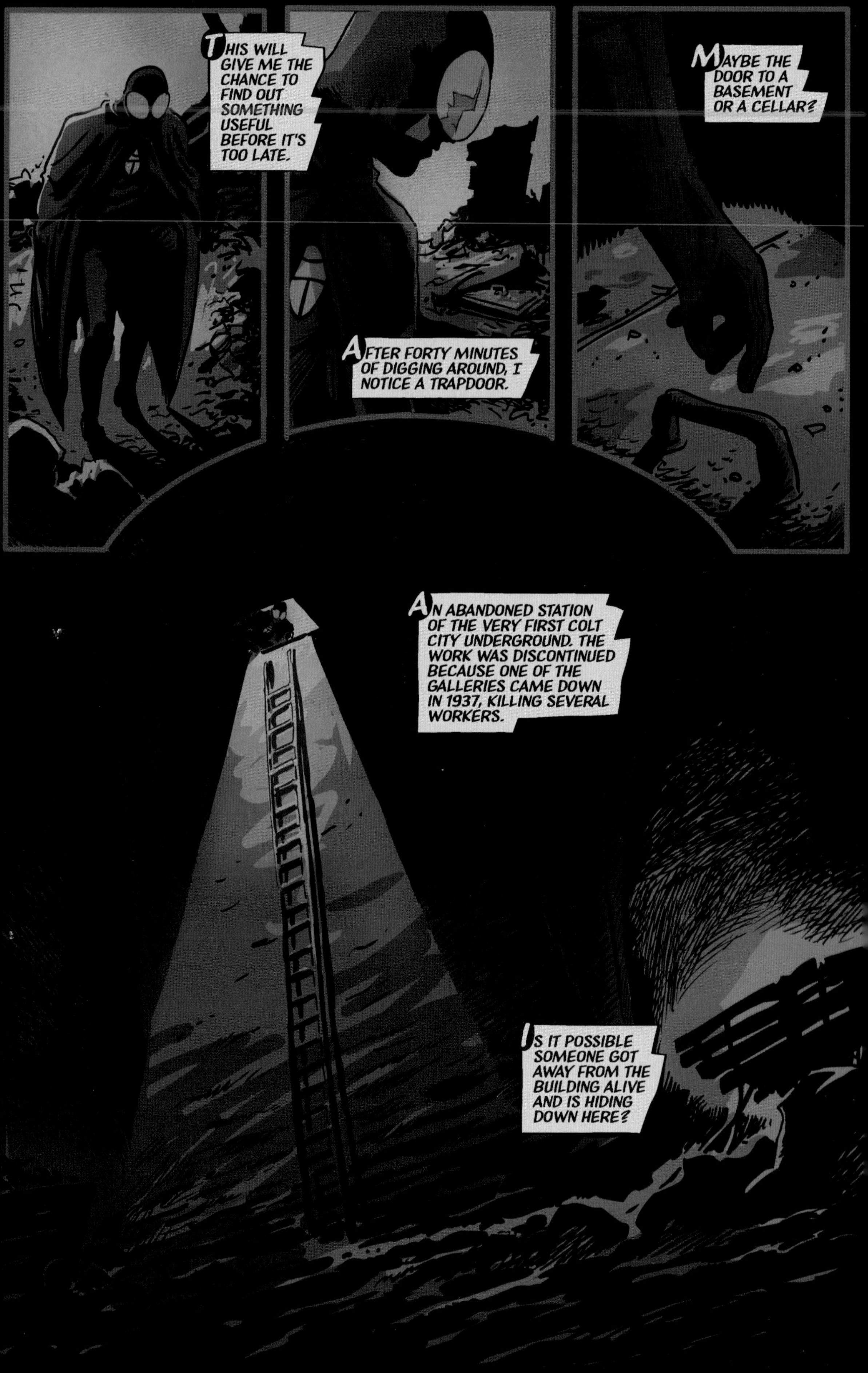
THIS WILL GIVE ME THE CHANCE TO FIND OUT SOMETHING USEFUL BEFORE IT'S TOO LATE.
AFTER FORTY MINUTES OF DIGGING AROUND, I NOTICE A TRAPDOOR.
MAYBE THE DOOR TO A BASEMENT OR A CELLAR?
AN ABANDONED STATION OF THE VERY FIRST COLT CITY UNDERGROUND. THE WORK WAS DISCONTINUED BECAUSE ONE OF THE GALLERIES CAME DOWN IN 1937, KILLING SEVERAL WORKERS.
IS IT POSSIBLE SOMEONE GOT AWAY FROM THE BUILDING ALIVE AND IS HIDING DOWN HERE?

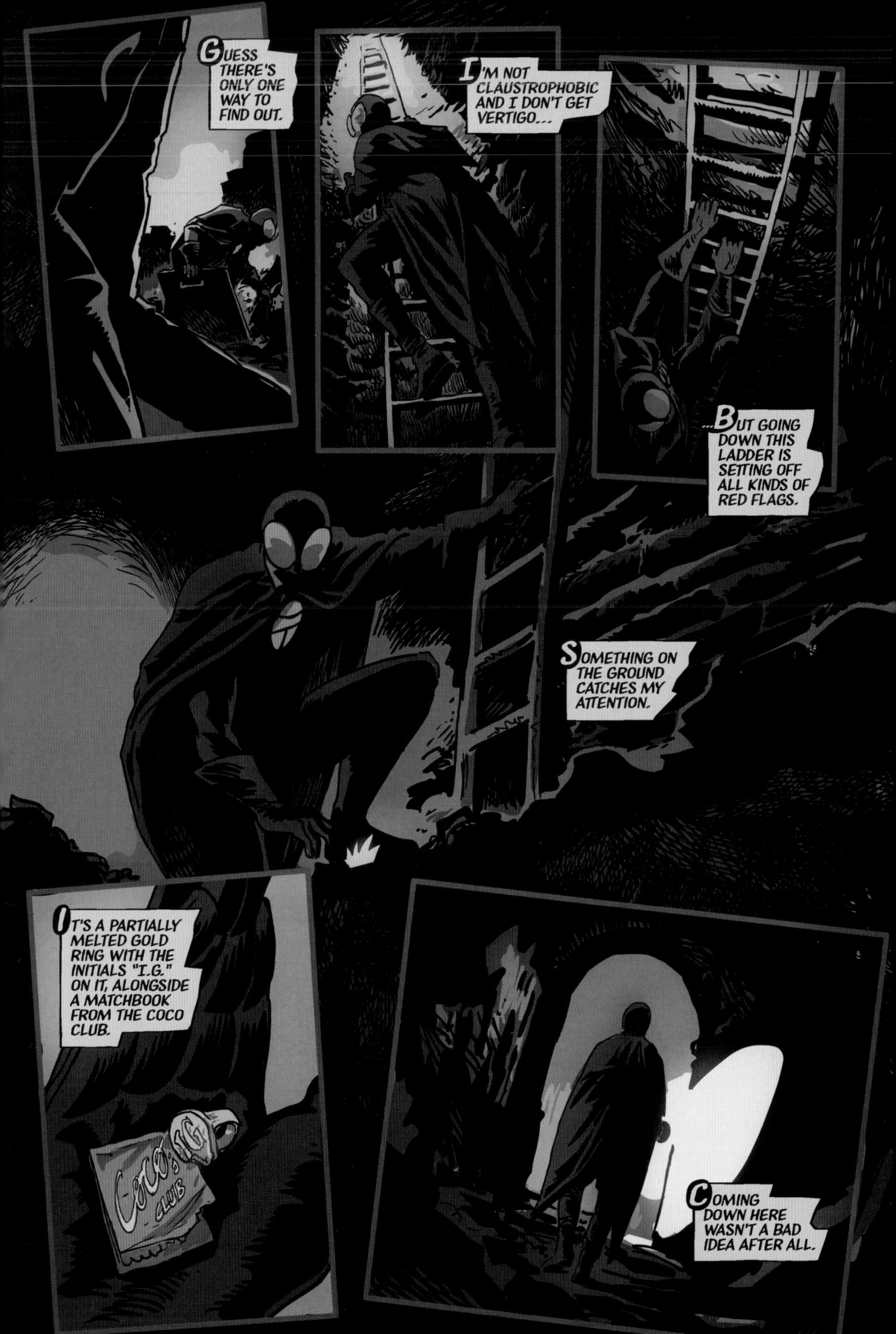
GUESS THERE'S ONLY ONE WAY TO FIND OUT.
I'M NOT CLAUSTROPHOBIC AND I DON'T GET VERTIGO...
...BUT GOING DOWN THIS LADDER IS SETTING OFF ALL KINDS OF RED FLAGS.
SOMETHING ON THE GROUND CATCHES MY ATTENTION.
IT'S A PARTIALLY MELTED GOLD RING WITH THE INITIALS "I.G." ON IT, ALONGSIDE A MATCHBOOK FROM THE COCO CLUB.
COCO's CLUB
COMING DOWN HERE WASN'T A BAD IDEA AFTER ALL.

MAYBE I'LL FIND SOMETHING ELSE.

BESIDES THE RATS. THIS PLACE IS FULL OF THEM.

NO SURPRISE THERE, THOUGH. THIS OLD UNDERGROUND STATION IS CONNECTED TO THE SEWER SYSTEM.

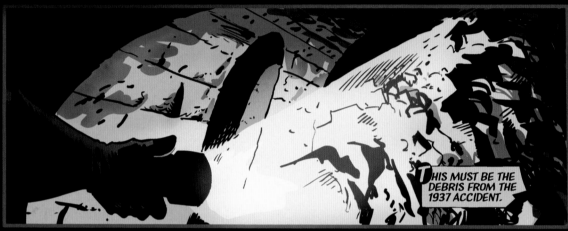

THIS MUST BE THE DEBRIS FROM THE 1937 ACCIDENT.

WELL, THERE'S ONLY ONE TUNNEL LEFT.

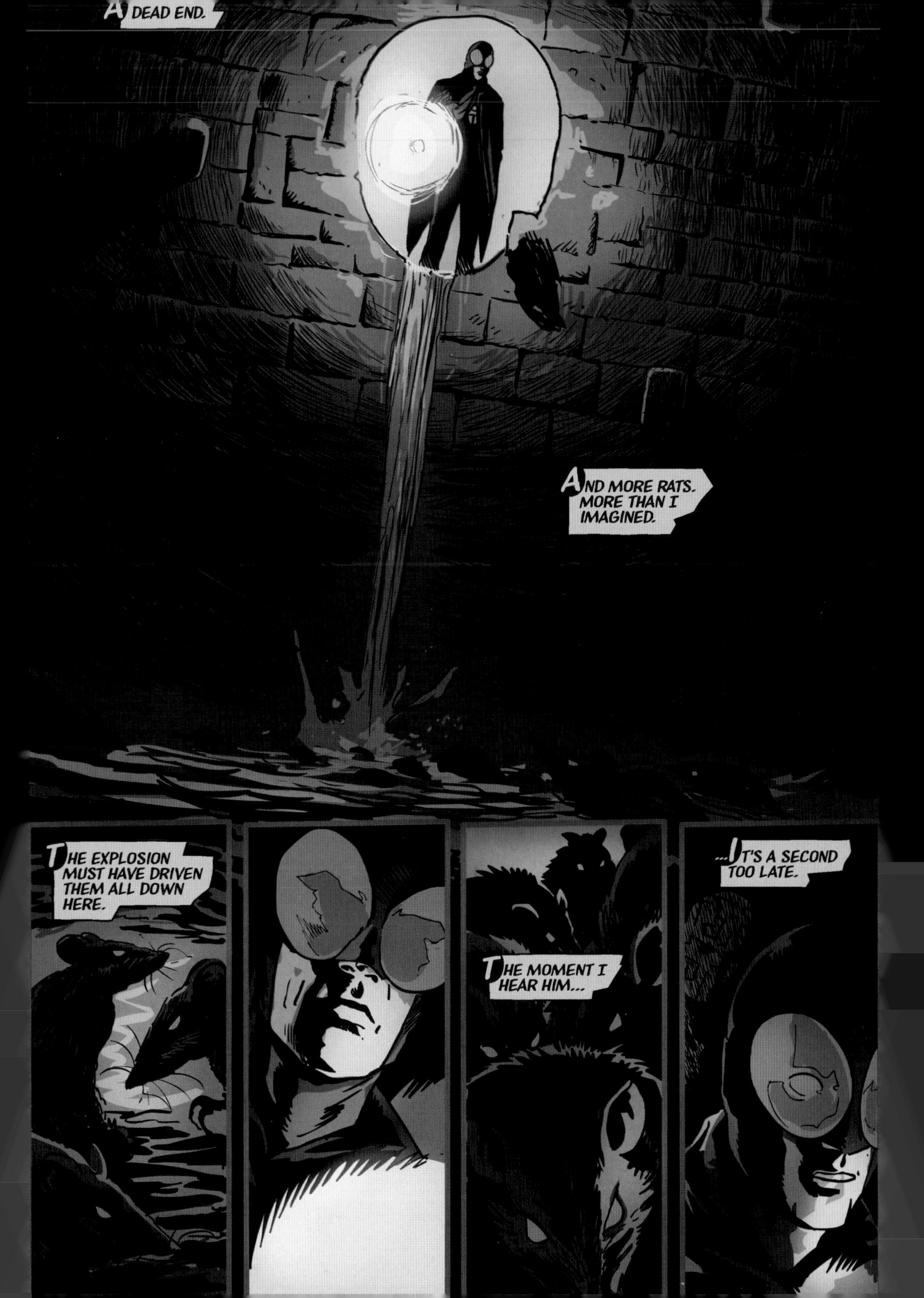
A DEAD END.
AND MORE RATS. MORE THAN I IMAGINED.
THE EXPLOSION MUST HAVE DRIVEN THEM ALL DOWN HERE.
THE MOMENT I HEAR HIM...
...IT'S A SECOND TOO LATE.

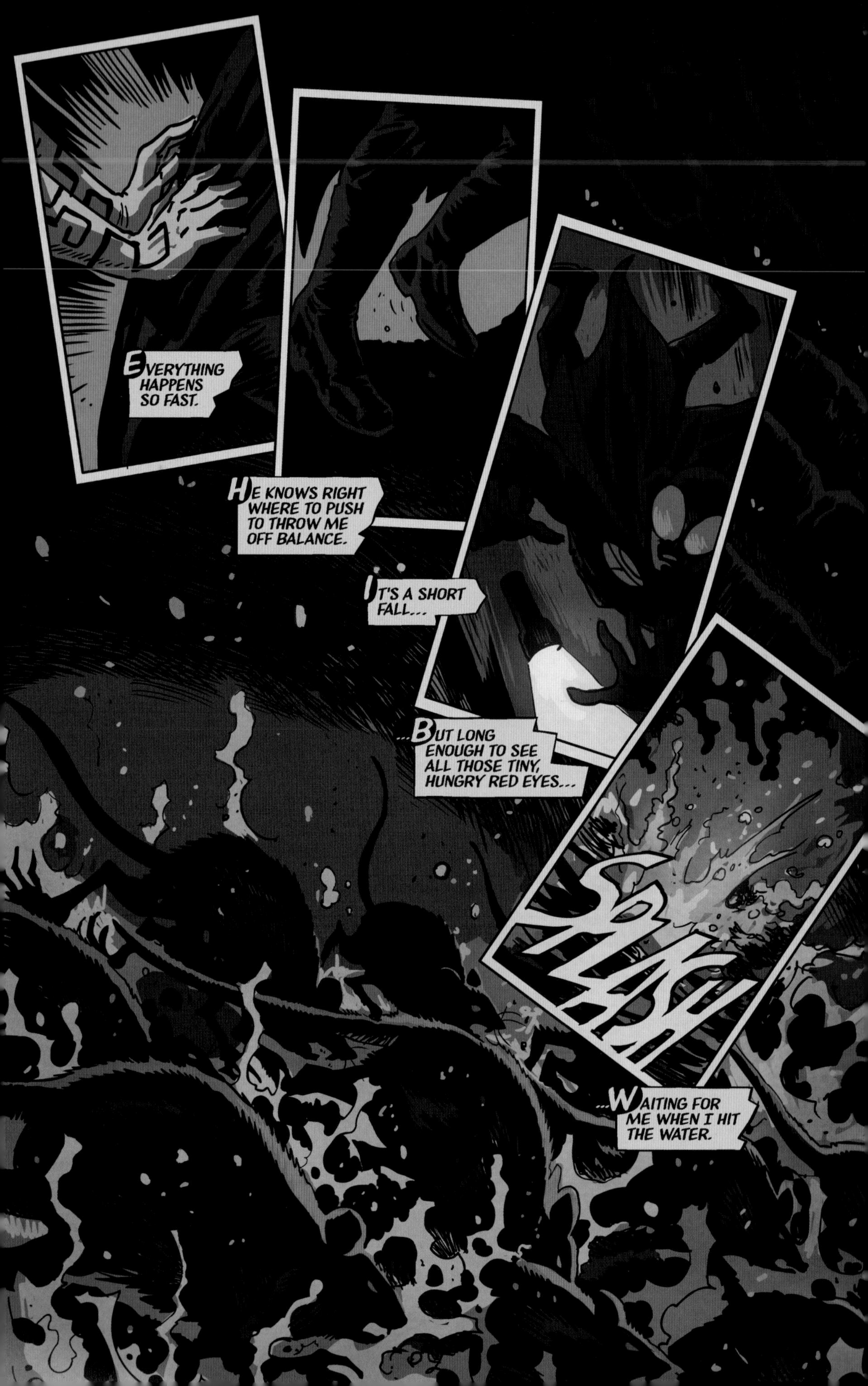
EVERYTHING HAPPENS SO FAST.
HE KNOWS RIGHT WHERE TO PUSH TO THROW ME OFF BALANCE.
IT'S A SHORT FALL...
...BUT LONG ENOUGH TO SEE ALL THOSE TINY, HUNGRY RED EYES...
SPLASH
...WAITING FOR ME WHEN I HIT THE WATER.

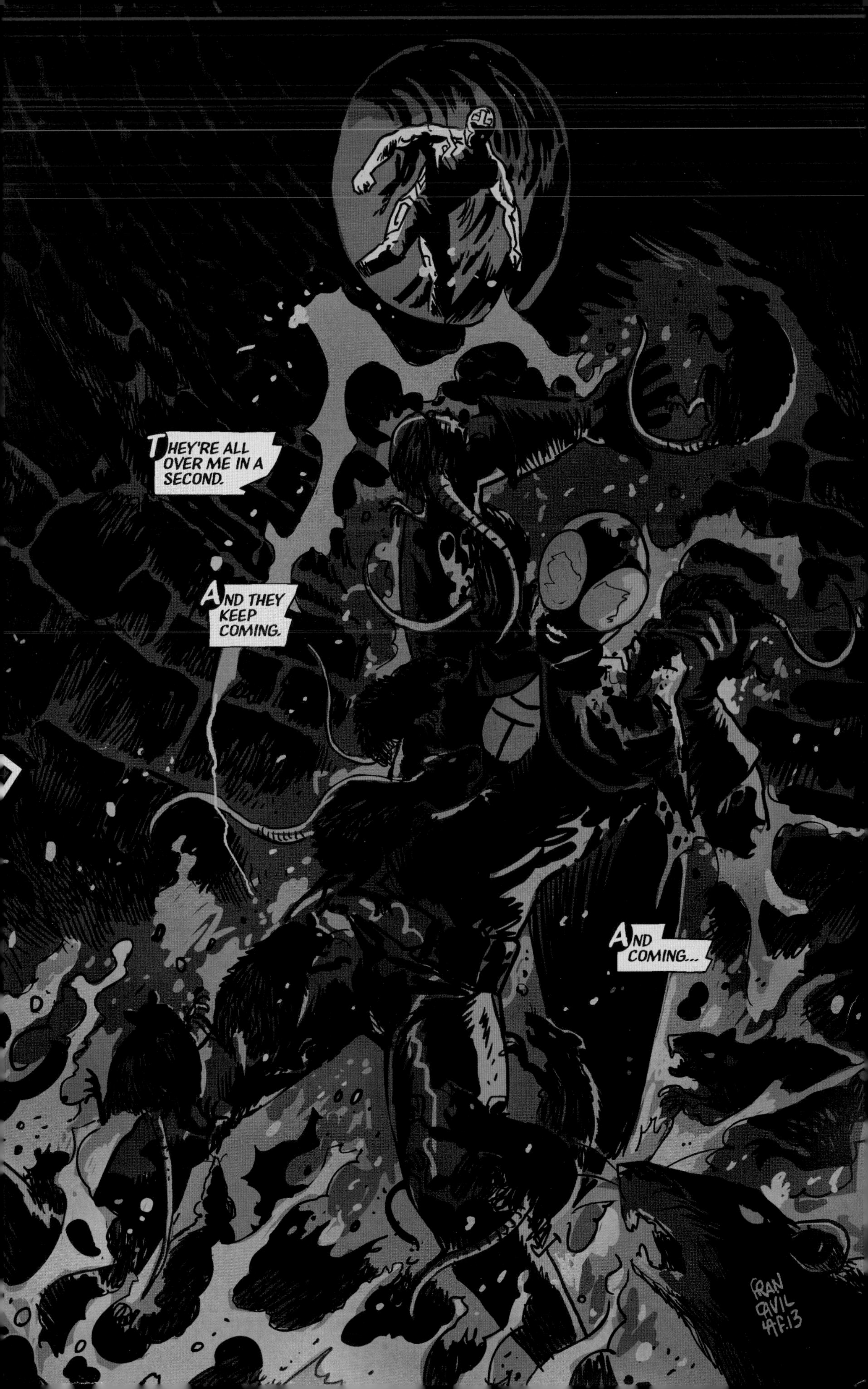
THEY'RE ALL OVER ME IN A SECOND.
AND THEY KEEP COMING.
AND COMING...
FRAN CAVIL 4 AF.13

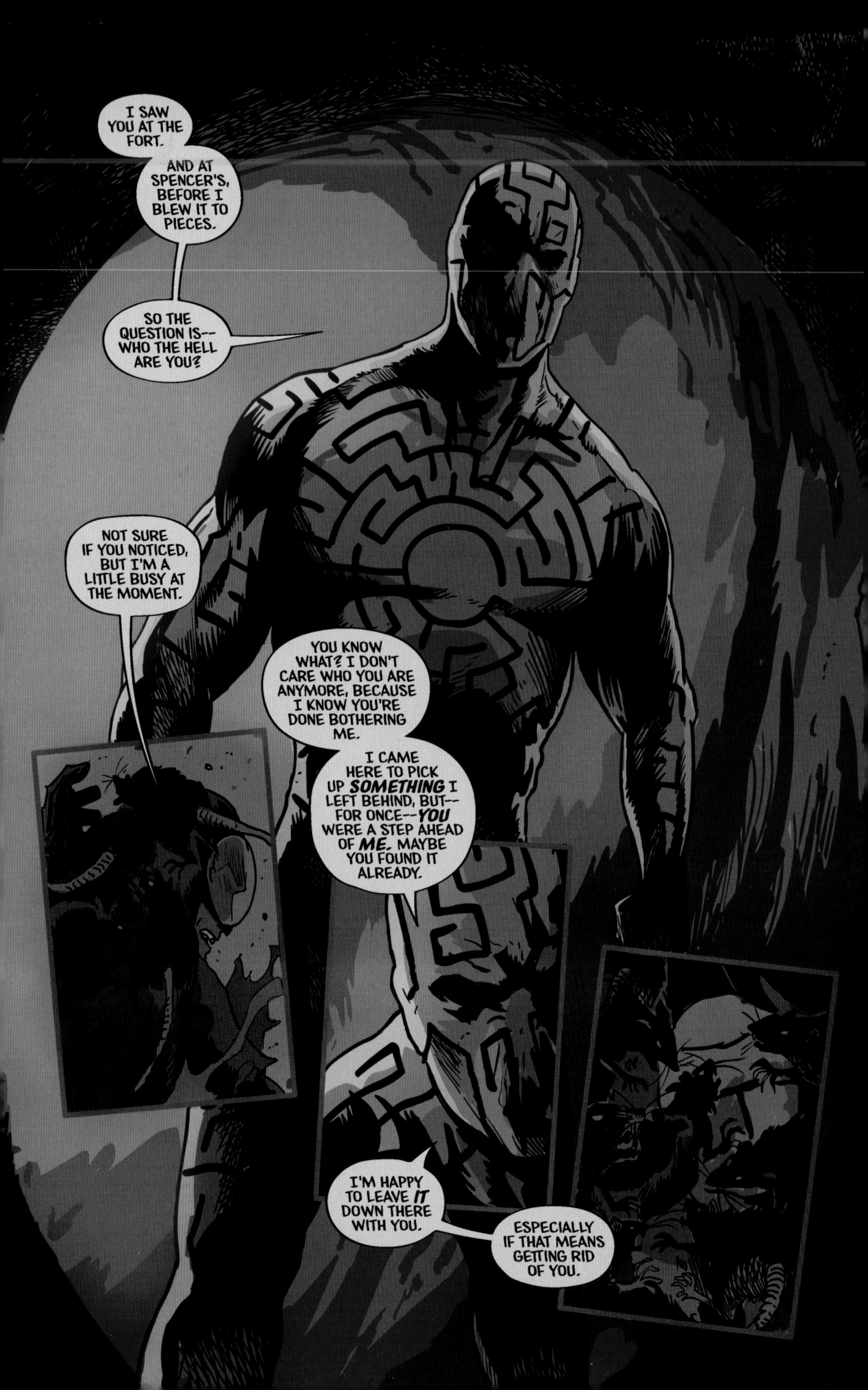
I SAW YOU AT THE FORT.
AND AT SPENCER'S, BEFORE I BLEW IT TO PIECES.
SO THE QUESTION IS-- WHO THE HELL ARE YOU?
NOT SURE IF YOU NOTICED, BUT I'M A LITTLE BUSY AT THE MOMENT.
YOU KNOW WHAT? I DON'T CARE WHO YOU ARE ANYMORE, BECAUSE I KNOW YOU'RE DONE BOTHERING ME.
I CAME HERE TO PICK UP SOMETHING I LEFT BEHIND, BUT-- FOR ONCE--YOU WERE A STEP AHEAD OF ME. MAYBE YOU FOUND IT ALREADY.
I'M HAPPY TO LEAVE IT DOWN THERE WITH YOU.
ESPECIALLY IF THAT MEANS GETTING RID OF YOU.

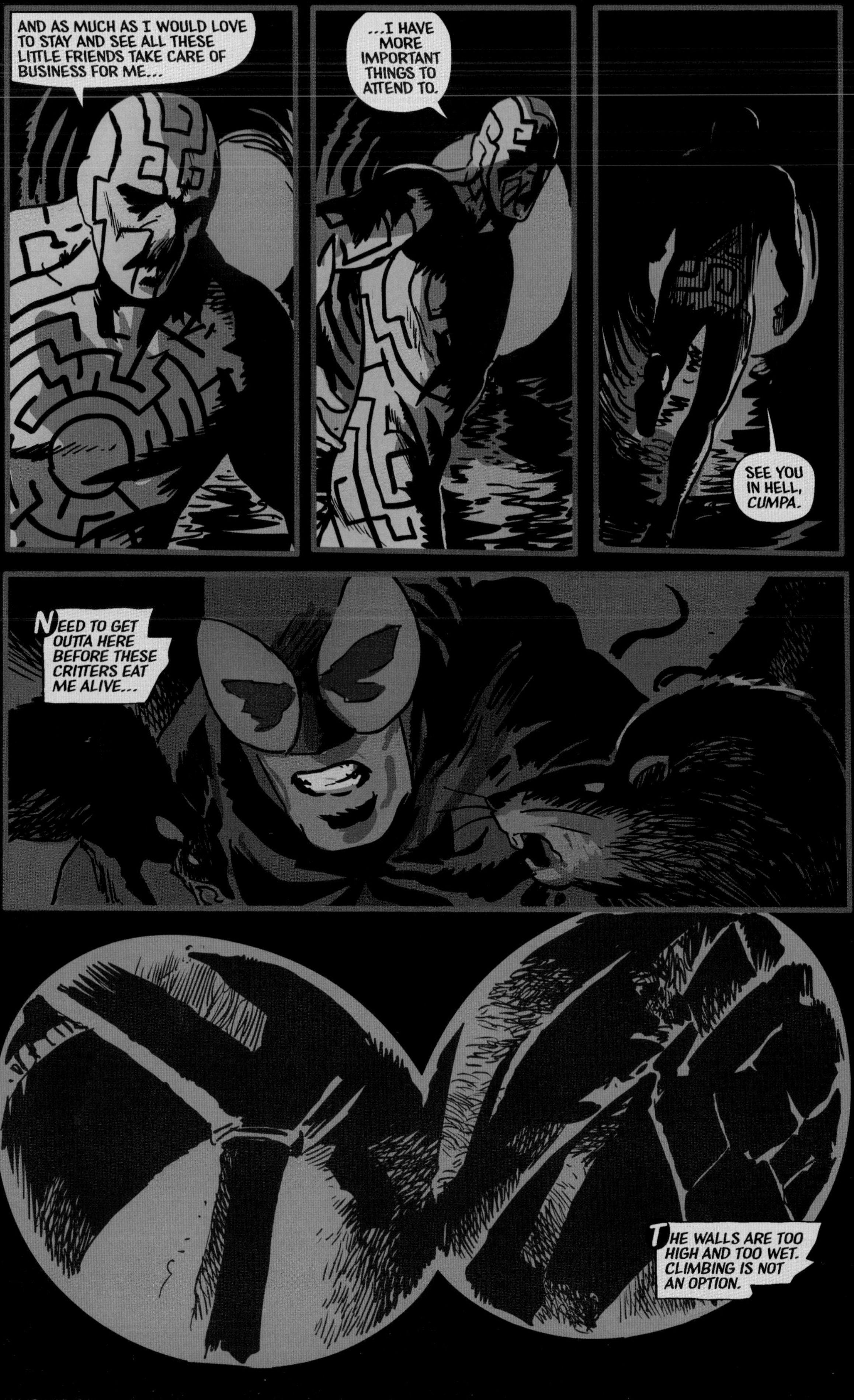
AND AS MUCH AS I WOULD LOVE TO STAY AND SEE ALL THESE LITTLE FRIENDS TAKE CARE OF BUSINESS FOR ME...
...I HAVE MORE IMPORTANT THINGS TO ATTEND TO.
SEE YOU IN HELL, CUMPA.
NEED TO GET OUTTA HERE BEFORE THESE CRITTERS EAT ME ALIVE...
THE WALLS ARE TOO HIGH AND TOO WET. CLIMBING IS NOT AN OPTION.

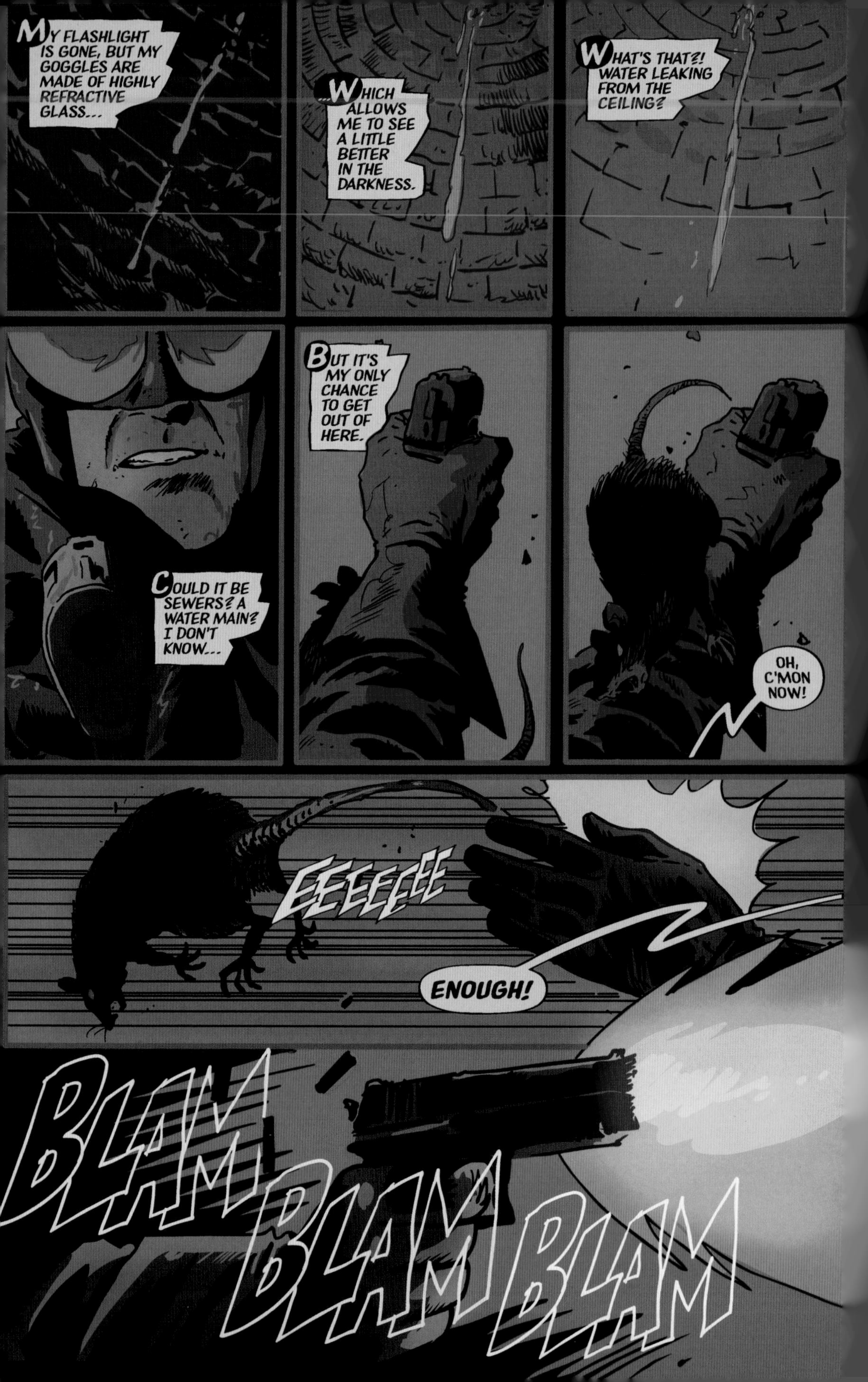
MY FLASHLIGHT IS GONE, BUT MY GOGGLES ARE MADE OF HIGHLY REFRACTIVE GLASS...
...WHICH ALLOWS ME TO SEE A LITTLE BETTER IN THE DARKNESS.
WHAT'S THAT?! WATER LEAKING FROM THE CEILING?
COULD IT BE SEWERS? A WATER MAIN? I DON'T KNOW...
BUT IT'S MY ONLY CHANCE TO GET OUT OF HERE.
OH, C'MON NOW!
EEEEEEE
ENOUGH!
BLAM BLAM BLAM

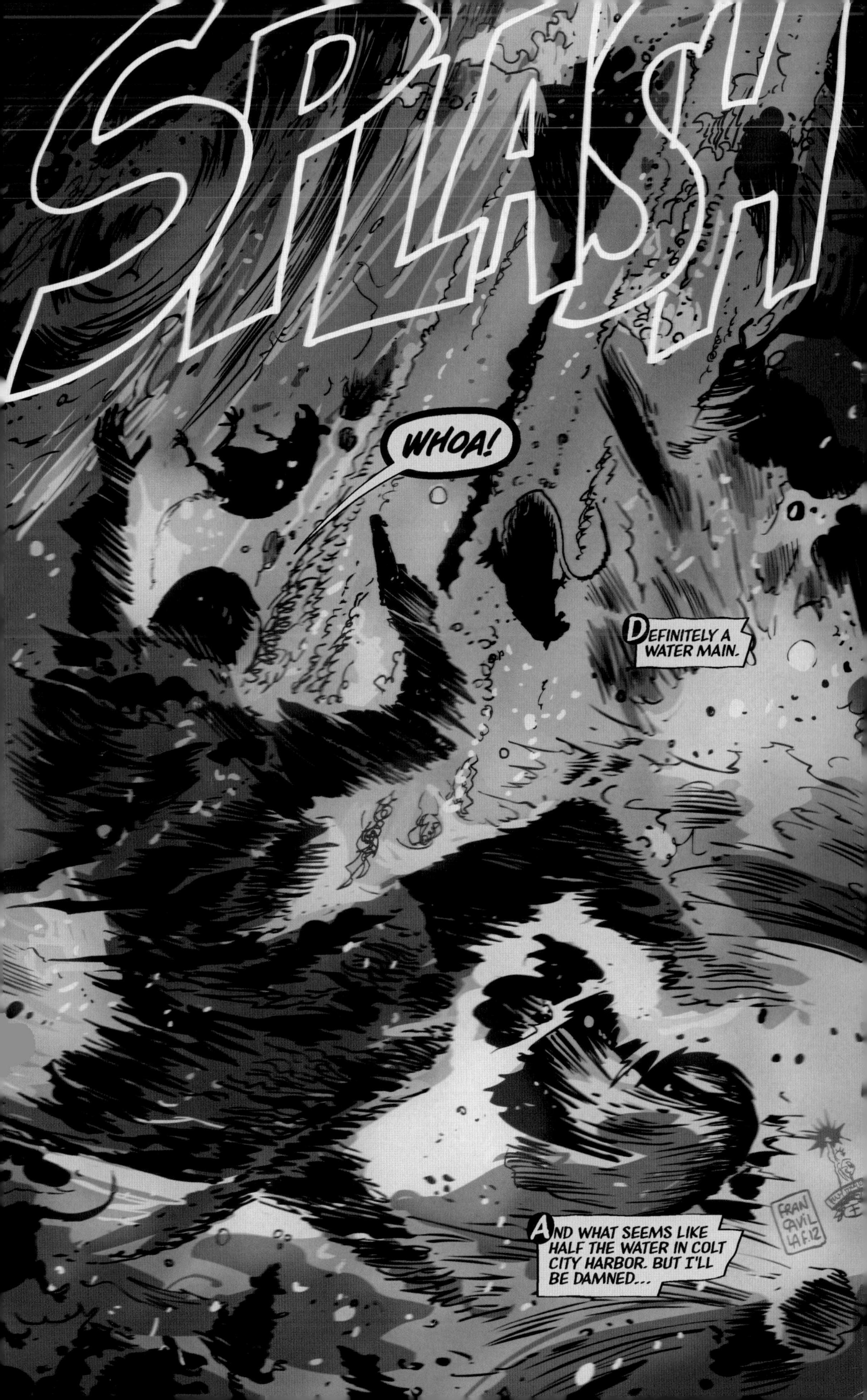
SPLASH
WHOA!
DEFINITELY A WATER MAIN.
AND WHAT SEEMS LIKE HALF THE WATER IN COLT CITY HARBOR. BUT I'LL BE DAMNED...
FRAN GAVIL

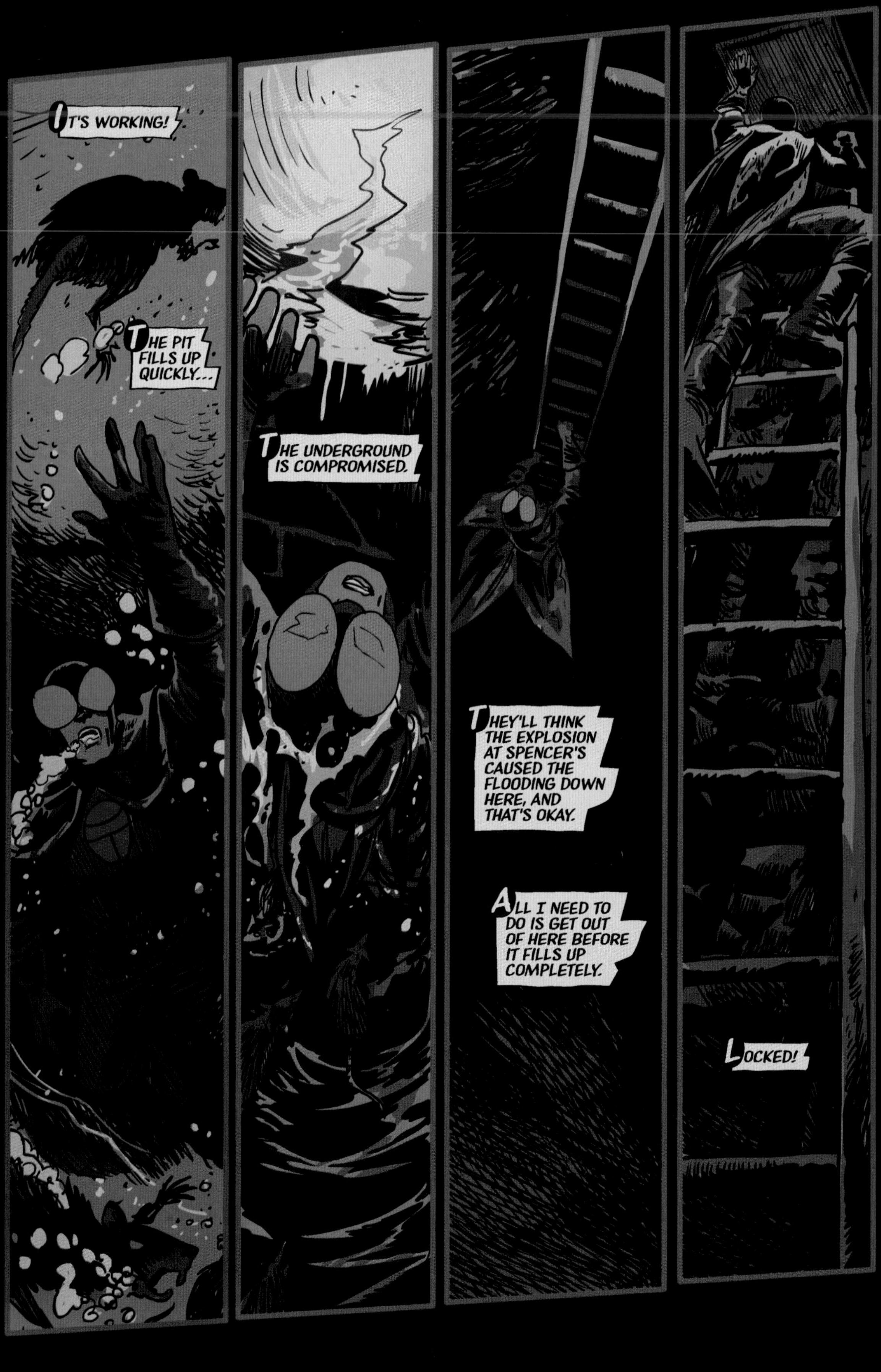
IT'S WORKING!
THE PIT FILLS UP QUICKLY...
THE UNDERGROUND IS COMPROMISED.
THEY'LL THINK THE EXPLOSION AT SPENCER'S CAUSED THE FLOODING DOWN HERE, AND THAT'S OKAY.
ALL I NEED TO DO IS GET OUT OF HERE BEFORE IT FILLS UP COMPLETELY.
LOCKED!

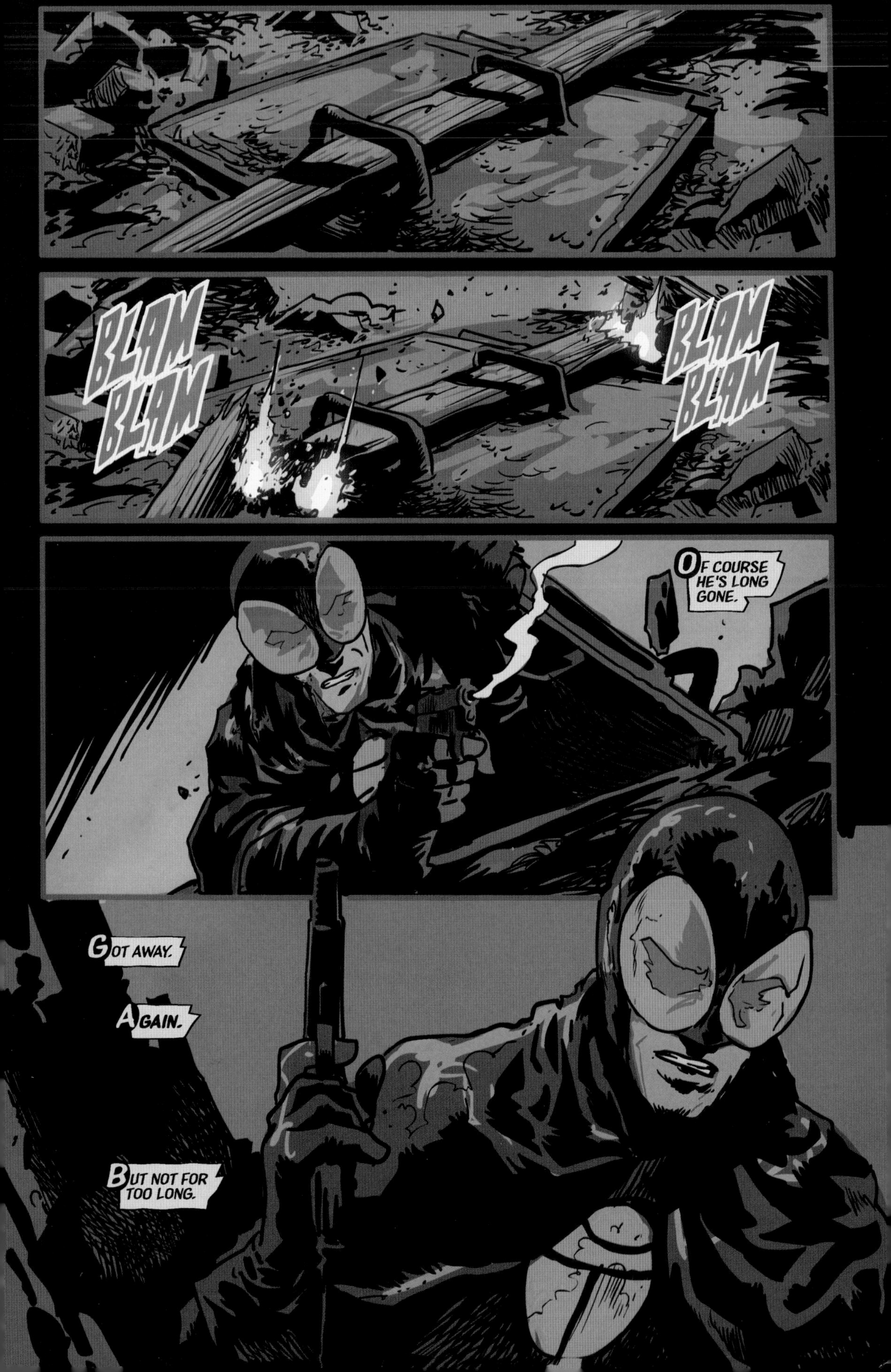
BLAM
BLAM
BLAM
BLAM
OF COURSE HE'S LONG GONE.
GOT AWAY.
AGAIN.
BUT NOT FOR TOO LONG.

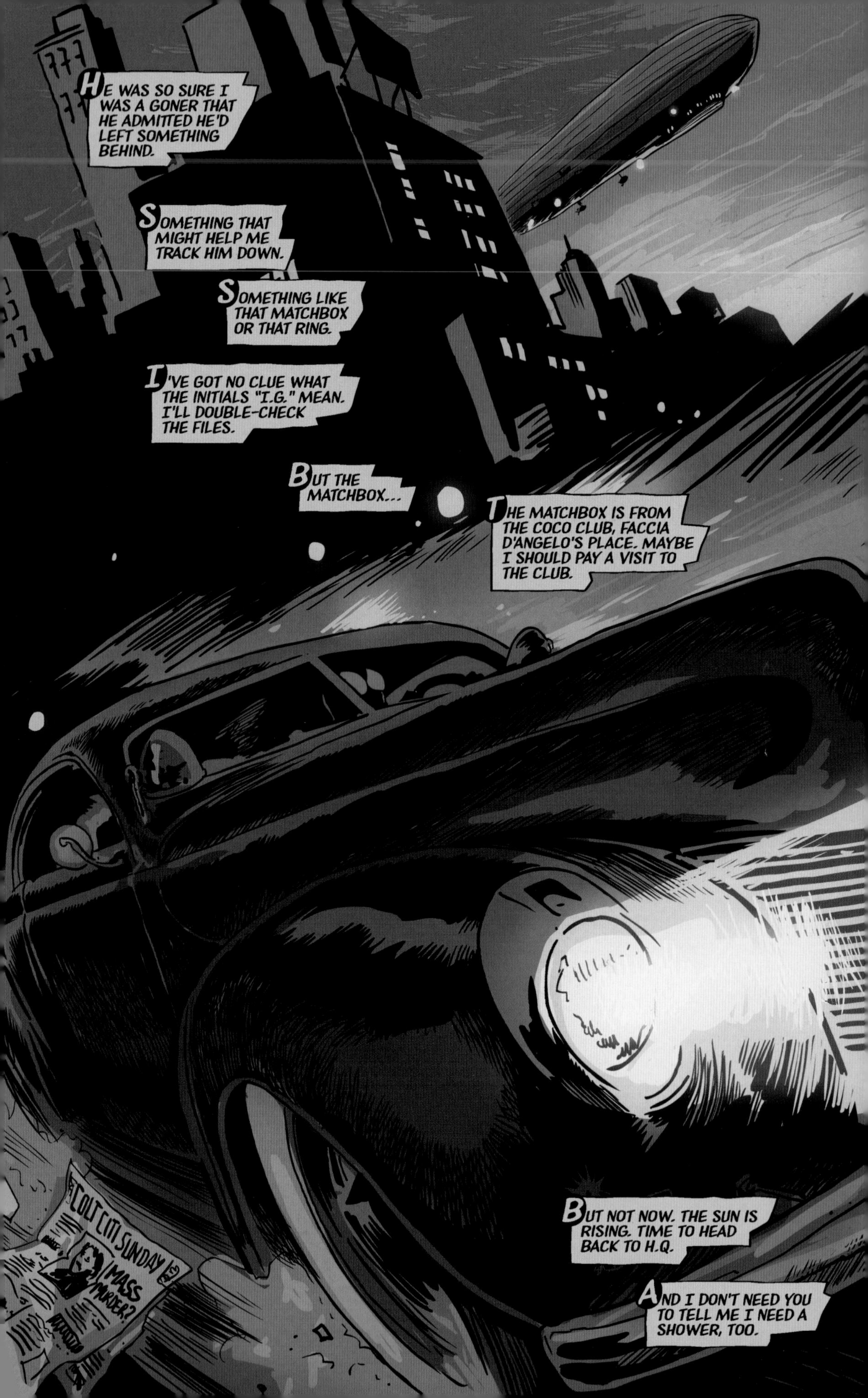
HE WAS SO SURE I WAS A GONER THAT HE ADMITTED HE'D LEFT SOMETHING BEHIND.
SOMETHING THAT MIGHT HELP ME TRACK HIM DOWN.
SOMETHING LIKE THAT MATCHBOX OR THAT RING.
I'VE GOT NO CLUE WHAT THE INITIALS "I.G." MEAN. I'LL DOUBLE-CHECK THE FILES.
BUT THE MATCHBOX...
THE MATCHBOX IS FROM THE COCO CLUB, FACCIA D'ANGELO'S PLACE. MAYBE I SHOULD PAY A VISIT TO THE CLUB.
COLT CITY SUNDAY
MASS MURDER?
BUT NOT NOW. THE SUN IS RISING. TIME TO HEAD BACK TO H.Q.
AND I DON'T NEED YOU TO TELL ME I NEED A SHOWER, TOO.

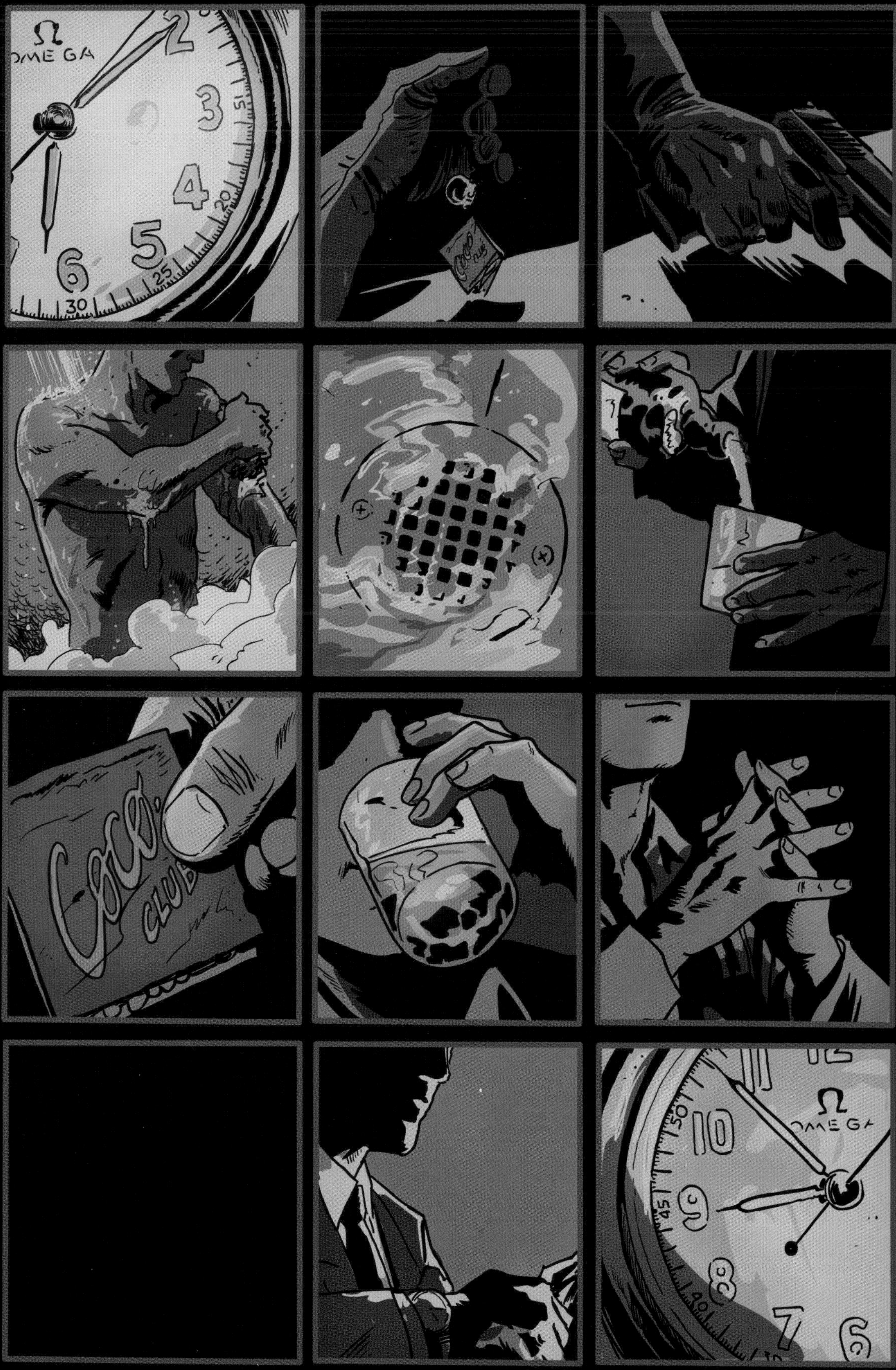
OMEGA
Coco CLUB
OMEGA

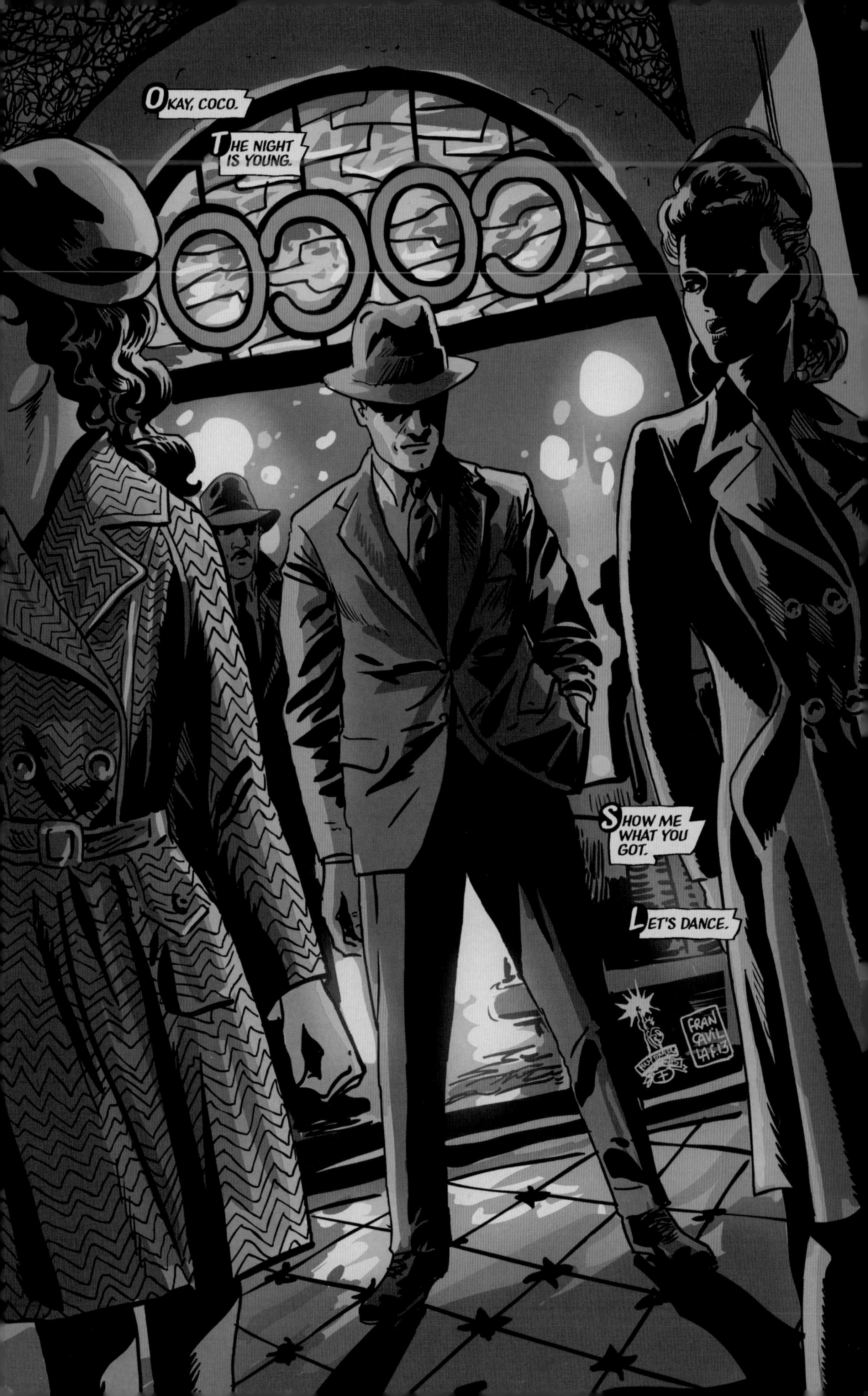
OKAY, COCO.
THE NIGHT IS YOUNG.
SHOW ME WHAT YOU GOT.
LET'S DANCE.

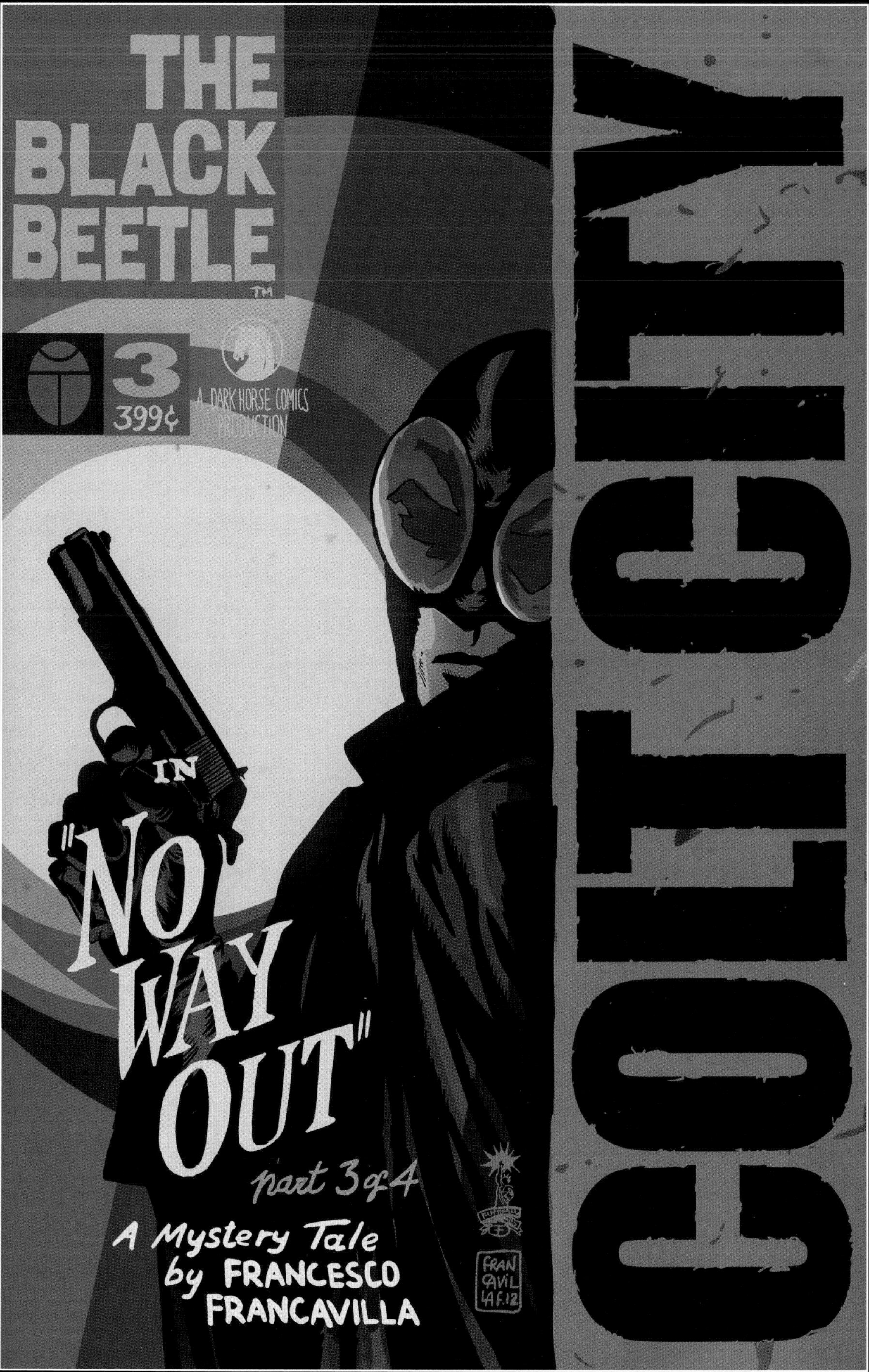
THE BLACK BEETLE ™
3
399¢
A DARK HORSE COMICS PRODUCTION
IN
"NO WAY OUT"
part 3 of 4
A Mystery Tale by FRANCESCO FRANCAVILLA
COLT CITY
FRAN CAVIL LA F.12

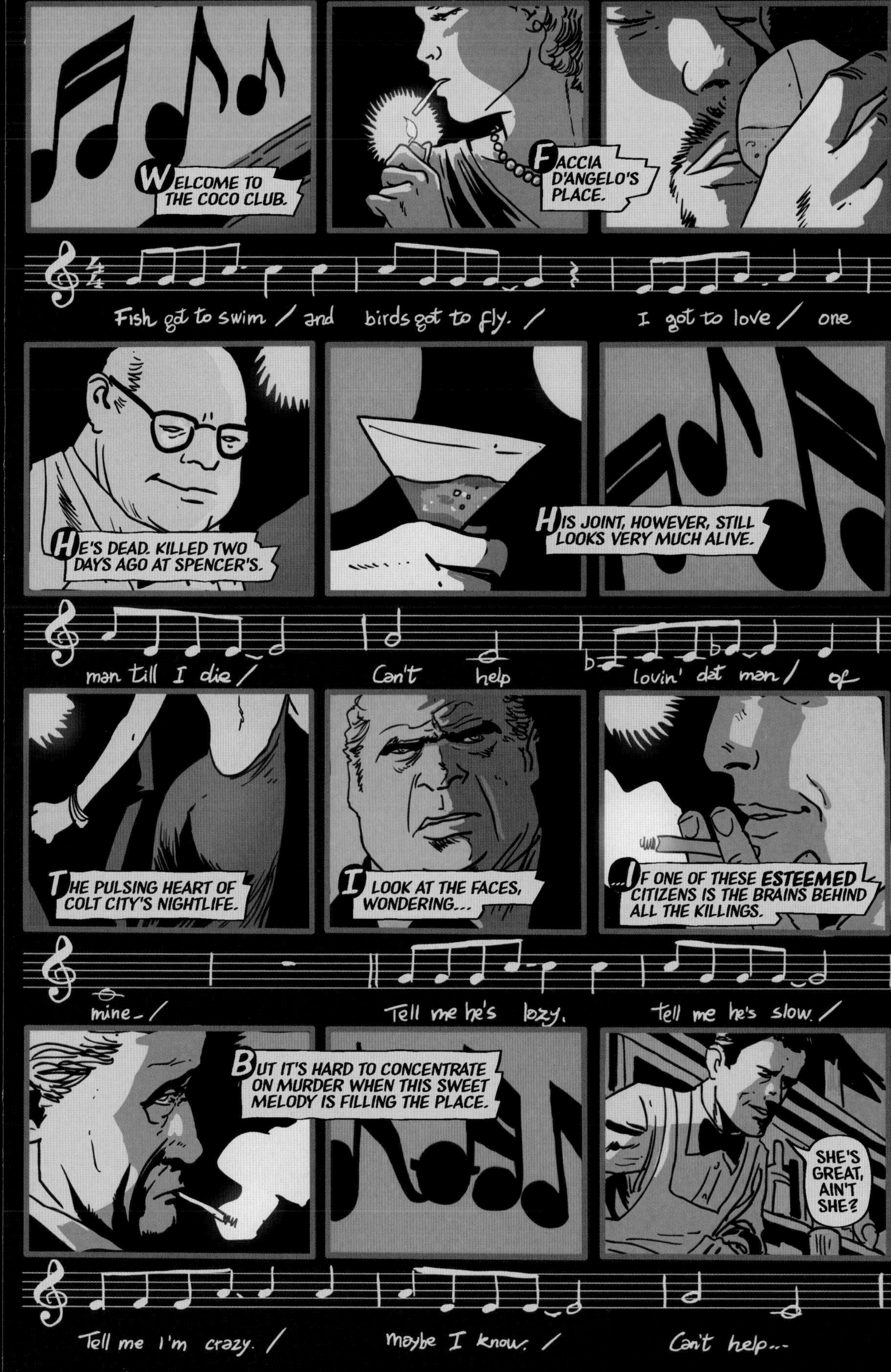
WELCOME TO THE COCO CLUB.
FACCIA D'ANGELO'S PLACE.
Fish got to swim / and birds got to fly. / I got to love / one
HE'S DEAD. KILLED TWO DAYS AGO AT SPENCER'S.
HIS JOINT, HOWEVER, STILL LOOKS VERY MUCH ALIVE.
man till I die / Can't help lovin' dat man / of
THE PULSING HEART OF COLT CITY'S NIGHTLIFE.
I LOOK AT THE FACES, WONDERING...
...IF ONE OF THESE ESTEEMED CITIZENS IS THE BRAINS BEHIND ALL THE KILLINGS.
mine_ / Tell me he's lazy. tell me he's slow. /
BUT IT'S HARD TO CONCENTRATE ON MURDER WHEN THIS SWEET MELODY IS FILLING THE PLACE.
SHE'S GREAT, AIN'T SHE?
Tell me I'm crazy. / maybe I know. / Can't help...

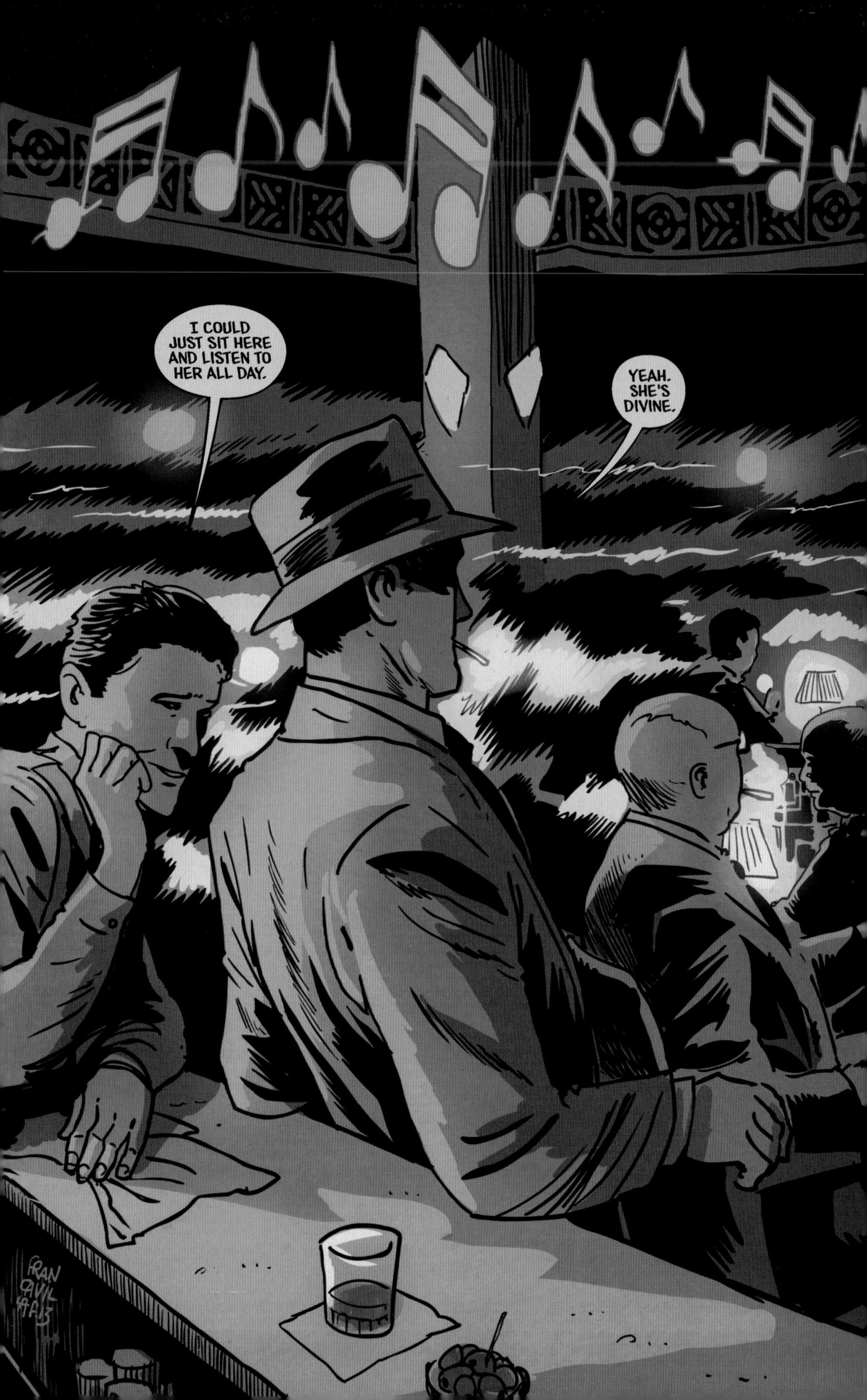
I COULD JUST SIT HERE AND LISTEN TO HER ALL DAY.
YEAH. SHE'S DIVINE.

♪ LOVIN' DAT MAN OF MINE. ♫
THE BLACK BEETLE™
"NO WAY OUT"
part 3 of 4
A Mystery Tale by FRANCESCO FRANCAVILLA
the BLACK BEETLE™ CREATED BY FRANCESCO FRANCAVILLA

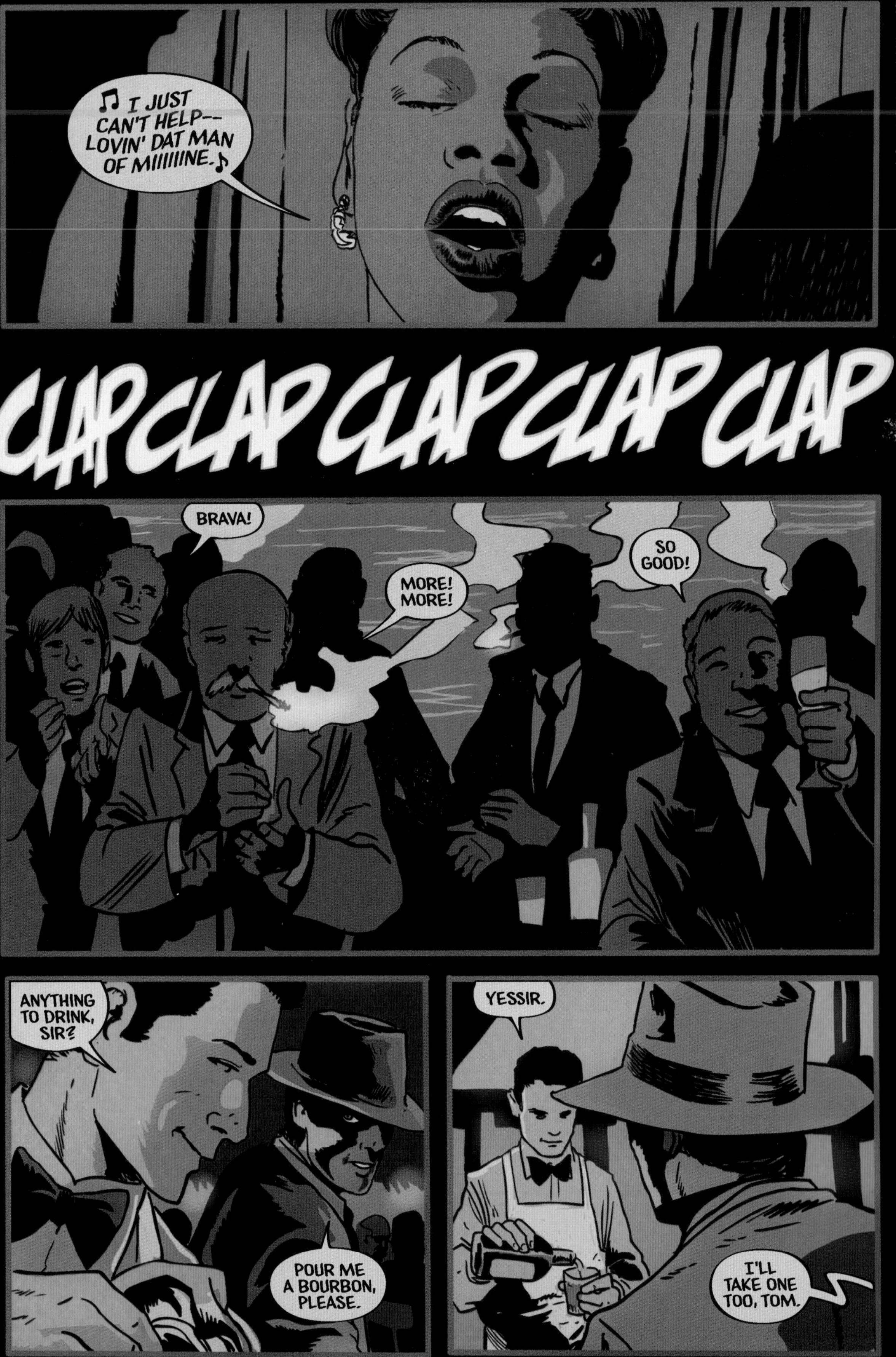

♫ I JUST CAN'T HELP-- LOVIN' DAT MAN OF MIIIIINE. ♪
CLAP CLAP CLAP CLAP CLAP
BRAVA!
MORE! MORE!
SO GOOD!
ANYTHING TO DRINK, SIR?
POUR ME A BOURBON, PLEASE.
YESSIR.
I'LL TAKE ONE TOO, TOM.

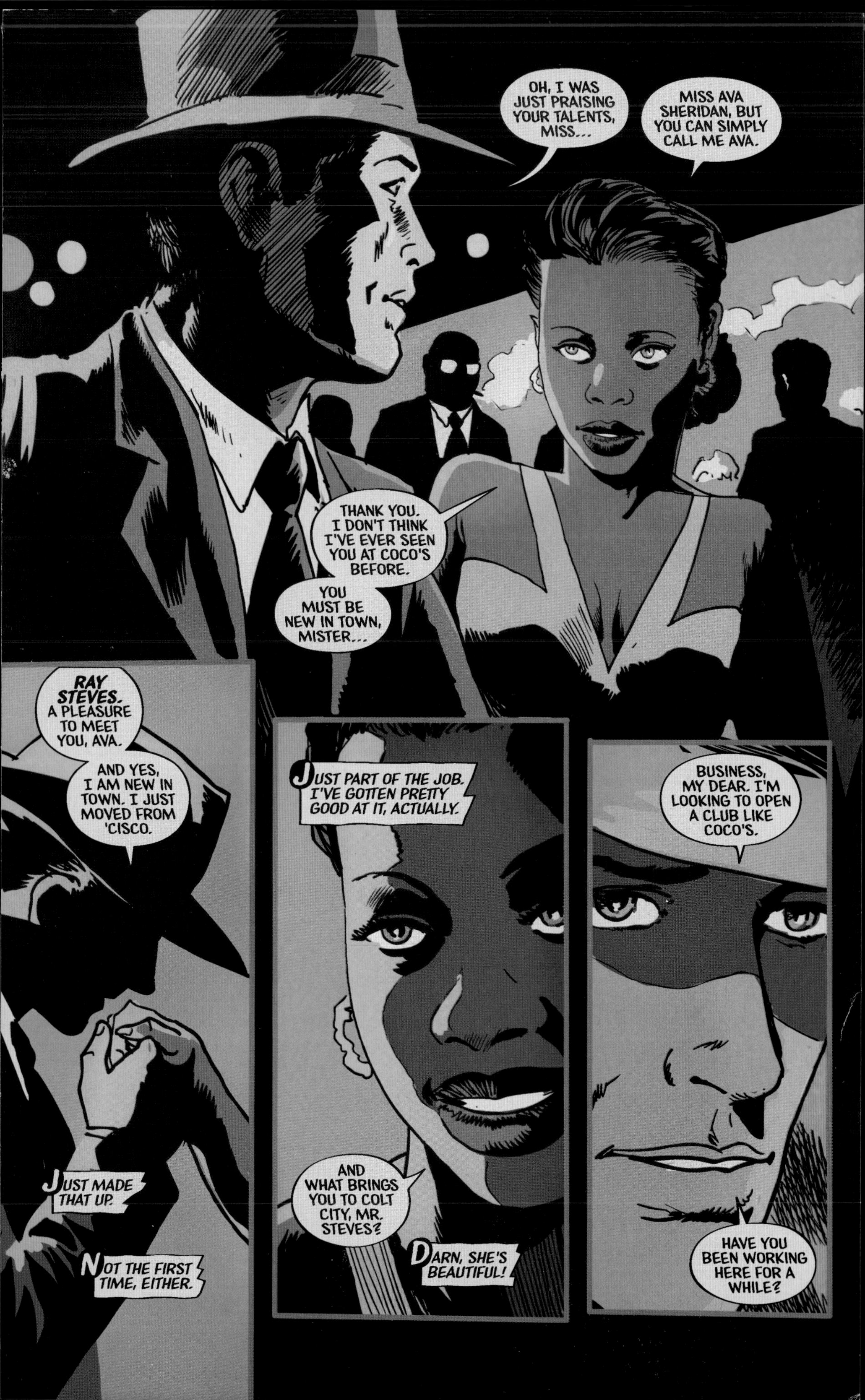
OH, I WAS JUST PRAISING YOUR TALENTS, MISS...
MISS AVA SHERIDAN, BUT YOU CAN SIMPLY CALL ME AVA.
THANK YOU. I DON'T THINK I'VE EVER SEEN YOU AT COCO'S BEFORE.
YOU MUST BE NEW IN TOWN, MISTER...
RAY STEVES. A PLEASURE TO MEET YOU, AVA.
AND YES, I AM NEW IN TOWN. I JUST MOVED FROM 'CISCO.
JUST MADE THAT UP.
NOT THE FIRST TIME, EITHER.
JUST PART OF THE JOB. I'VE GOTTEN PRETTY GOOD AT IT, ACTUALLY.
AND WHAT BRINGS YOU TO COLT CITY, MR. STEVES?
DARN, SHE'S BEAUTIFUL!
BUSINESS, MY DEAR. I'M LOOKING TO OPEN A CLUB LIKE COCO'S.
HAVE YOU BEEN WORKING HERE FOR A WHILE?

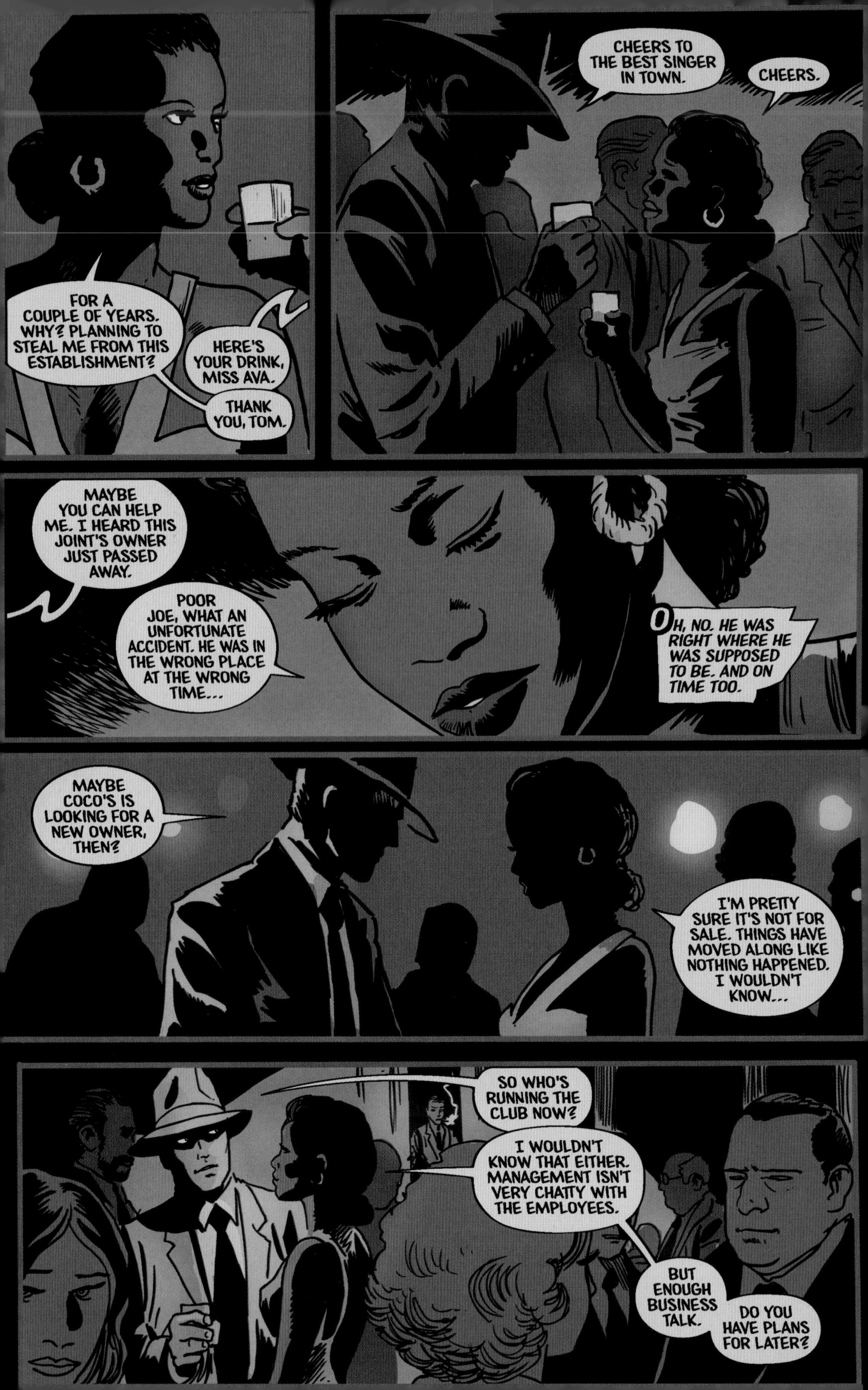
FOR A COUPLE OF YEARS. WHY? PLANNING TO STEAL ME FROM THIS ESTABLISHMENT?
HERE'S YOUR DRINK, MISS AVA.
THANK YOU, TOM.
CHEERS TO THE BEST SINGER IN TOWN.
CHEERS.
MAYBE YOU CAN HELP ME. I HEARD THIS JOINT'S OWNER JUST PASSED AWAY.
POOR JOE, WHAT AN UNFORTUNATE ACCIDENT. HE WAS IN THE WRONG PLACE AT THE WRONG TIME...
OH, NO. HE WAS RIGHT WHERE HE WAS SUPPOSED TO BE. AND ON TIME TOO.
MAYBE COCO'S IS LOOKING FOR A NEW OWNER, THEN?
I'M PRETTY SURE IT'S NOT FOR SALE. THINGS HAVE MOVED ALONG LIKE NOTHING HAPPENED. I WOULDN'T KNOW...
SO WHO'S RUNNING THE CLUB NOW?
I WOULDN'T KNOW THAT EITHER. MANAGEMENT ISN'T VERY CHATTY WITH THE EMPLOYEES.
BUT ENOUGH BUSINESS TALK.
DO YOU HAVE PLANS FOR LATER?

I HAD A COUPLA THINGS, BUT YOU MADE ME FORGET THEM, SWEETHEART.

WAIT! THAT GUY LOOKS LIKE FIERRO! HOW IS THAT POSSIBLE?!

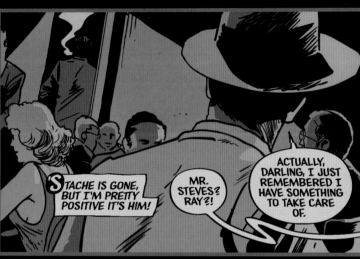

STACHE IS GONE, BUT I'M PRETTY POSITIVE IT'S HIM!

MR. STEVES? RAY?!

ACTUALLY, DARLING, I JUST REMEMBERED I HAVE SOMETHING TO TAKE CARE OF.

RAIN CHECK?

BUT...

I'LL SEE YOU AGAIN. I PROMISE.

WHERE DID HE GO? I CAN'T LOSE HIM.

THE BACK DOOR! THAT'S THE ONLY WAY OUT.

LET'S SEE IF IT'S REALLY YOU, FACCIA D'AN--

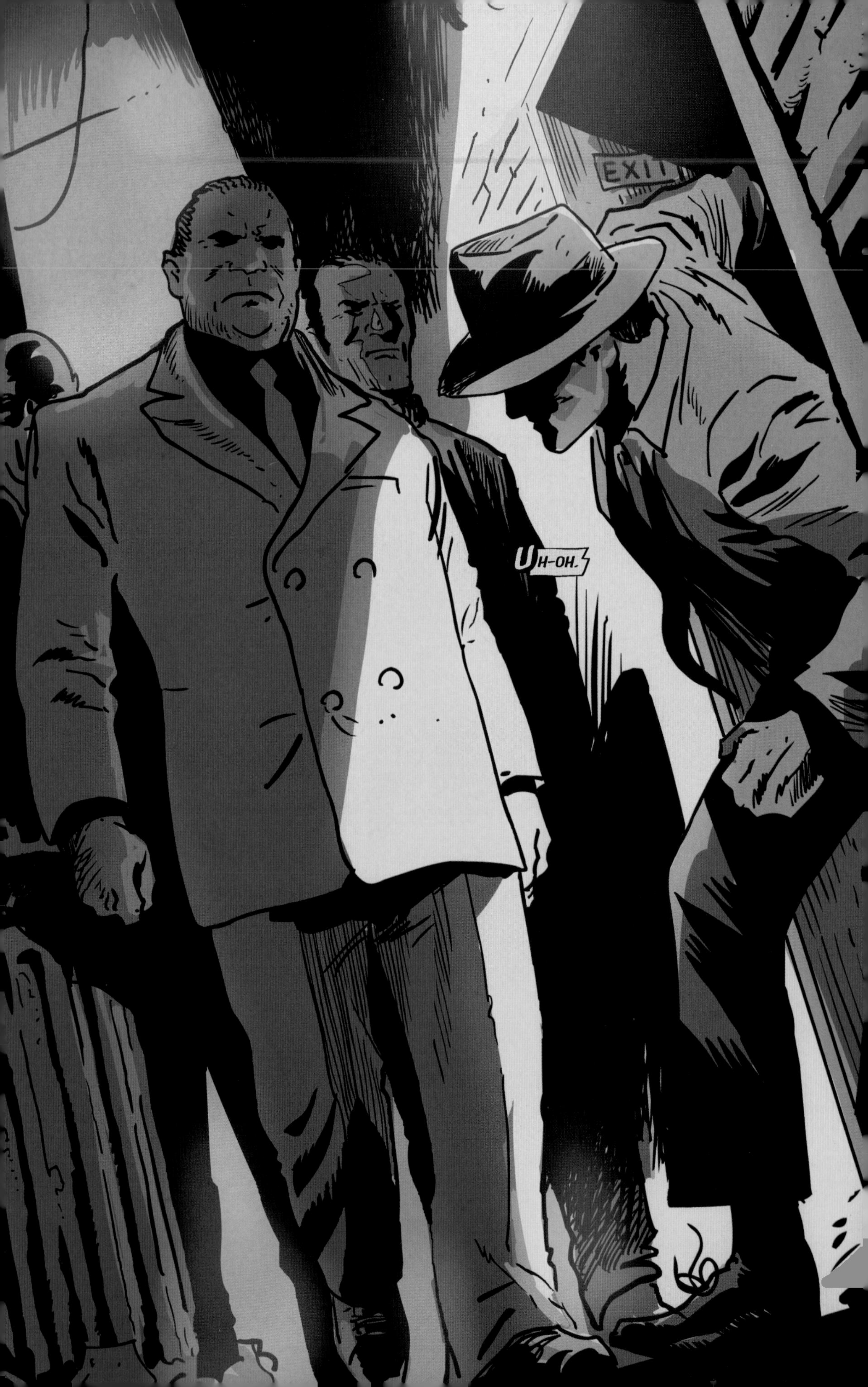
EXIT
UH-OH.

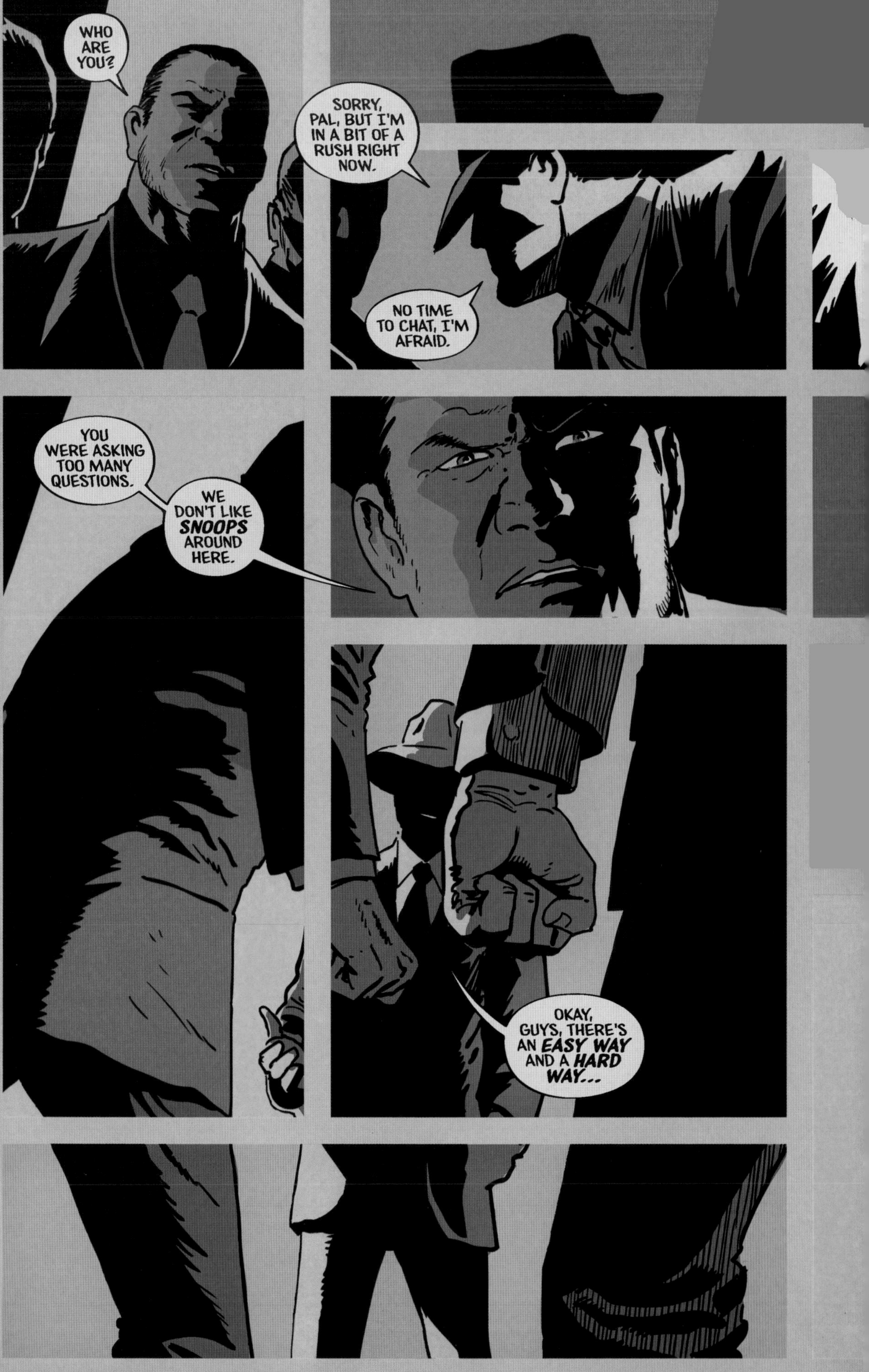
WHO ARE YOU?
SORRY, PAL, BUT I'M IN A BIT OF A RUSH RIGHT NOW.
NO TIME TO CHAT, I'M AFRAID.
YOU WERE ASKING TOO MANY QUESTIONS.
WE DON'T LIKE SNOOPS AROUND HERE.
OKAY, GUYS, THERE'S AN EASY WAY AND A HARD WAY...

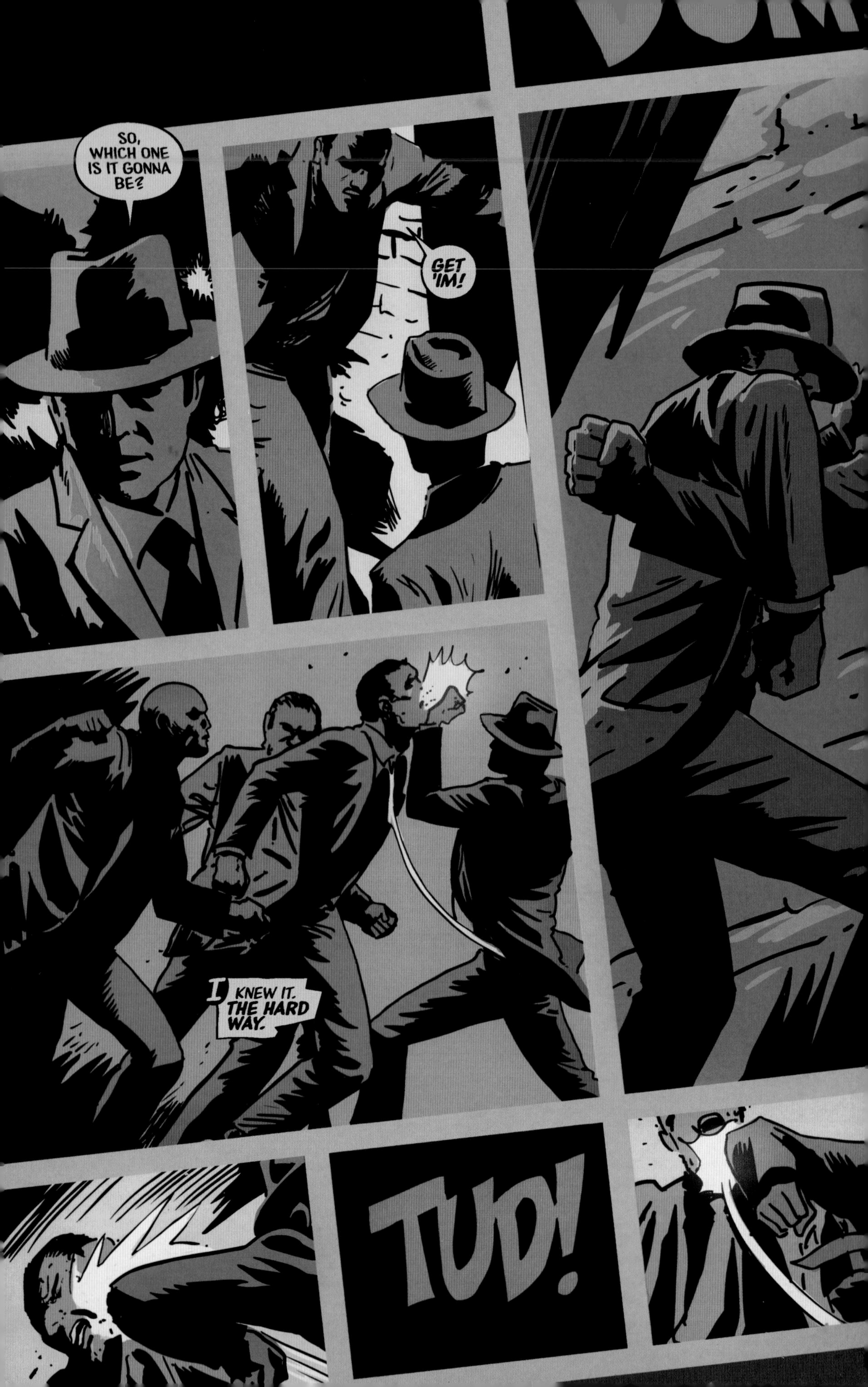
SO, WHICH ONE IS IT GONNA BE?
GET 'IM!
I KNEW IT. THE HARD WAY.
TUD!

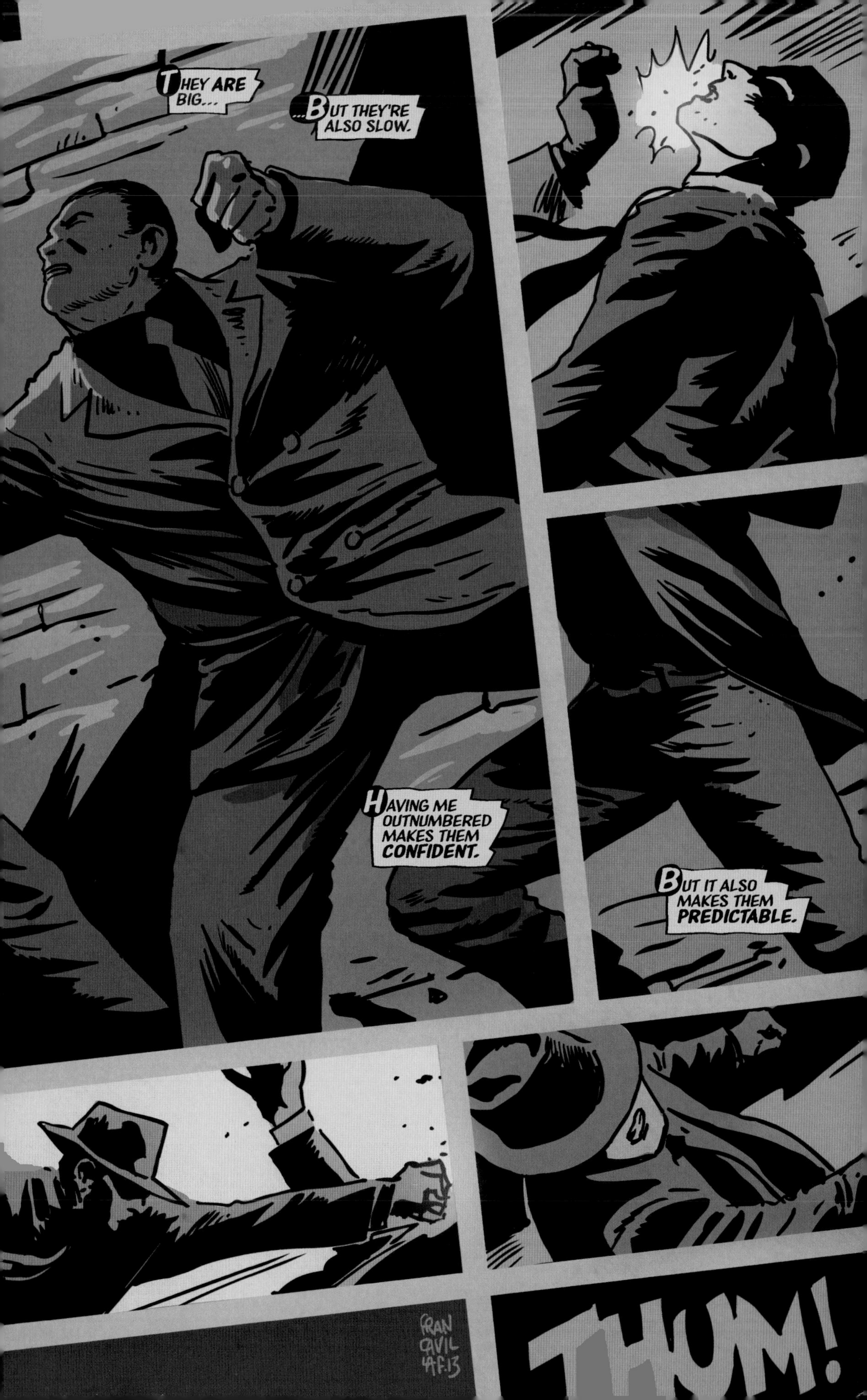
THEY ARE BIG...
...BUT THEY'RE ALSO SLOW.
HAVING ME OUTNUMBERED MAKES THEM CONFIDENT.
BUT IT ALSO MAKES THEM PREDICTABLE.
FRAN GALVIL 4 F.13
THUM!

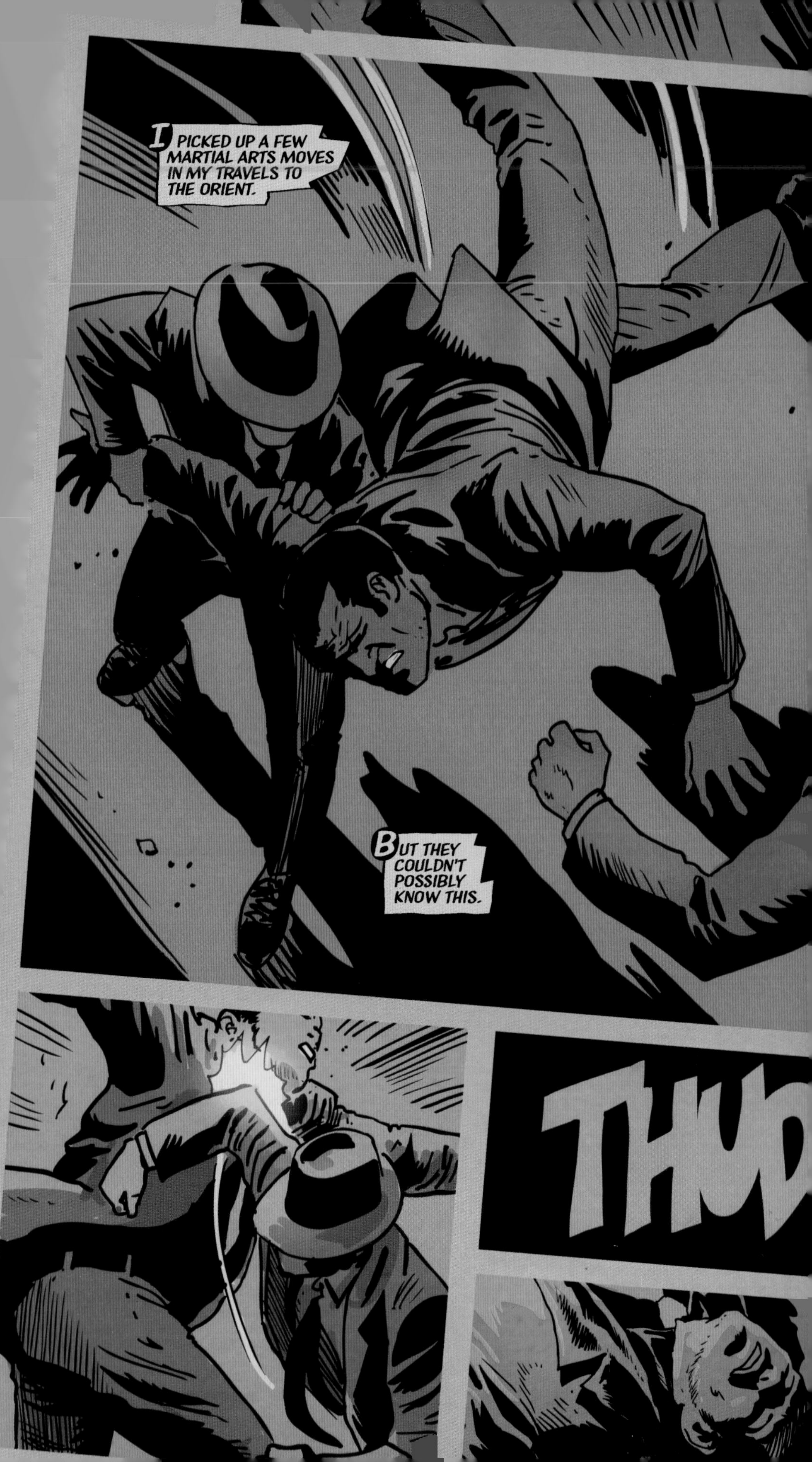
I PICKED UP A FEW MARTIAL ARTS MOVES IN MY TRAVELS TO THE ORIENT.
BUT THEY COULDN'T POSSIBLY KNOW THIS.
THUD

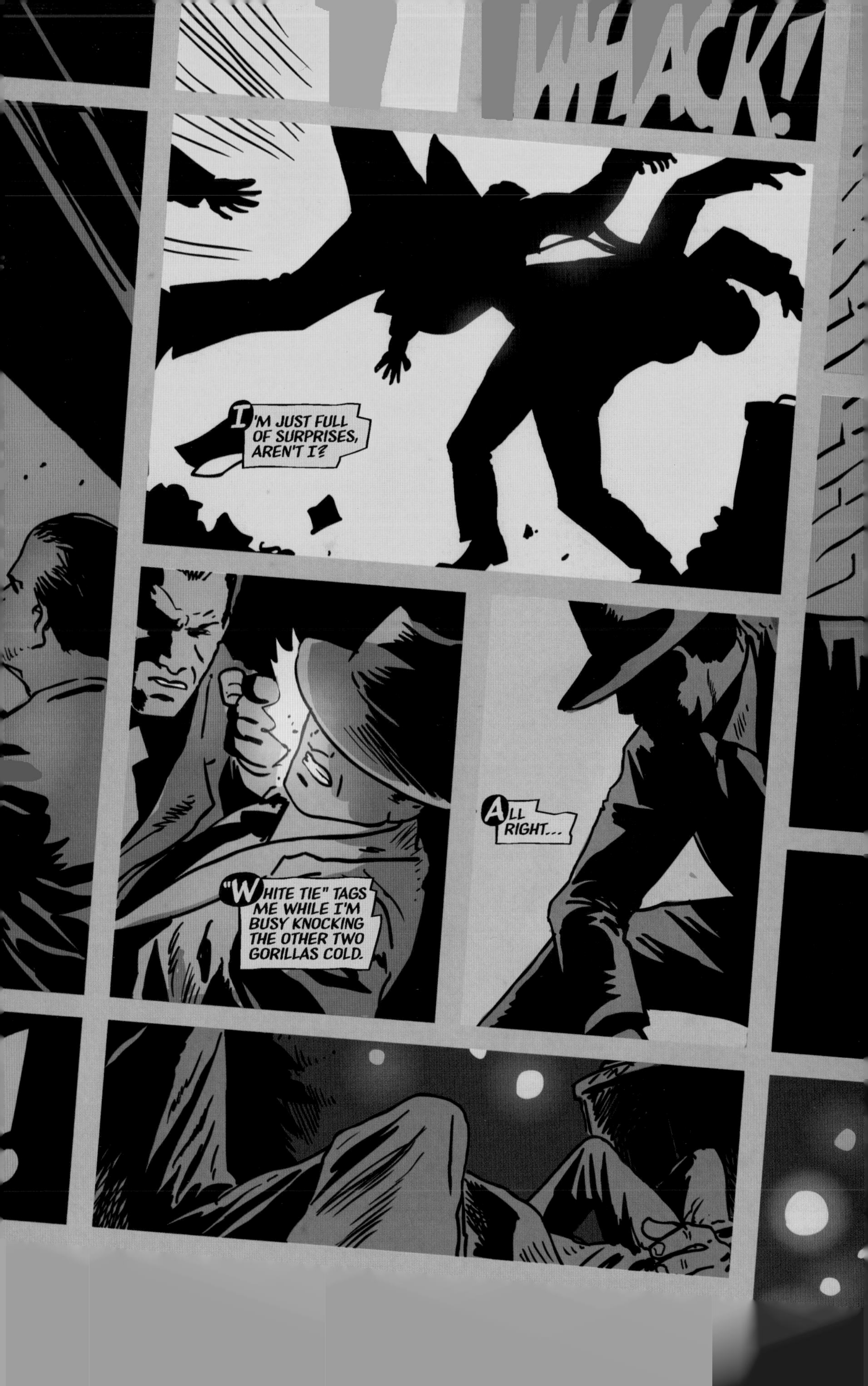
WHACK!
I'M JUST FULL OF SURPRISES, AREN'T I?
"WHITE TIE" TAGS ME WHILE I'M BUSY KNOCKING THE OTHER TWO GORILLAS COLD.
ALL RIGHT...

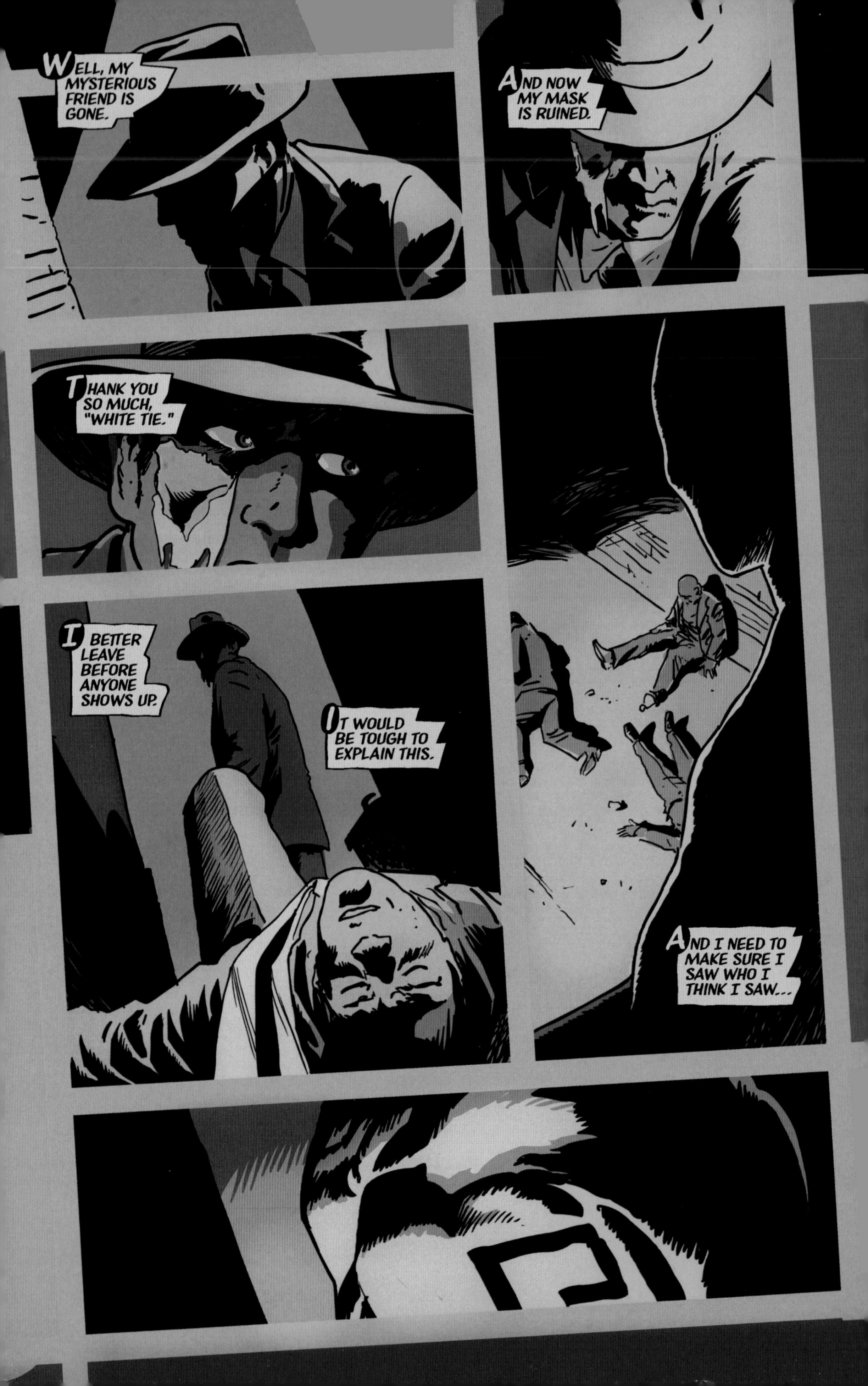
WELL, MY MYSTERIOUS FRIEND IS GONE.
AND NOW MY MASK IS RUINED.
THANK YOU SO MUCH, "WHITE TIE."
I BETTER LEAVE BEFORE ANYONE SHOWS UP.
IT WOULD BE TOUGH TO EXPLAIN THIS.
AND I NEED TO MAKE SURE I SAW WHO I THINK I SAW...

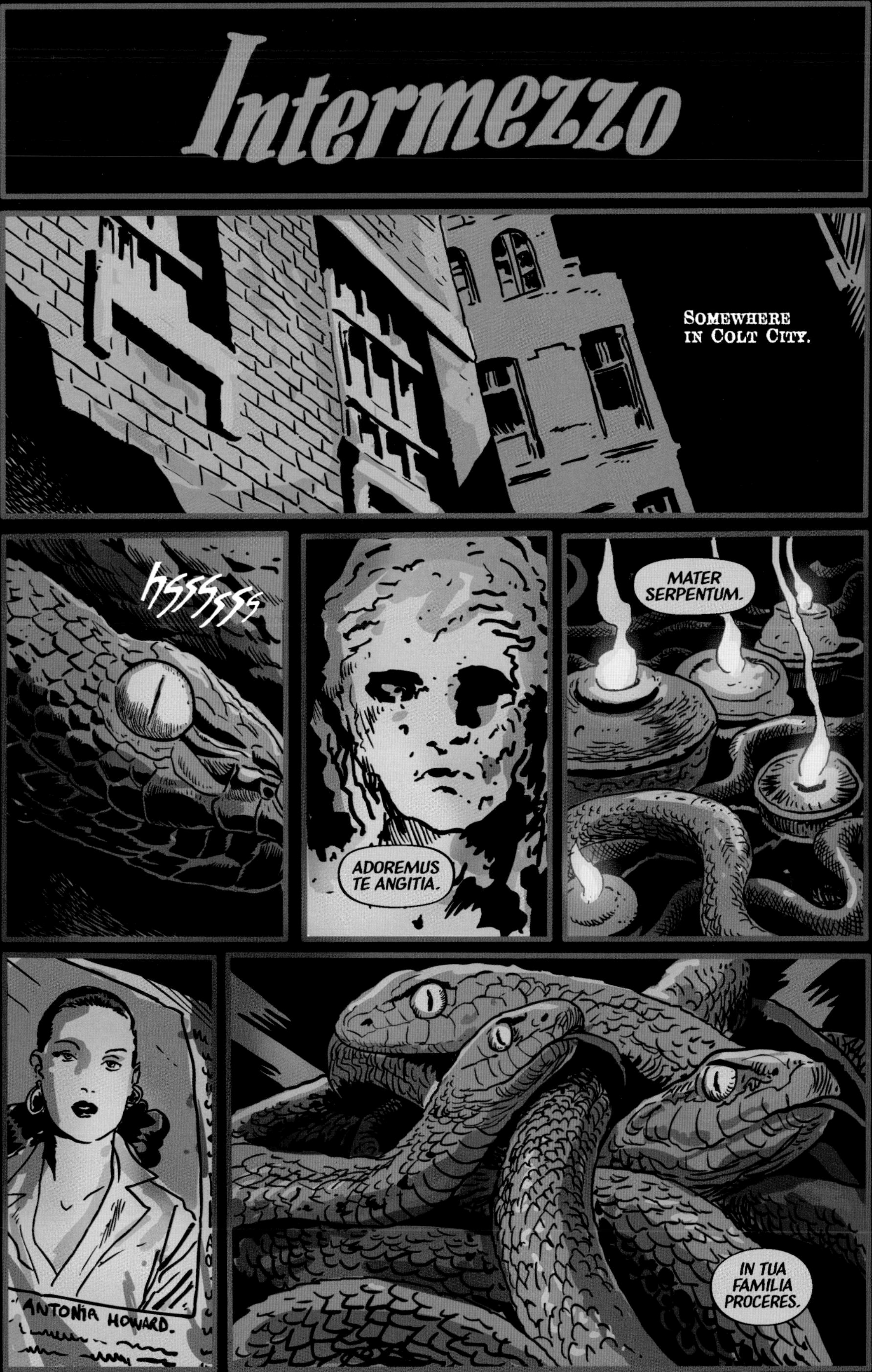
Intermezzo
SOMEWHERE IN COLT CITY.
hsssssss
ADOREMUS TE ANGITIA.
MATER SERPENTUM.
ANTONIA HOWARD.
IN TUA FAMILIA PROCERES.

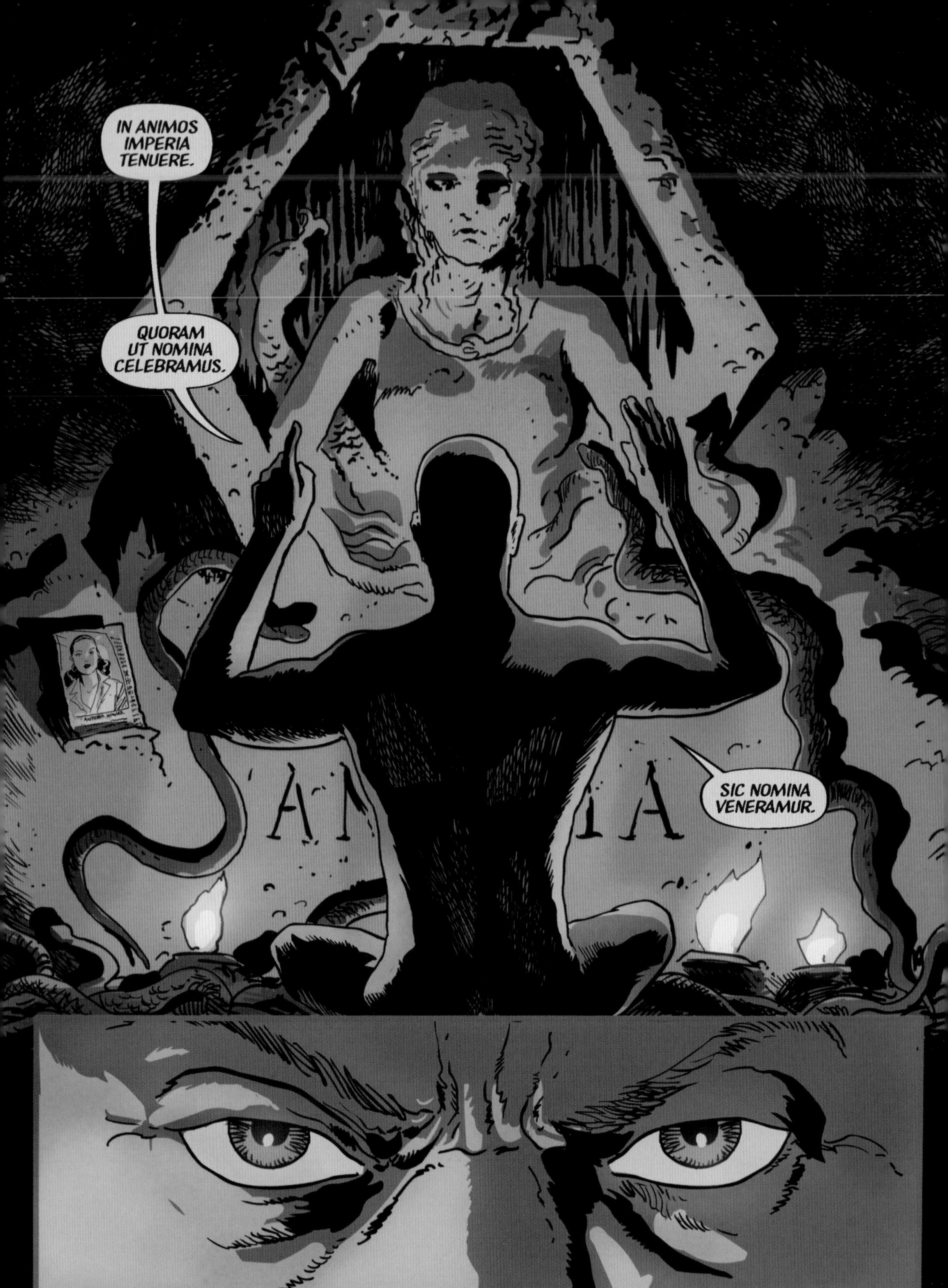
IN ANIMOS IMPERIA TENUERE.
QUORAM UT NOMINA CELEBRAMUS.
SIC NOMINA VENERAMUR.

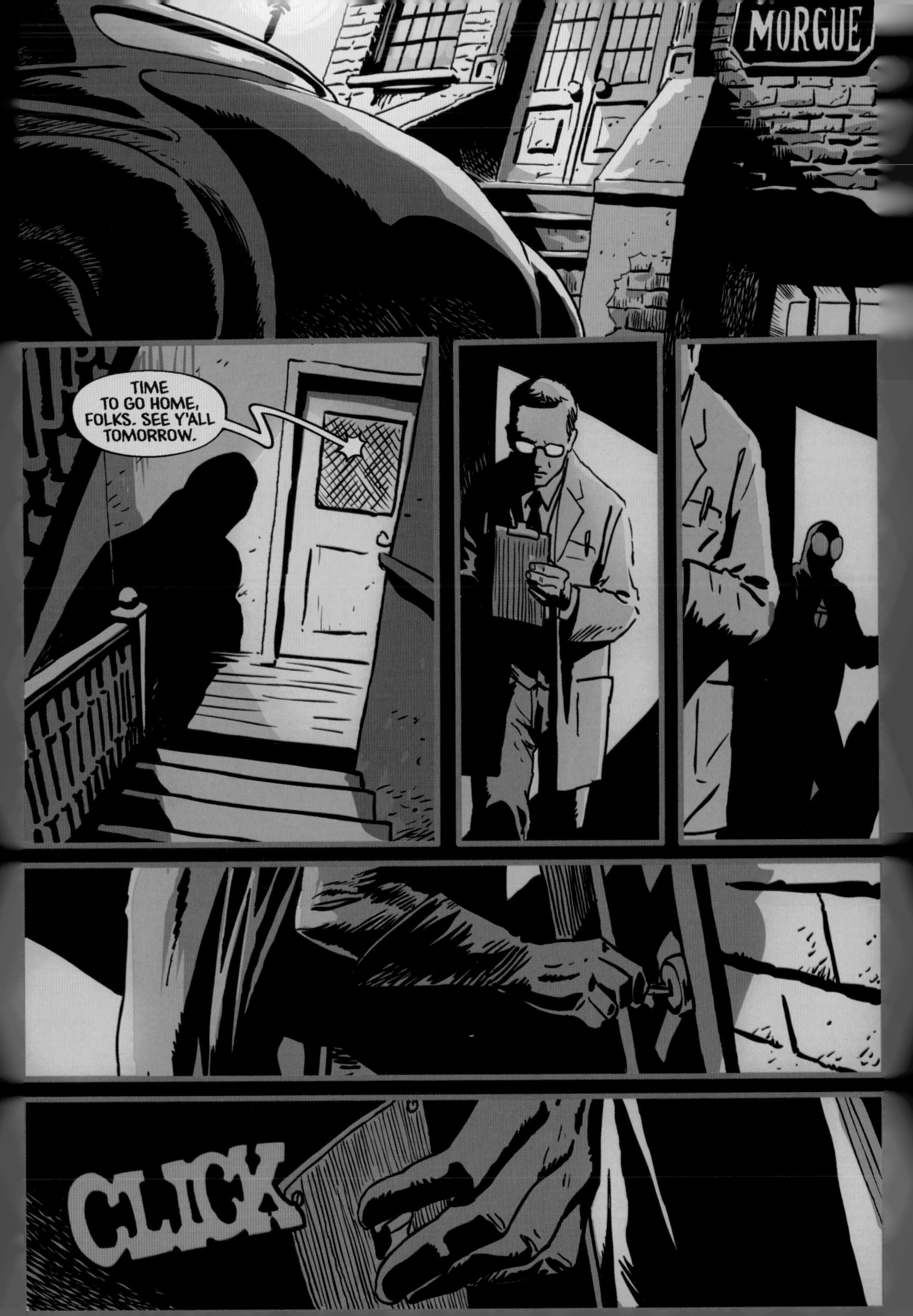
MORGUE
TIME TO GO HOME, FOLKS. SEE Y'ALL TOMORROW.
CLICK

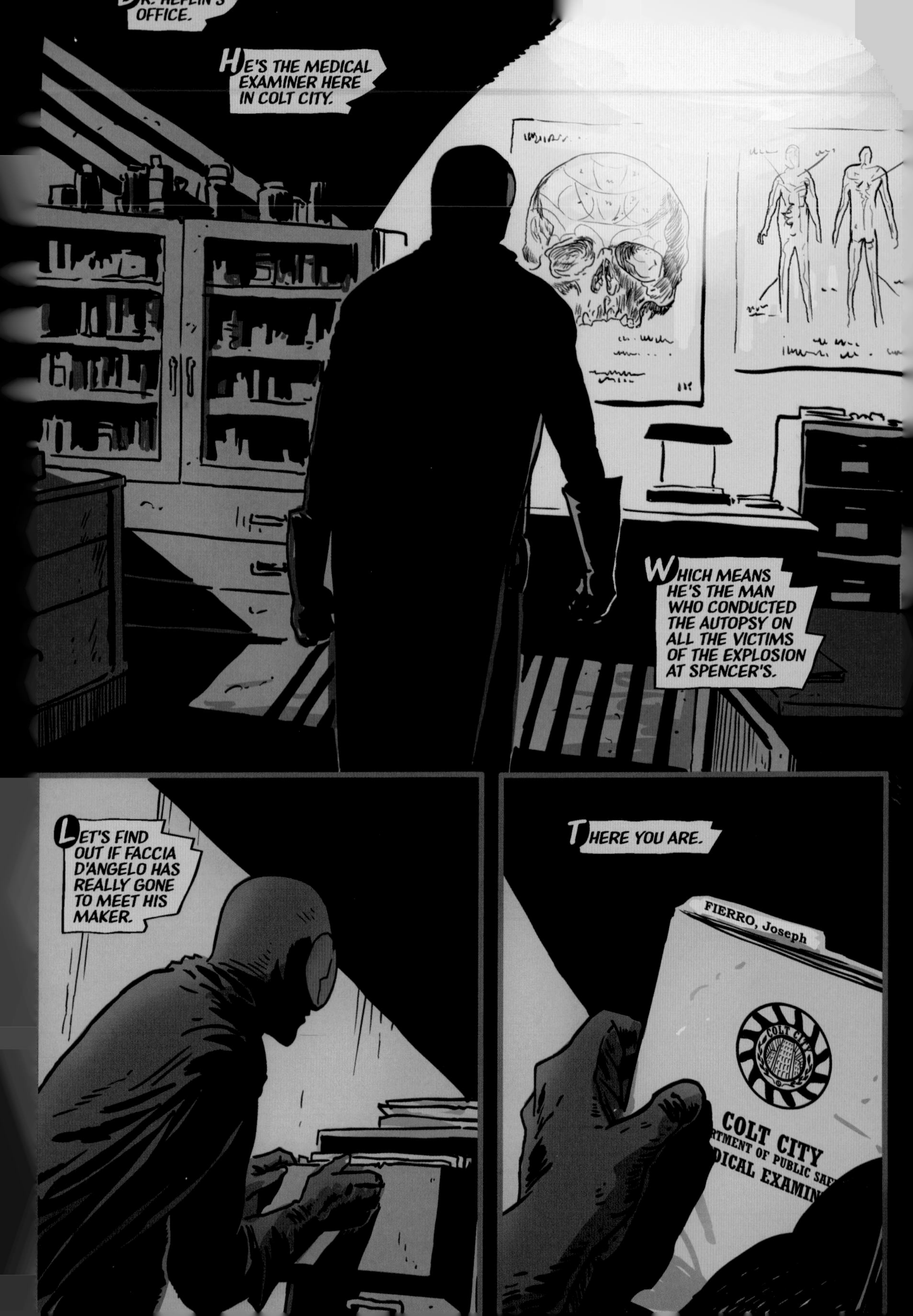
OFFICE.
HE'S THE MEDICAL EXAMINER HERE IN COLT CITY.
WHICH MEANS HE'S THE MAN WHO CONDUCTED THE AUTOPSY ON ALL THE VICTIMS OF THE EXPLOSION AT SPENCER'S.
LET'S FIND OUT IF FACCIA D'ANGELO HAS REALLY GONE TO MEET HIS MAKER.
THERE YOU ARE.
FIERRO, Joseph
COLT CITY
COLT CITY

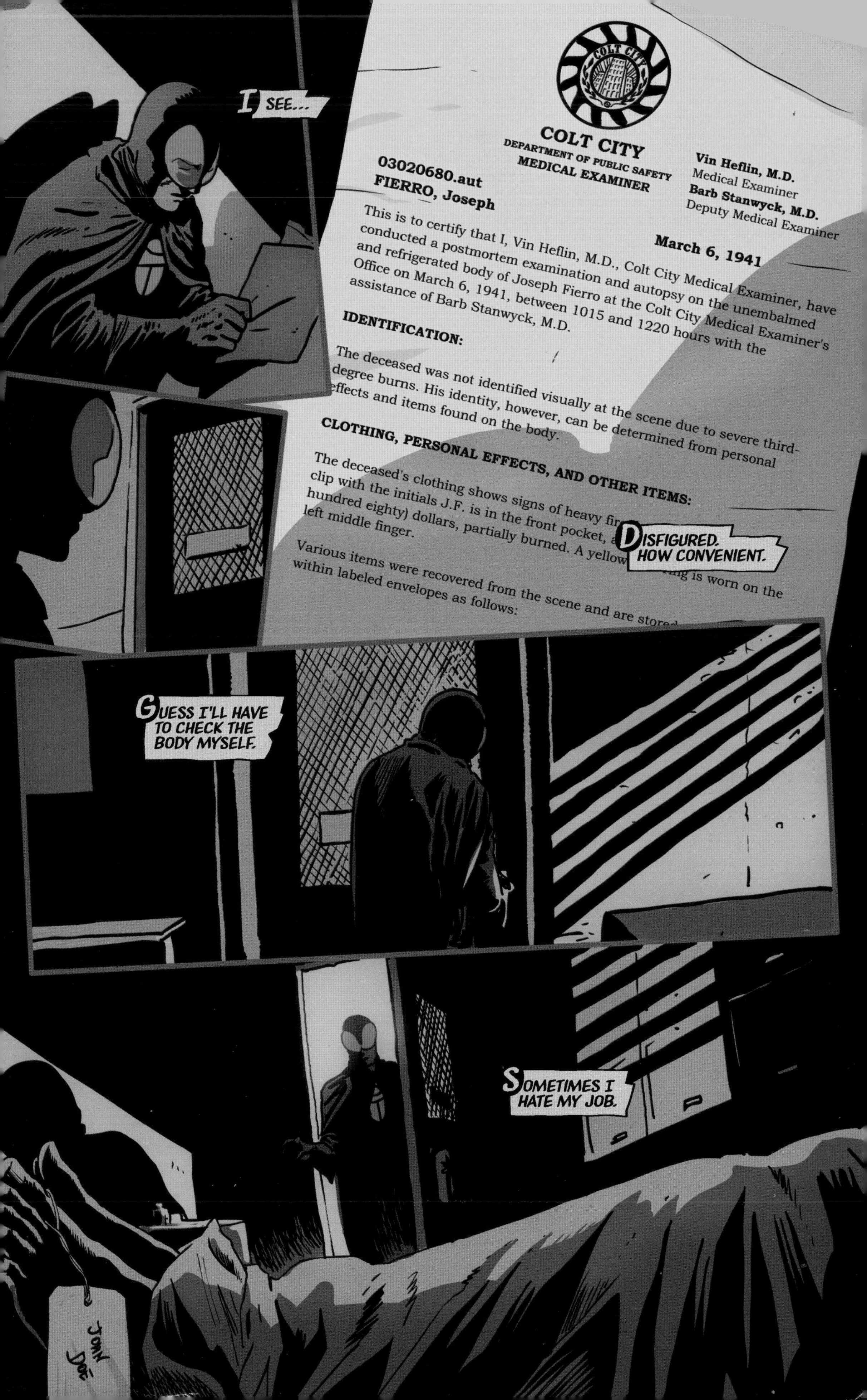
I SEE...
COLT CITY
COLT CITY
DEPARTMENT OF PUBLIC SAFETY
MEDICAL EXAMINER
Vin Heflin, M.D.
Medical Examiner
Barb Stanwyck, M.D.
Deputy Medical Examiner
03020680.aut
FIERRO, Joseph
March 6, 1941
This is to certify that I, Vin Heflin, M.D., Colt City Medical Examiner, have conducted a postmortem examination and autopsy on the unembalmed and refrigerated body of Joseph Fierro at the Colt City Medical Examiner's Office on March 6, 1941, between 1015 and 1220 hours with the assistance of Barb Stanwyck, M.D.
IDENTIFICATION:
The deceased was not identified visually at the scene due to severe third-degree burns. His identity, however, can be determined from personal effects and items found on the body.
CLOTHING, PERSONAL EFFECTS, AND OTHER ITEMS:
The deceased's clothing shows signs of heavy fir
clip with the initials J.F. is in the front pocket, a
hundred eighty) dollars, partially burned. A yellow
ing is worn on the
left middle finger.
Various items were recovered from the scene and are stored
within labeled envelopes as follows:
DISFIGURED. HOW CONVENIENT.
GUESS I'LL HAVE TO CHECK THE BODY MYSELF.
SOMETIMES I HATE MY JOB.
JOHN DOE

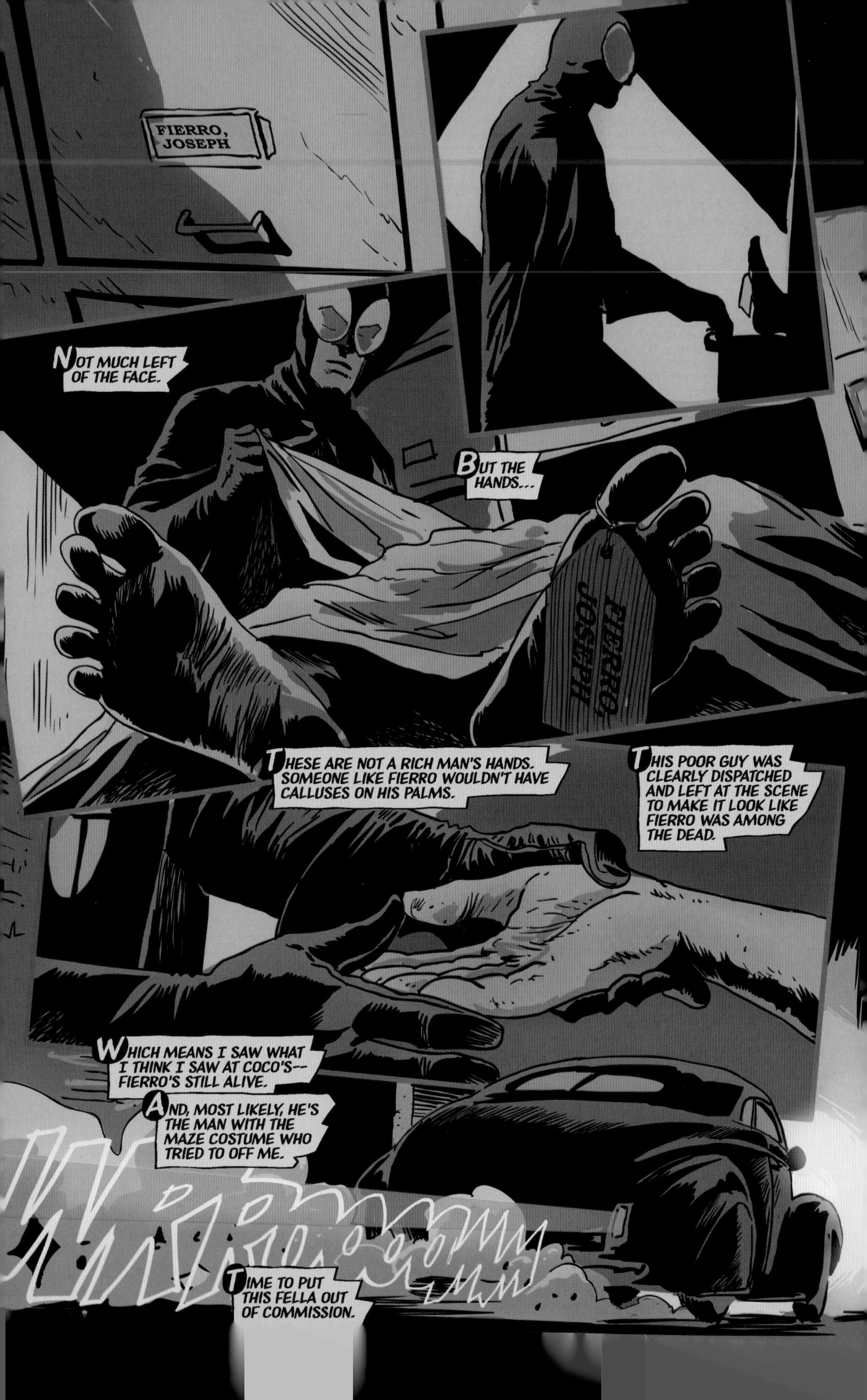
FIERRO, JOSEPH
NOT MUCH LEFT OF THE FACE.
BUT THE HANDS...
FIERRO, JOSEPH
THESE ARE NOT A RICH MAN'S HANDS. SOMEONE LIKE FIERRO WOULDN'T HAVE CALLUSES ON HIS PALMS.
THIS POOR GUY WAS CLEARLY DISPATCHED AND LEFT AT THE SCENE TO MAKE IT LOOK LIKE FIERRO WAS AMONG THE DEAD.
WHICH MEANS I SAW WHAT I THINK I SAW AT COCO'S-- FIERRO'S STILL ALIVE.
AND, MOST LIKELY, HE'S THE MAN WITH THE MAZE COSTUME WHO TRIED TO OFF ME.
TIME TO PUT THIS FELLA OUT OF COMMISSION.

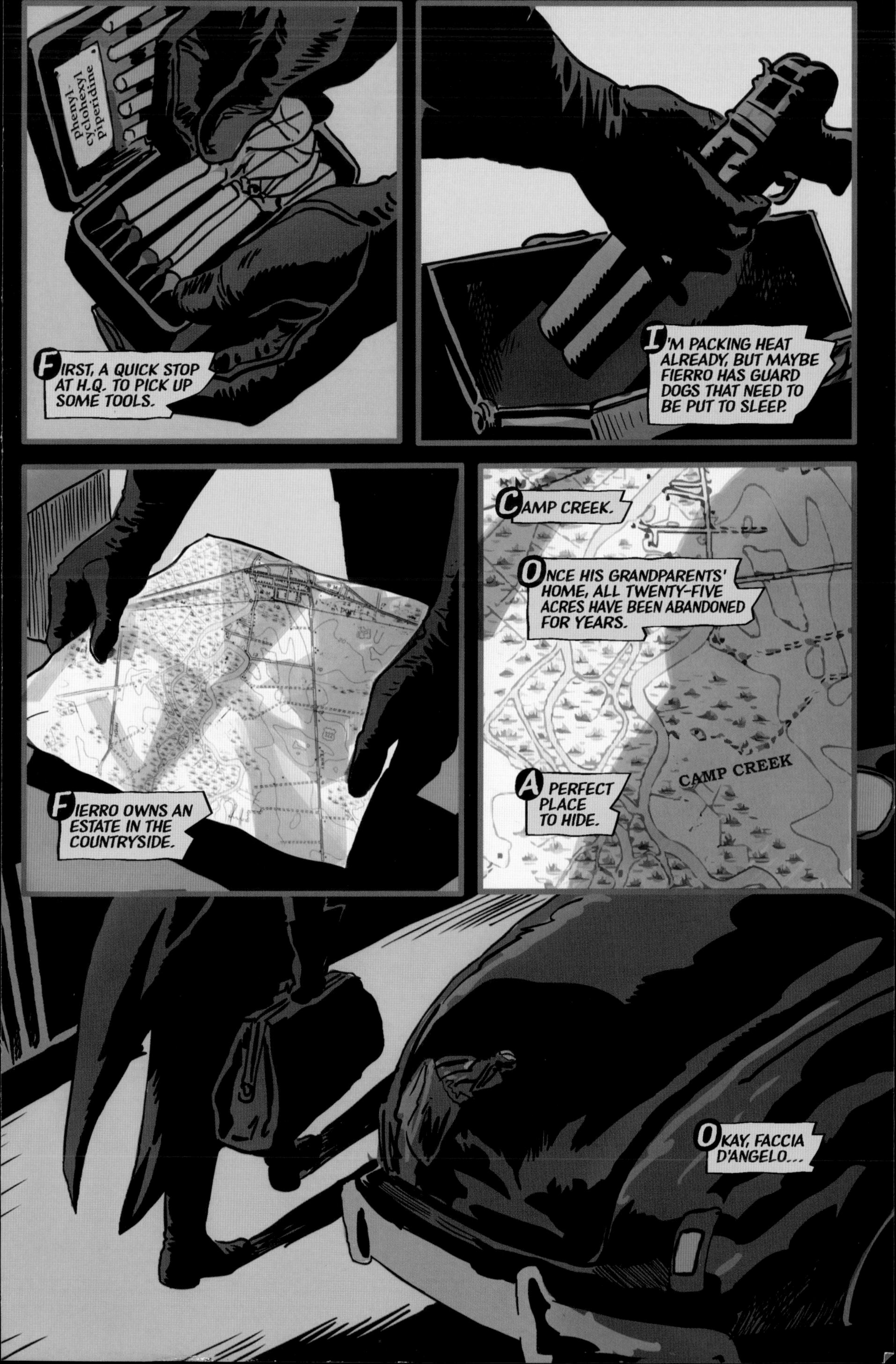
phenyl-
cyclohexyl
piperidine
FIRST, A QUICK STOP AT H.Q. TO PICK UP SOME TOOLS.
I'M PACKING HEAT ALREADY, BUT MAYBE FIERRO HAS GUARD DOGS THAT NEED TO BE PUT TO SLEEP.
FIERRO OWNS AN ESTATE IN THE COUNTRYSIDE.
CAMP CREEK.
ONCE HIS GRANDPARENTS' HOME, ALL TWENTY-FIVE ACRES HAVE BEEN ABANDONED FOR YEARS.
CAMP CREEK
A PERFECT PLACE TO HIDE.
OKAY, FACCIA D'ANGELO...

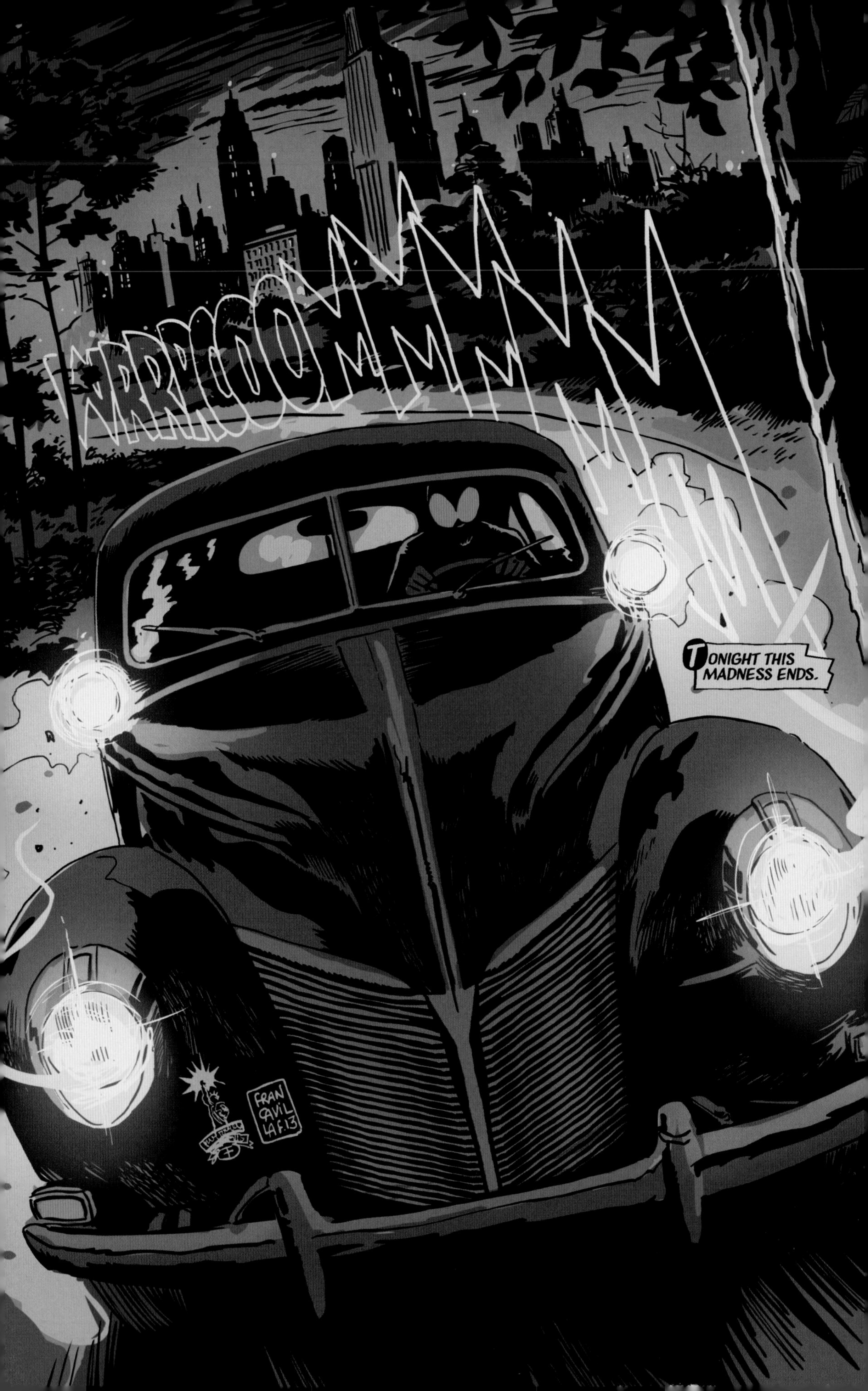
VRRRROOOMMMMMMMMMMM
TONIGHT THIS MADNESS ENDS.

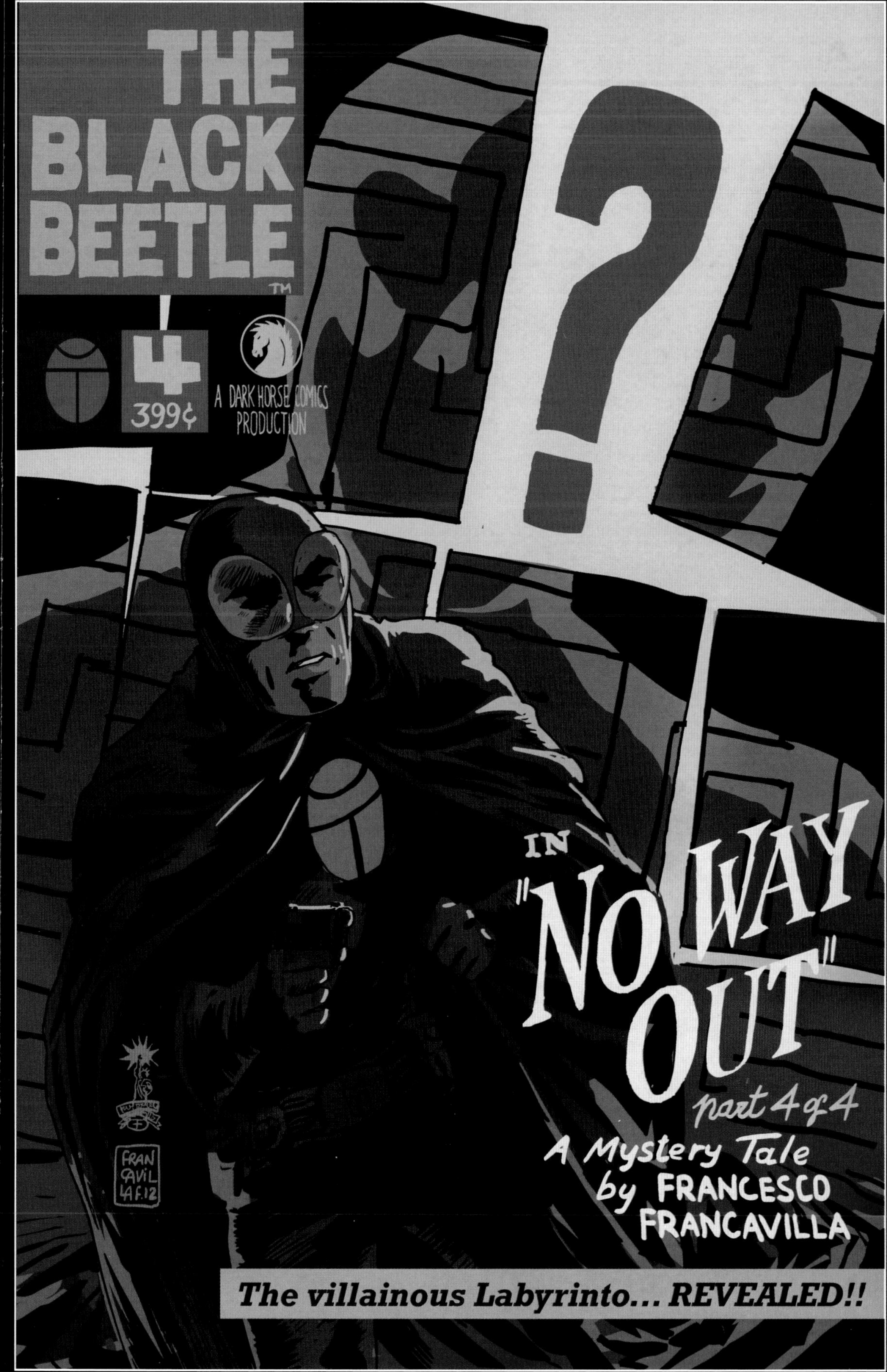
THE BLACK BEETLE
TM
4
399¢
A DARK HORSE COMICS PRODUCTION
IN "NO WAY OUT"
part 4 of 4
A Mystery Tale by FRANCESCO FRANCAVILLA
FRAN CAVIL LA F.12
The villainous Labyrinto... REVEALED!!

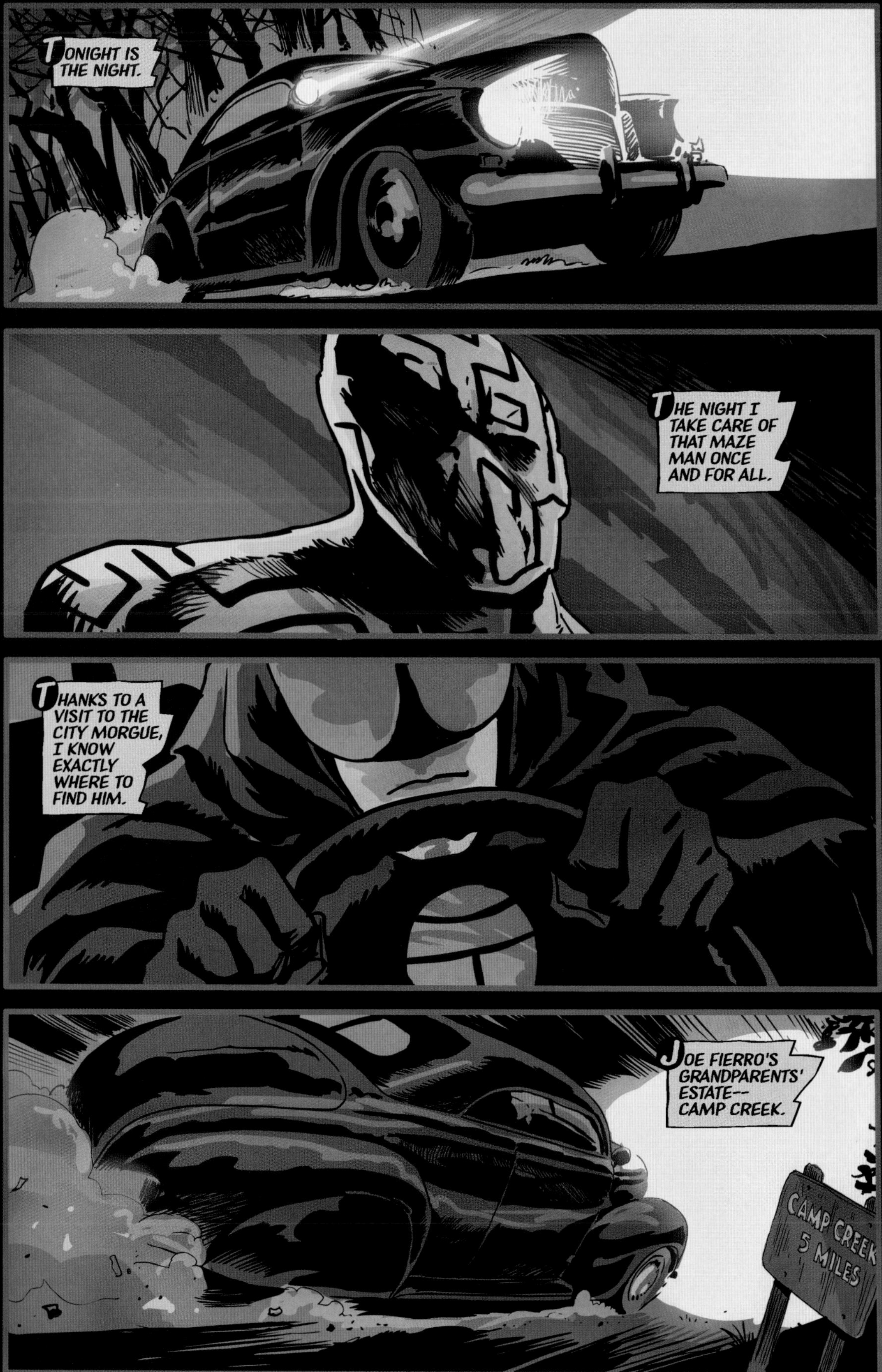
TONIGHT IS THE NIGHT.
THE NIGHT I TAKE CARE OF THAT MAZE MAN ONCE AND FOR ALL.
THANKS TO A VISIT TO THE CITY MORGUE, I KNOW EXACTLY WHERE TO FIND HIM.
JOE FIERRO'S GRANDPARENTS' ESTATE-- CAMP CREEK.
CAMP CREEK 5 MILES

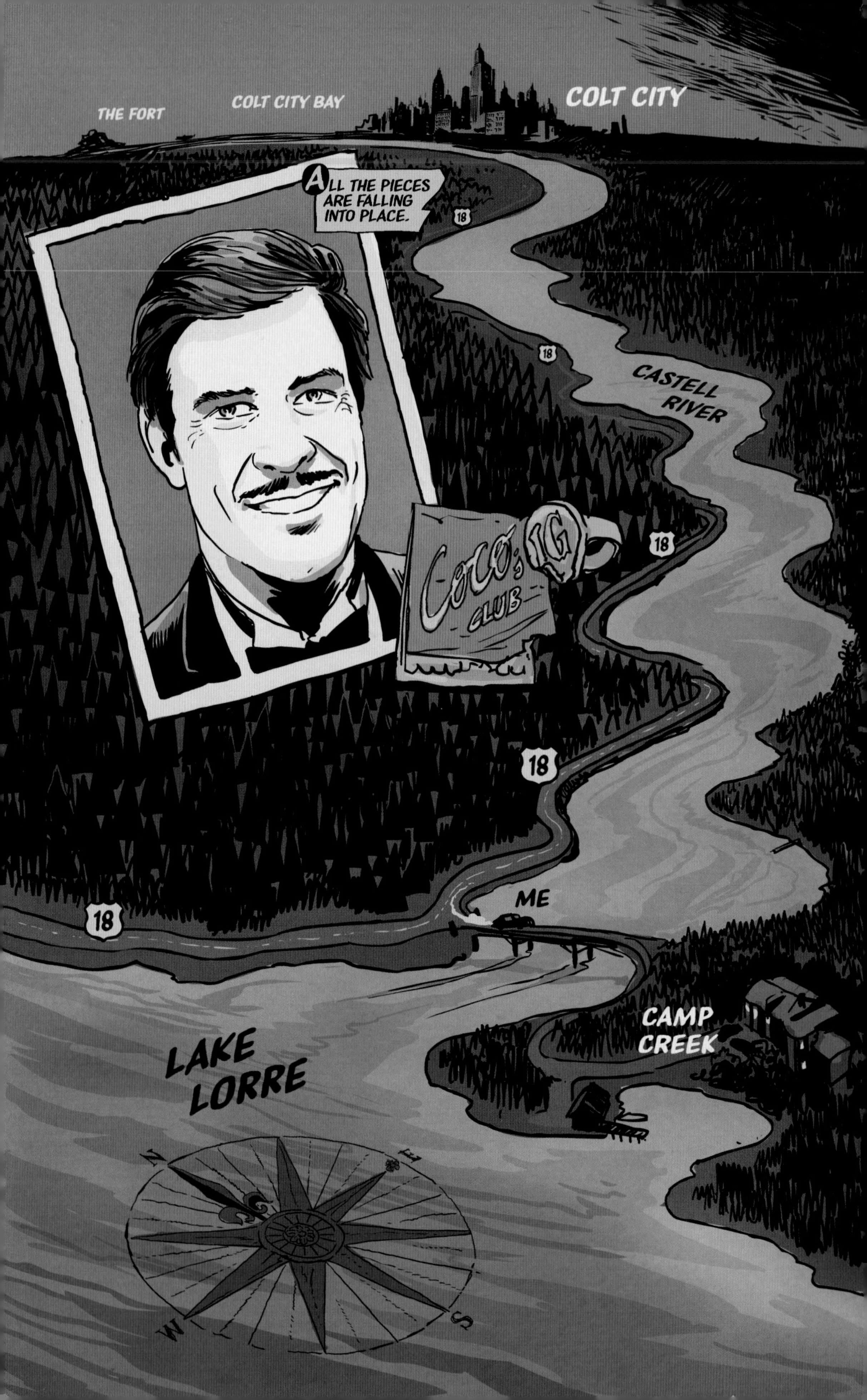
THE FORT
COLT CITY BAY
COLT CITY
ALL THE PIECES ARE FALLING INTO PLACE.
18
CASTELL RIVER
COCO'S CLUB
ME
CAMP CREEK
LAKE LORRE
N
E
S
W

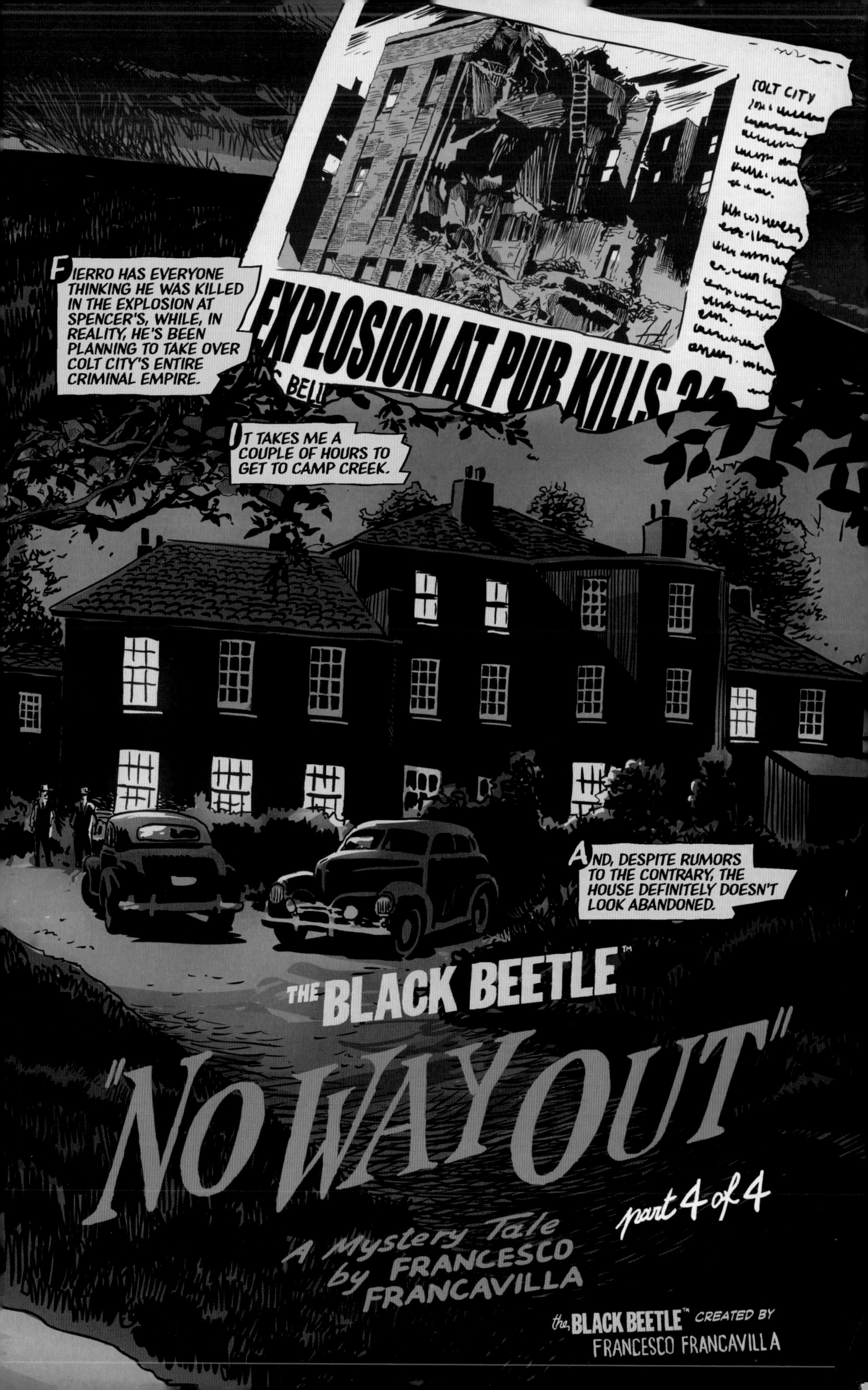
FIERRO HAS EVERYONE THINKING HE WAS KILLED IN THE EXPLOSION AT SPENCER'S, WHILE, IN REALITY, HE'S BEEN PLANNING TO TAKE OVER COLT CITY'S ENTIRE CRIMINAL EMPIRE.
COLT CITY
EXPLOSION AT PUB KILLS 2
IT TAKES ME A COUPLE OF HOURS TO GET TO CAMP CREEK.
AND, DESPITE RUMORS TO THE CONTRARY, THE HOUSE DEFINITELY DOESN'T LOOK ABANDONED.
THE BLACK BEETLE™
"NO WAY OUT"
part 4 of 4
A Mystery Tale by FRANCESCO FRANCAVILLA
the BLACK BEETLE™ CREATED BY FRANCESCO FRANCAVILLA

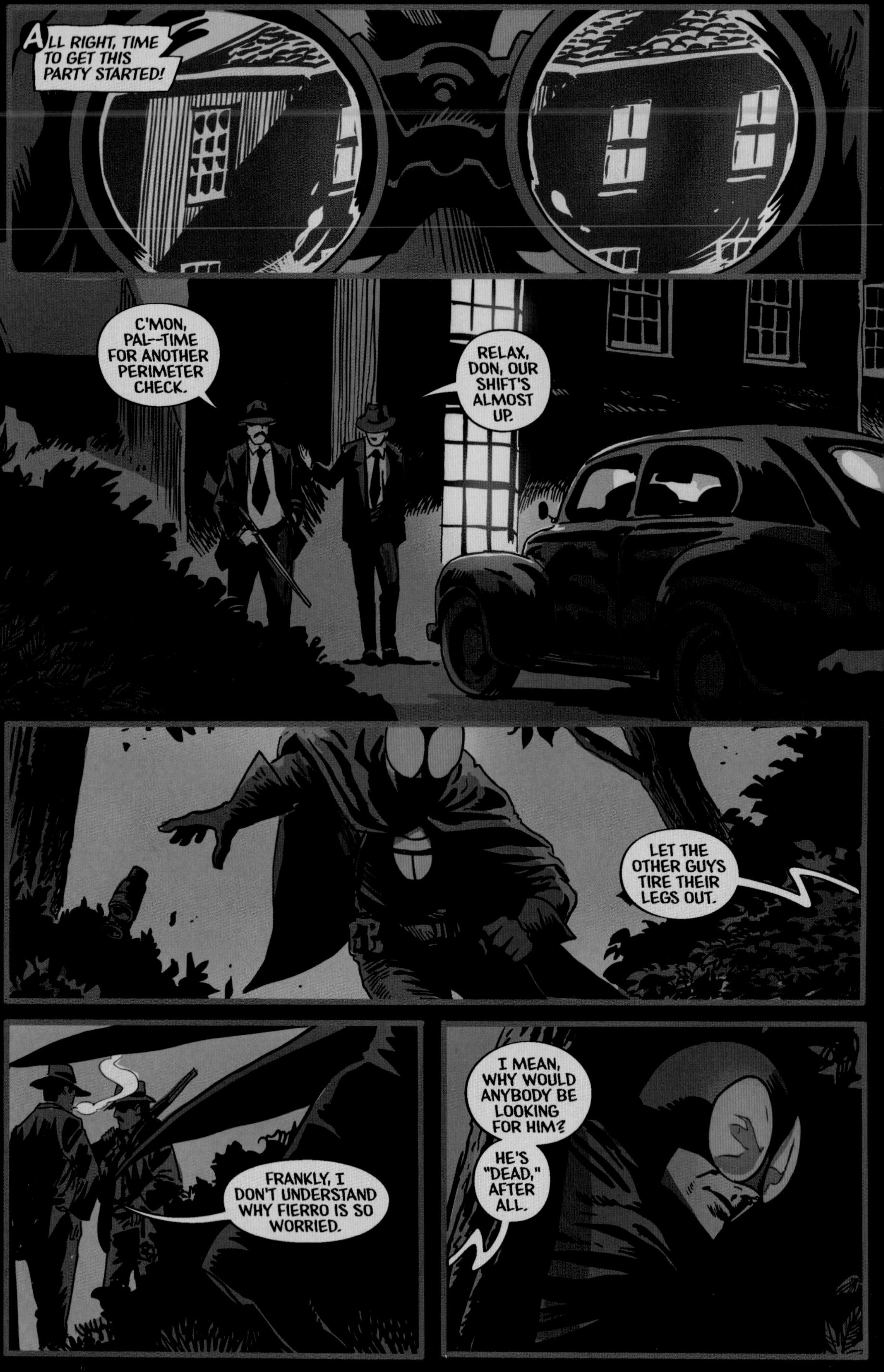
ALL RIGHT, TIME TO GET THIS PARTY STARTED!
C'MON, PAL--TIME FOR ANOTHER PERIMETER CHECK.
RELAX, DON, OUR SHIFT'S ALMOST UP.
LET THE OTHER GUYS TIRE THEIR LEGS OUT.
FRANKLY, I DON'T UNDERSTAND WHY FIERRO IS SO WORRIED.
I MEAN, WHY WOULD ANYBODY BE LOOKING FOR HIM?
HE'S "DEAD," AFTER ALL.

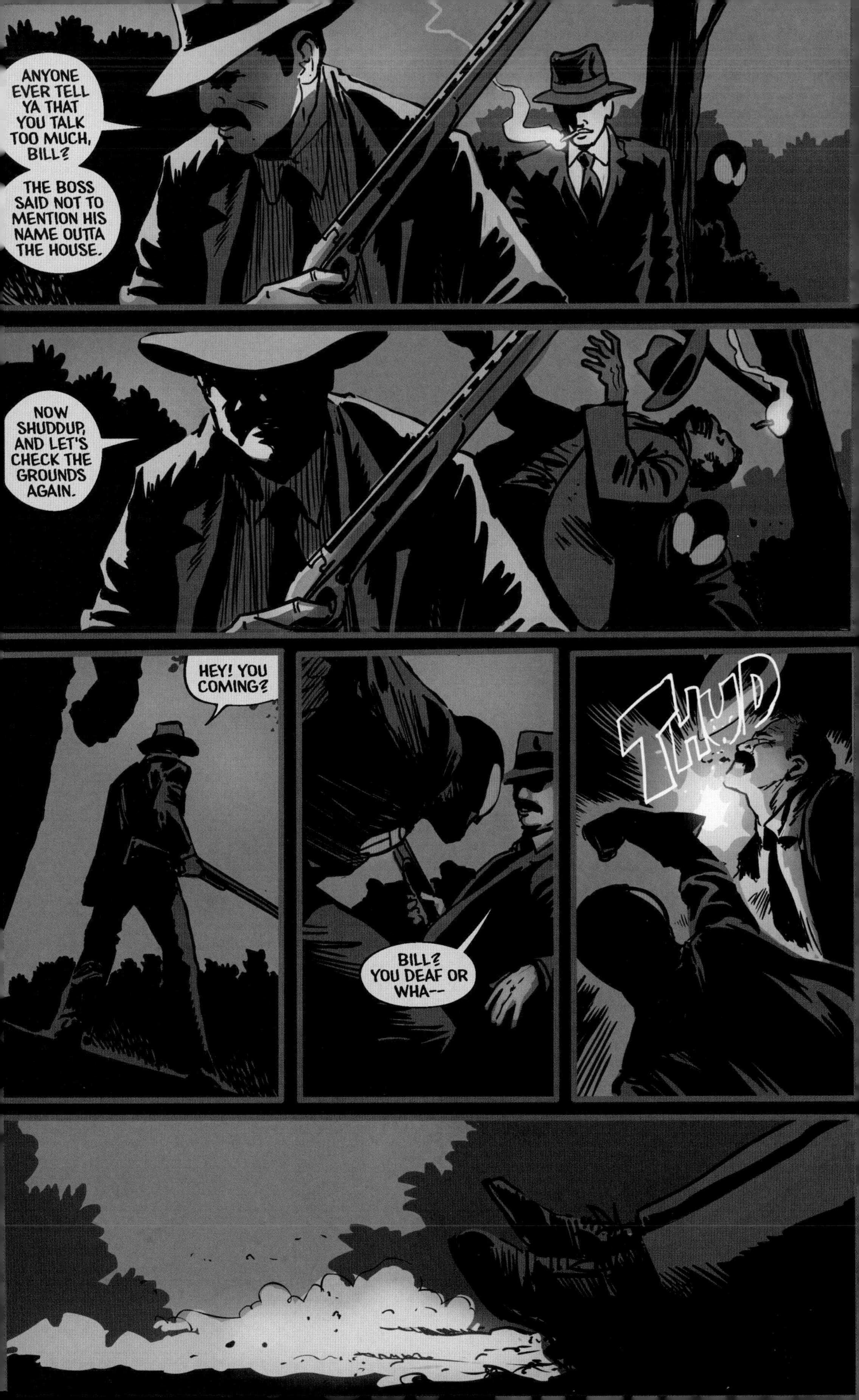
ANYONE EVER TELL YA THAT YOU TALK TOO MUCH, BILL?
THE BOSS SAID NOT TO MENTION HIS NAME OUTTA THE HOUSE.
NOW SHUDDUP, AND LET'S CHECK THE GROUNDS AGAIN.
HEY! YOU COMING?
BILL? YOU DEAF OR WHA--
THUD

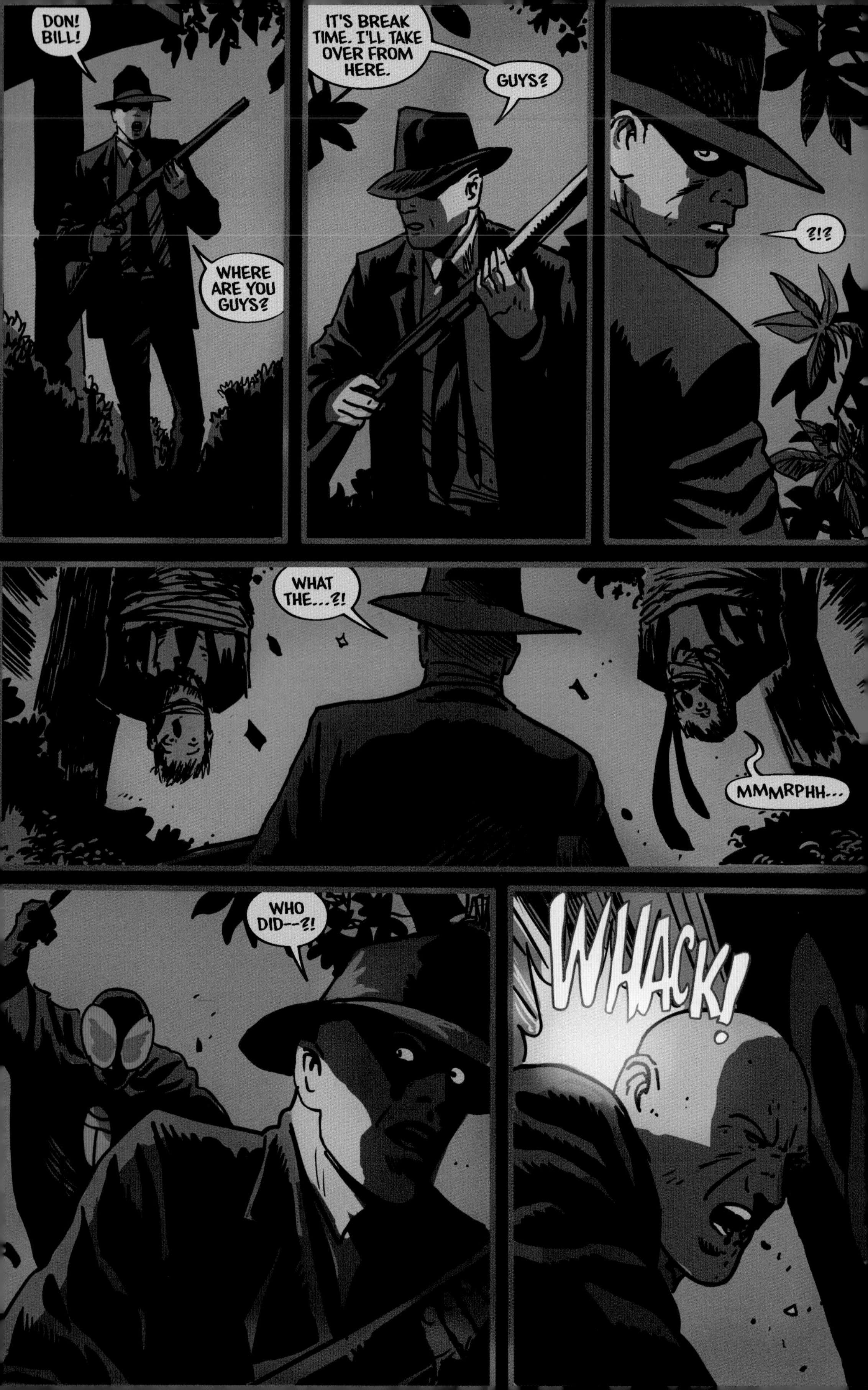
DON! BILL!
WHERE ARE YOU GUYS?
IT'S BREAK TIME. I'LL TAKE OVER FROM HERE.
GUYS?
?!?
WHAT THE...?!
MMMRPHH...
WHO DID--?!
WHACK!

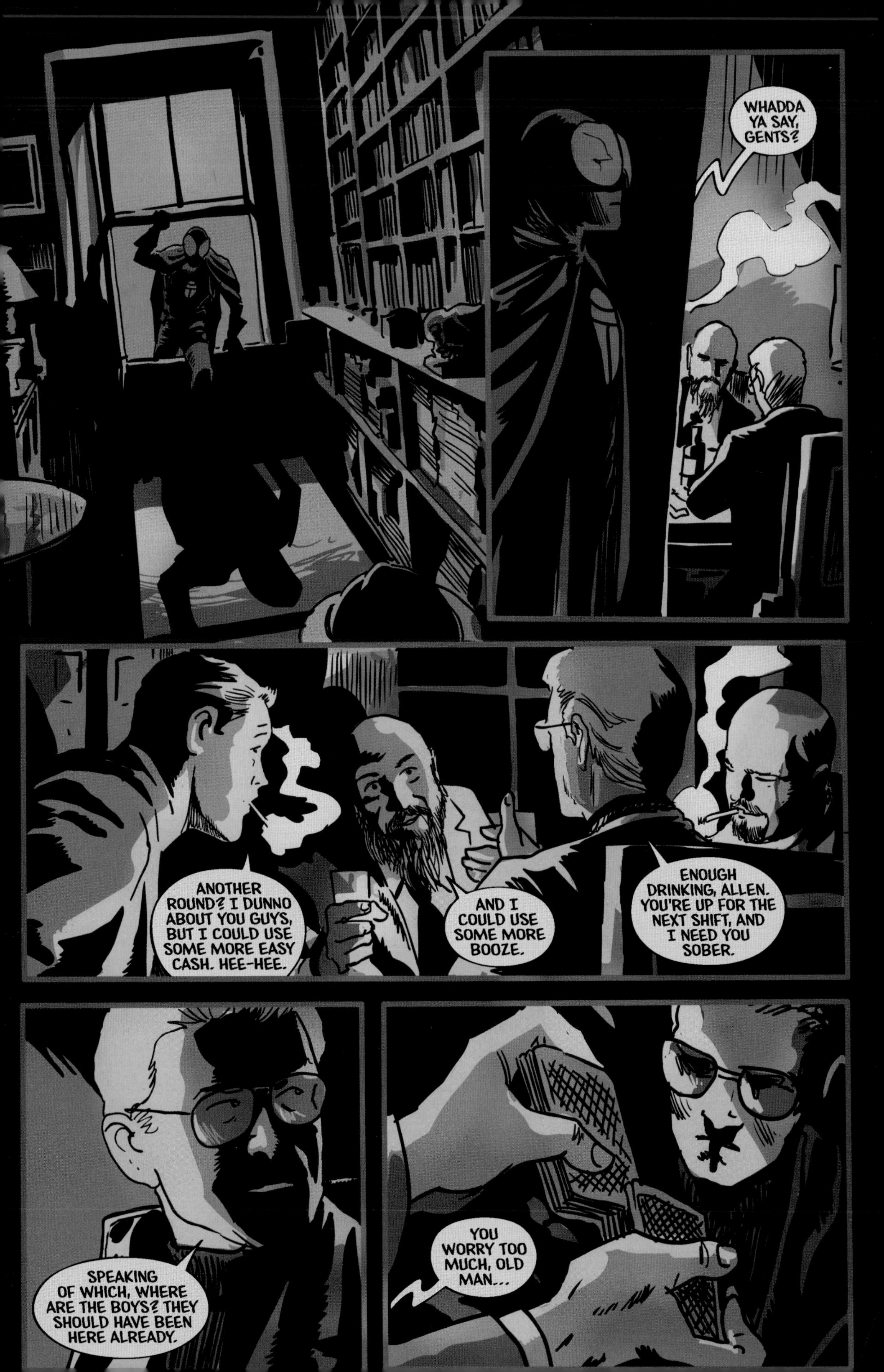
WHADDA YA SAY, GENTS?
ANOTHER ROUND? I DUNNO ABOUT YOU GUYS, BUT I COULD USE SOME MORE EASY CASH. HEE-HEE.
AND I COULD USE SOME MORE BOOZE.
ENOUGH DRINKING, ALLEN. YOU'RE UP FOR THE NEXT SHIFT, AND I NEED YOU SOBER.
SPEAKING OF WHICH, WHERE ARE THE BOYS? THEY SHOULD HAVE BEEN HERE ALREADY.
YOU WORRY TOO MUCH, OLD MAN...

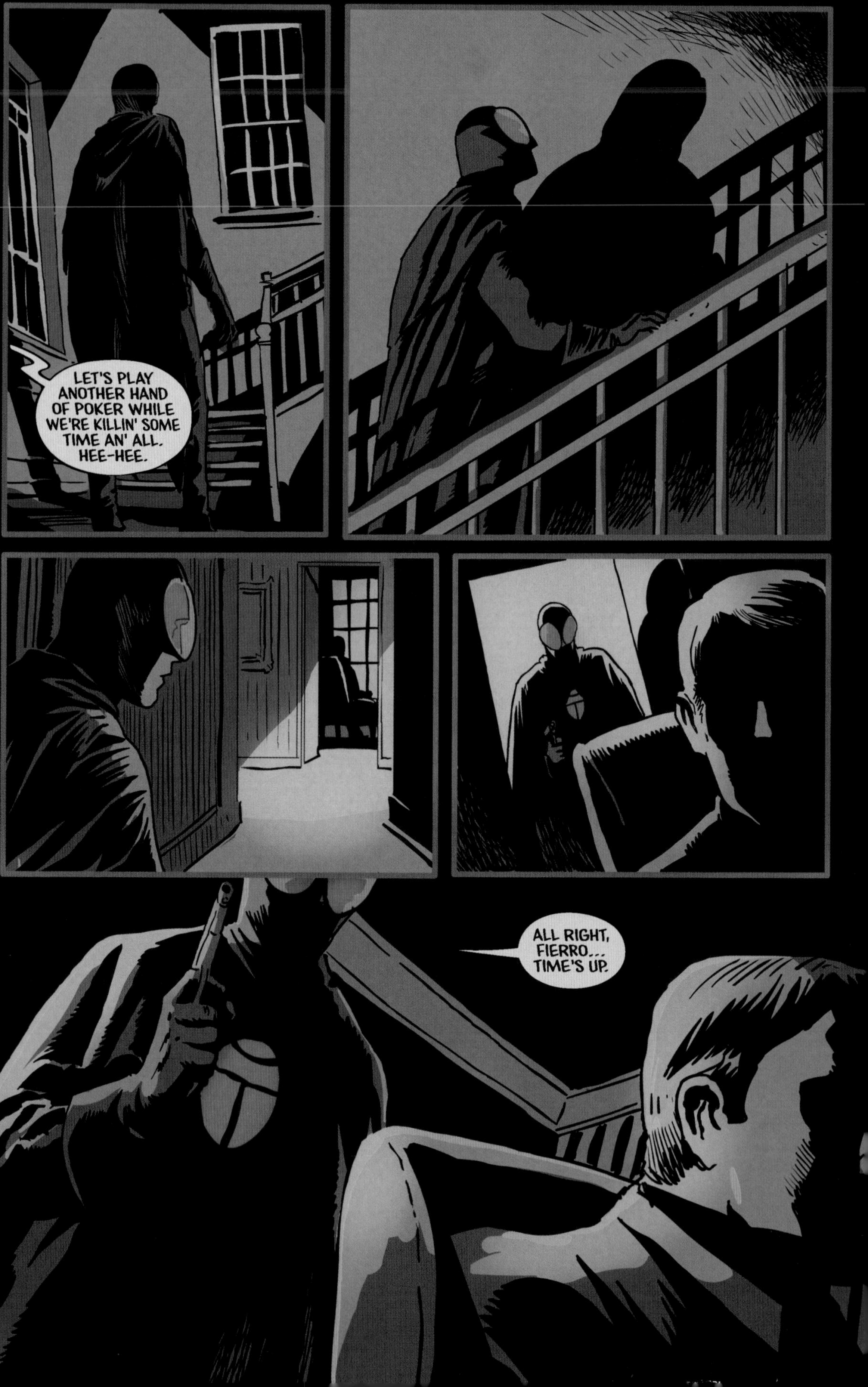
LET'S PLAY ANOTHER HAND OF POKER WHILE WE'RE KILLIN' SOME TIME AN' ALL. HEE-HEE.
ALL RIGHT, FIERRO... TIME'S UP.

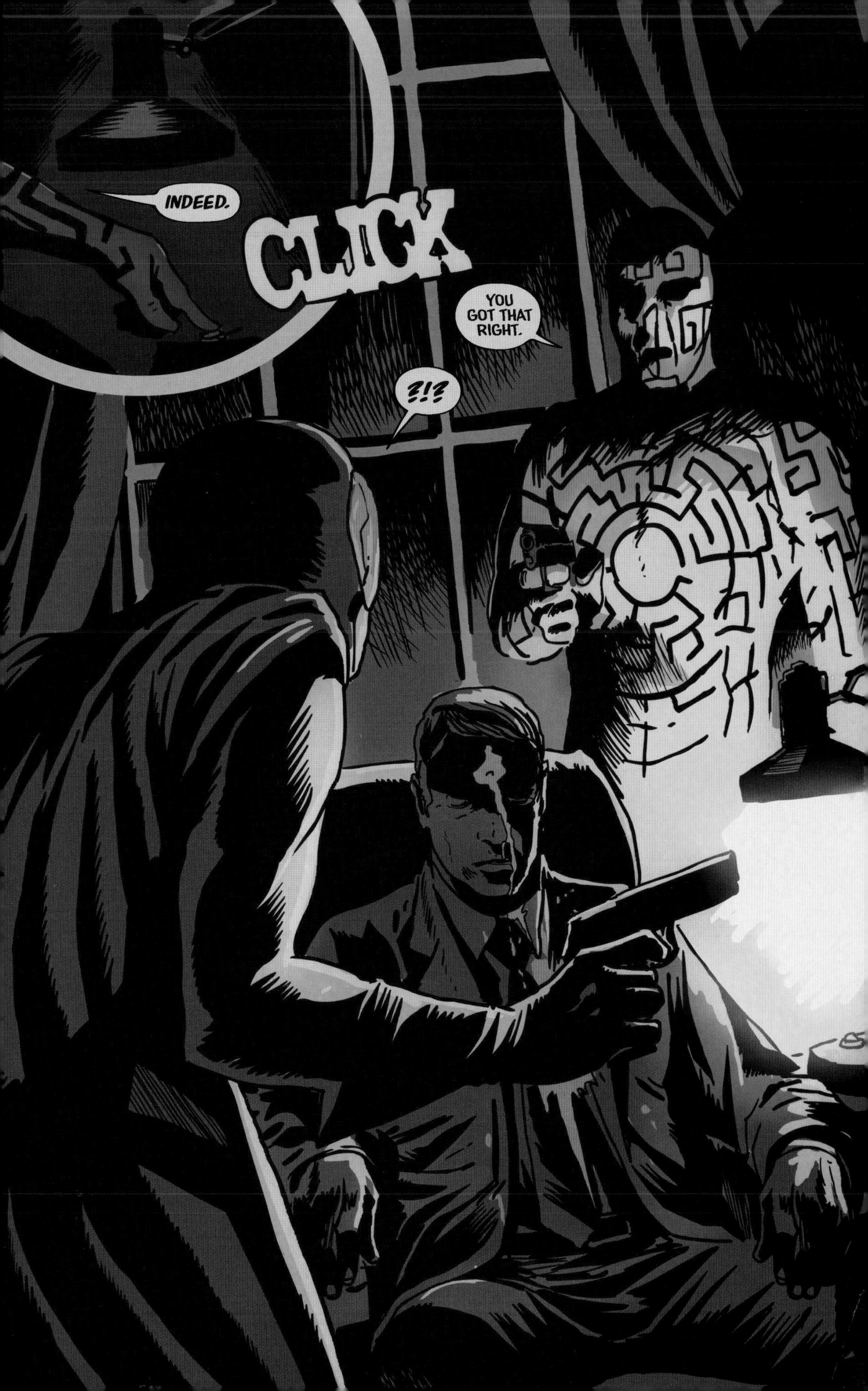
INDEED.
CLICK
YOU GOT THAT RIGHT.
?!?

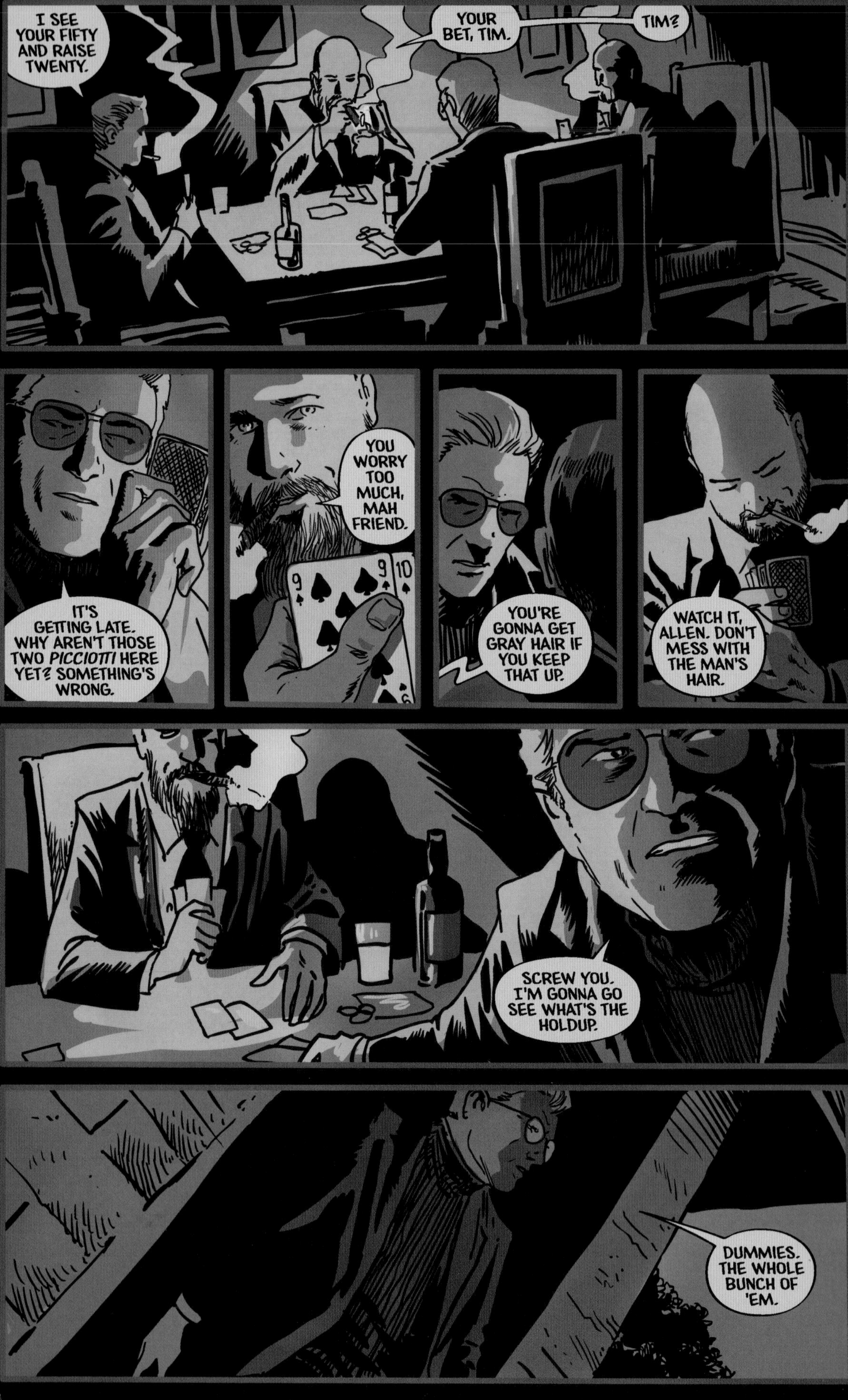
I SEE YOUR FIFTY AND RAISE TWENTY.
YOUR BET, TIM.
TIM?
IT'S GETTING LATE. WHY AREN'T THOSE TWO *PICCIOTTI* HERE YET? SOMETHING'S WRONG.
YOU WORRY TOO MUCH, MAH FRIEND.
YOU'RE GONNA GET GRAY HAIR IF YOU KEEP THAT UP.
WATCH IT, ALLEN. DON'T MESS WITH THE MAN'S HAIR.
SCREW YOU. I'M GONNA GO SEE WHAT'S THE HOLDUP.
DUMMIES. THE WHOLE BUNCH OF 'EM.

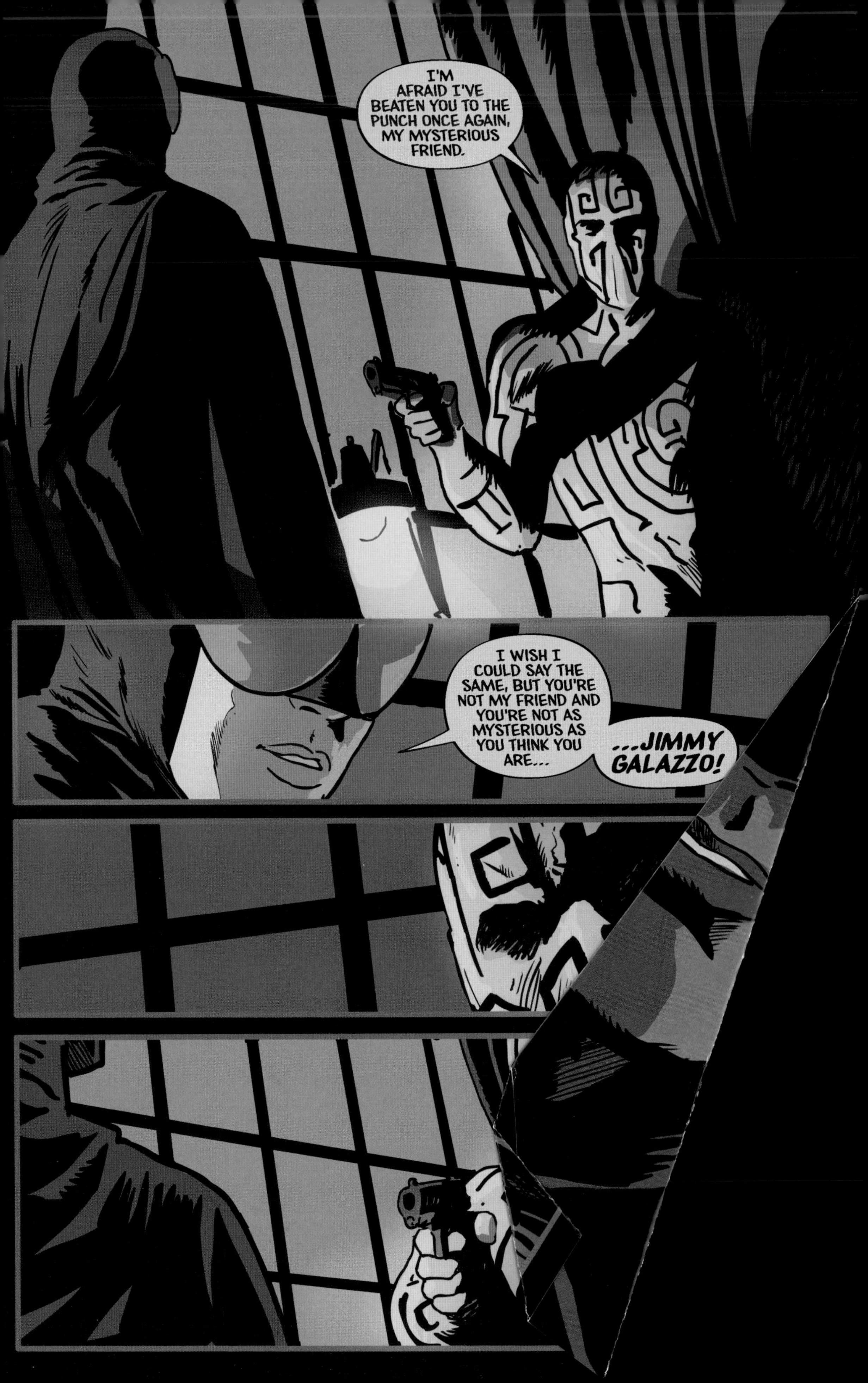
I'M AFRAID I'VE BEATEN YOU TO THE PUNCH ONCE AGAIN, MY MYSTERIOUS FRIEND.
I WISH I COULD SAY THE SAME, BUT YOU'RE NOT MY FRIEND AND YOU'RE NOT AS MYSTERIOUS AS YOU THINK YOU ARE...
...JIMMY GALAZZO!

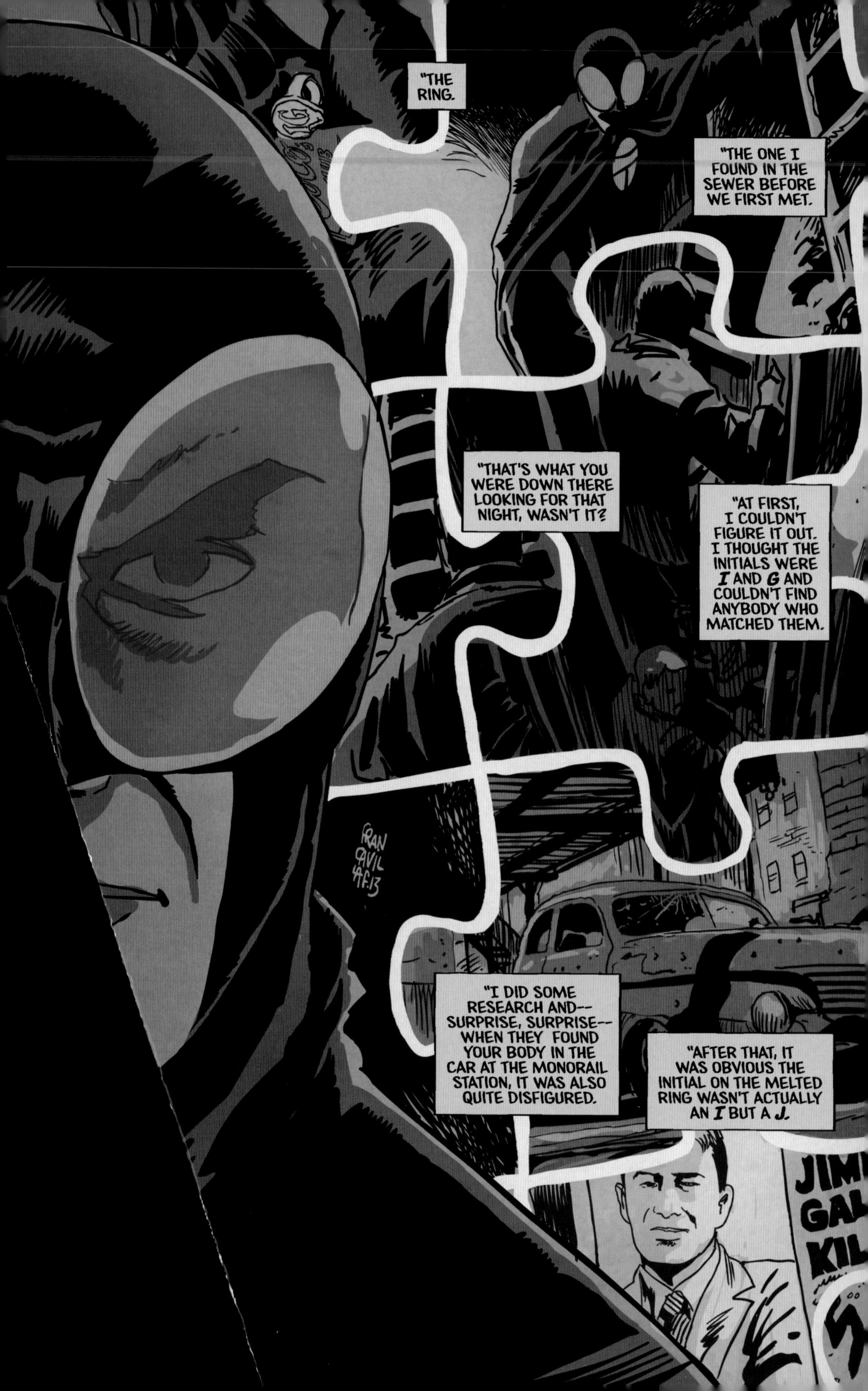
"THE RING.
"THE ONE I FOUND IN THE SEWER BEFORE WE FIRST MET.
"THAT'S WHAT YOU WERE DOWN THERE LOOKING FOR THAT NIGHT, WASN'T IT?
"AT FIRST, I COULDN'T FIGURE IT OUT. I THOUGHT THE INITIALS WERE *I* AND *G* AND COULDN'T FIND ANYBODY WHO MATCHED THEM.
"I DID SOME RESEARCH AND-- SURPRISE, SURPRISE-- WHEN THEY FOUND YOUR BODY IN THE CAR AT THE MONORAIL STATION, IT WAS ALSO QUITE DISFIGURED.
"AFTER THAT, IT WAS OBVIOUS THE INITIAL ON THE MELTED RING WASN'T ACTUALLY AN *I* BUT A *J*.
FRAN CAVIL

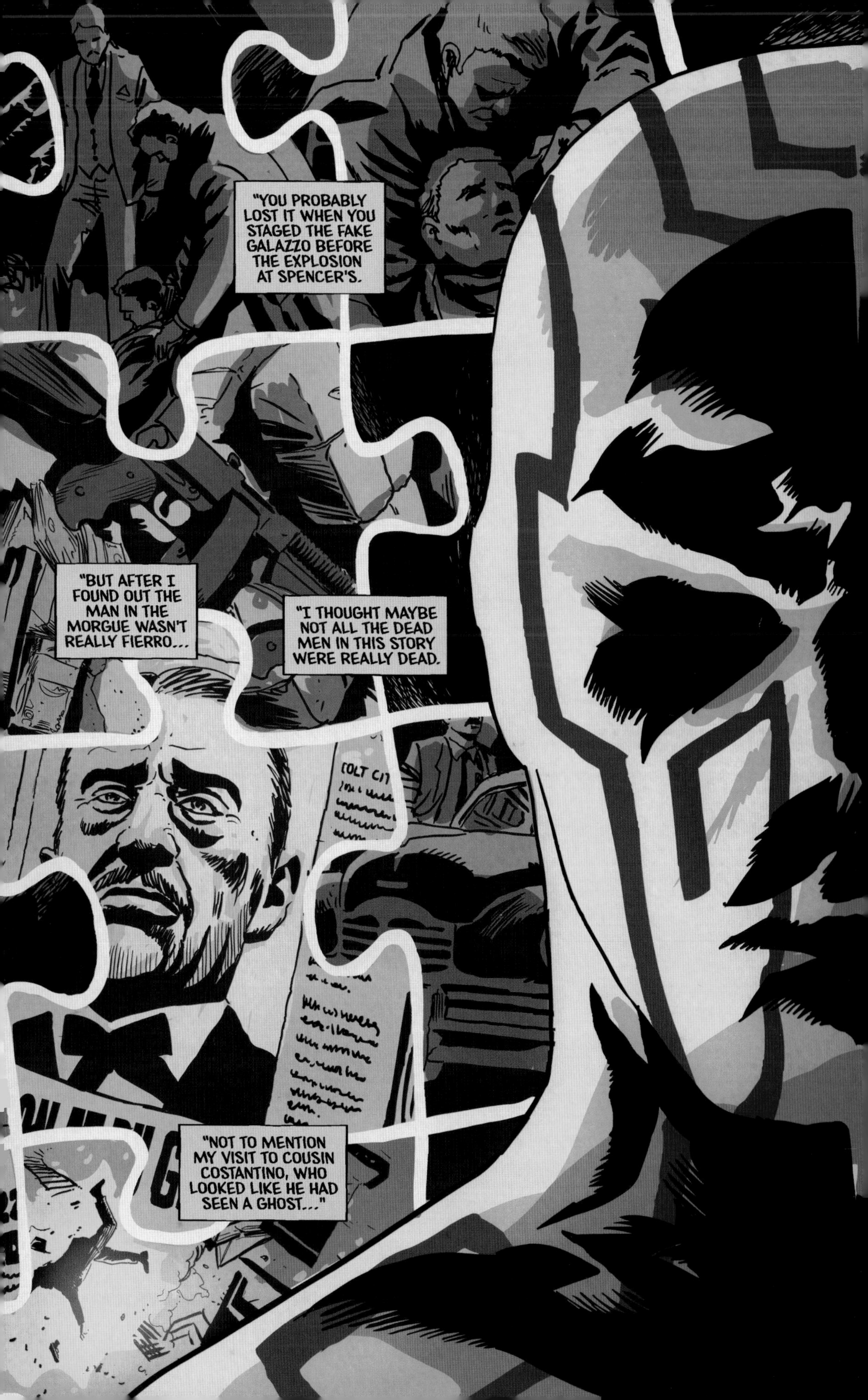
"YOU PROBABLY LOST IT WHEN YOU STAGED THE FAKE GALAZZO BEFORE THE EXPLOSION AT SPENCER'S.
"BUT AFTER I FOUND OUT THE MAN IN THE MORGUE WASN'T REALLY FIERRO...
"I THOUGHT MAYBE NOT ALL THE DEAD MEN IN THIS STORY WERE REALLY DEAD.
"NOT TO MENTION MY VISIT TO COUSIN COSTANTINO, WHO LOOKED LIKE HE HAD SEEN A GHOST..."
COLT CIT

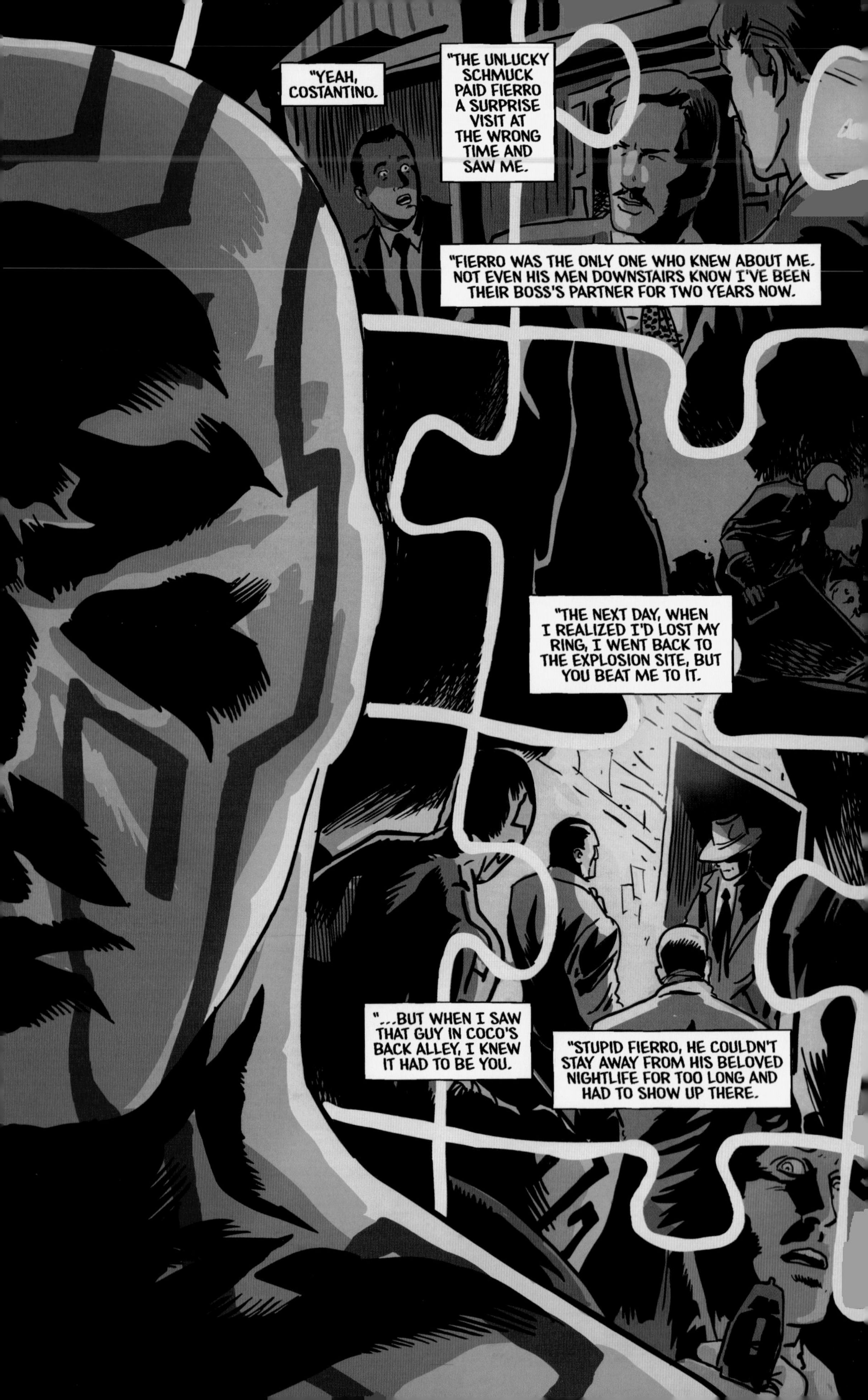
"YEAH, COSTANTINO.
"THE UNLUCKY SCHMUCK PAID FIERRO A SURPRISE VISIT AT THE WRONG TIME AND SAW ME.
"FIERRO WAS THE ONLY ONE WHO KNEW ABOUT ME. NOT EVEN HIS MEN DOWNSTAIRS KNOW I'VE BEEN THEIR BOSS'S PARTNER FOR TWO YEARS NOW.
"THE NEXT DAY, WHEN I REALIZED I'D LOST MY RING, I WENT BACK TO THE EXPLOSION SITE, BUT YOU BEAT ME TO IT.
"...BUT WHEN I SAW THAT GUY IN COCO'S BACK ALLEY, I KNEW IT HAD TO BE YOU.
"STUPID FIERRO, HE COULDN'T STAY AWAY FROM HIS BELOVED NIGHTLIFE FOR TOO LONG AND HAD TO SHOW UP THERE.

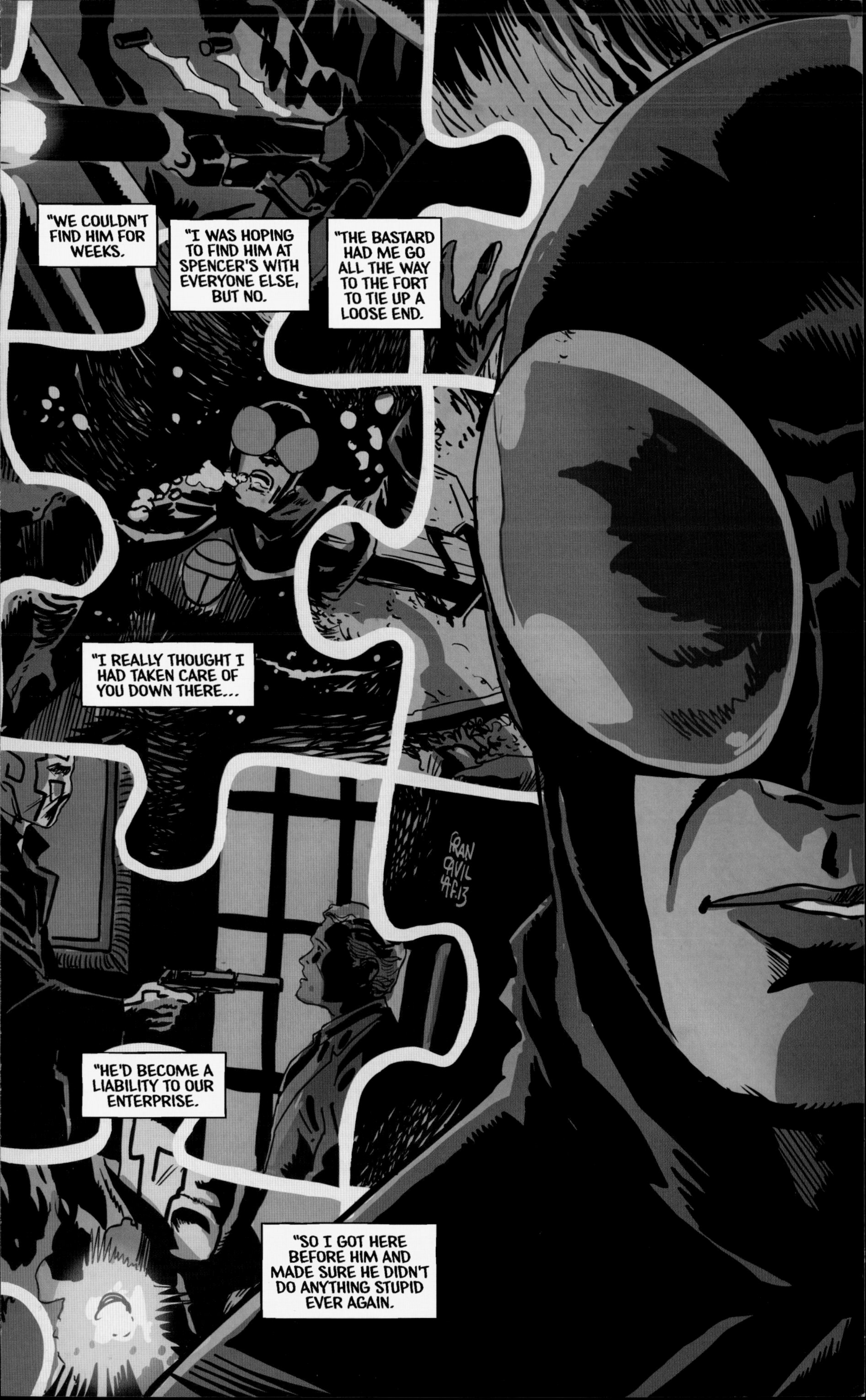
"WE COULDN'T FIND HIM FOR WEEKS.
"I WAS HOPING TO FIND HIM AT SPENCER'S WITH EVERYONE ELSE, BUT NO.
"THE BASTARD HAD ME GO ALL THE WAY TO THE FORT TO TIE UP A LOOSE END.
"I REALLY THOUGHT I HAD TAKEN CARE OF YOU DOWN THERE...
FRAN CAVIL 13
"HE'D BECOME A LIABILITY TO OUR ENTERPRISE.
"SO I GOT HERE BEFORE HIM AND MADE SURE HE DIDN'T DO ANYTHING STUPID EVER AGAIN.

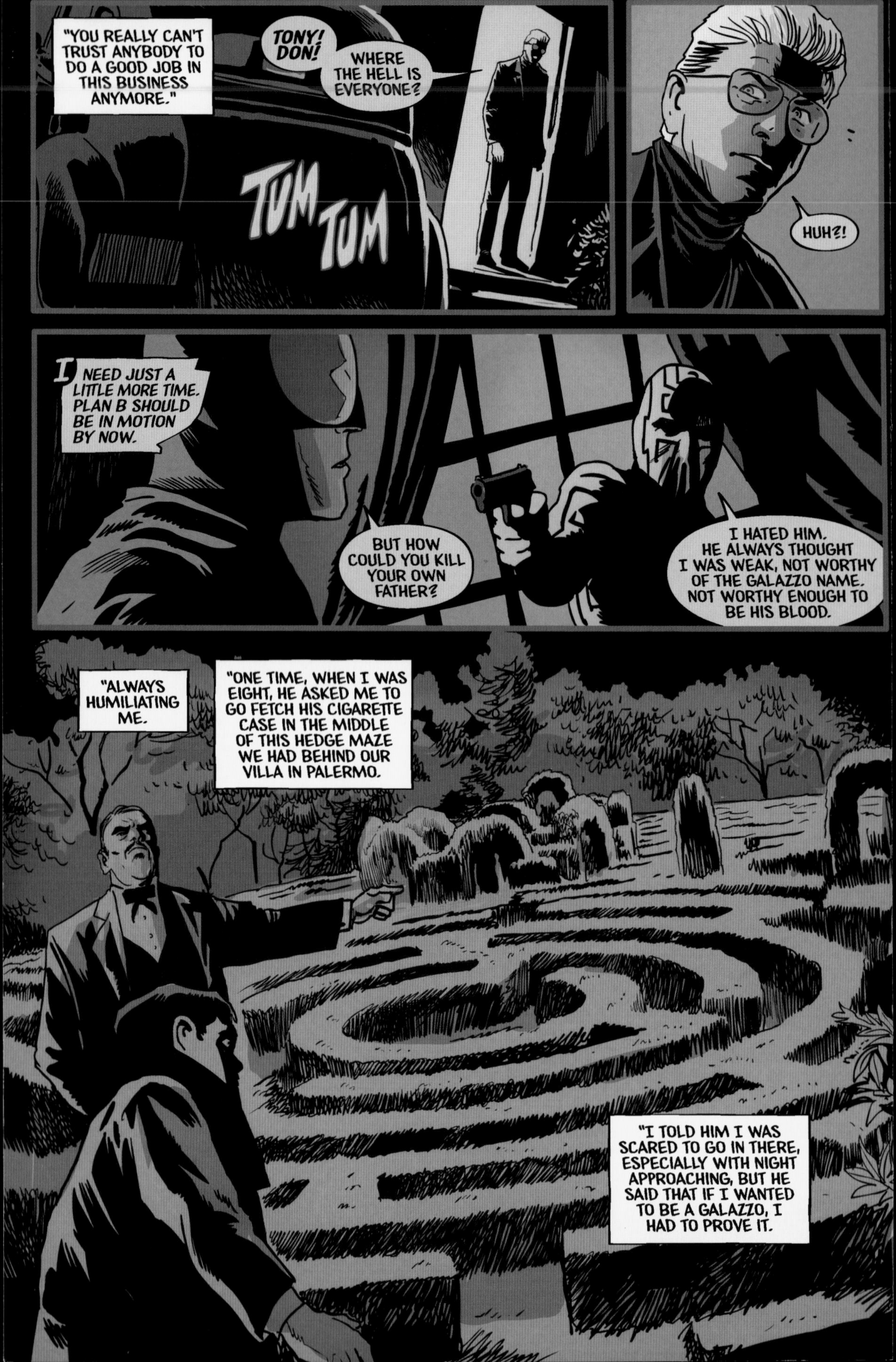
"YOU REALLY CAN'T TRUST ANYBODY TO DO A GOOD JOB IN THIS BUSINESS ANYMORE."
TONY! DON!
WHERE THE HELL IS EVERYONE?
TUM TUM
HUH?!
I NEED JUST A LITTLE MORE TIME. PLAN B SHOULD BE IN MOTION BY NOW.
BUT HOW COULD YOU KILL YOUR OWN FATHER?
I HATED HIM. HE ALWAYS THOUGHT I WAS WEAK, NOT WORTHY OF THE GALAZZO NAME. NOT WORTHY ENOUGH TO BE HIS BLOOD.
"ALWAYS HUMILIATING ME.
"ONE TIME, WHEN I WAS EIGHT, HE ASKED ME TO GO FETCH HIS CIGARETTE CASE IN THE MIDDLE OF THIS HEDGE MAZE WE HAD BEHIND OUR VILLA IN PALERMO.
"I TOLD HIM I WAS SCARED TO GO IN THERE, ESPECIALLY WITH NIGHT APPROACHING, BUT HE SAID THAT IF I WANTED TO BE A GALAZZO, I HAD TO PROVE IT.

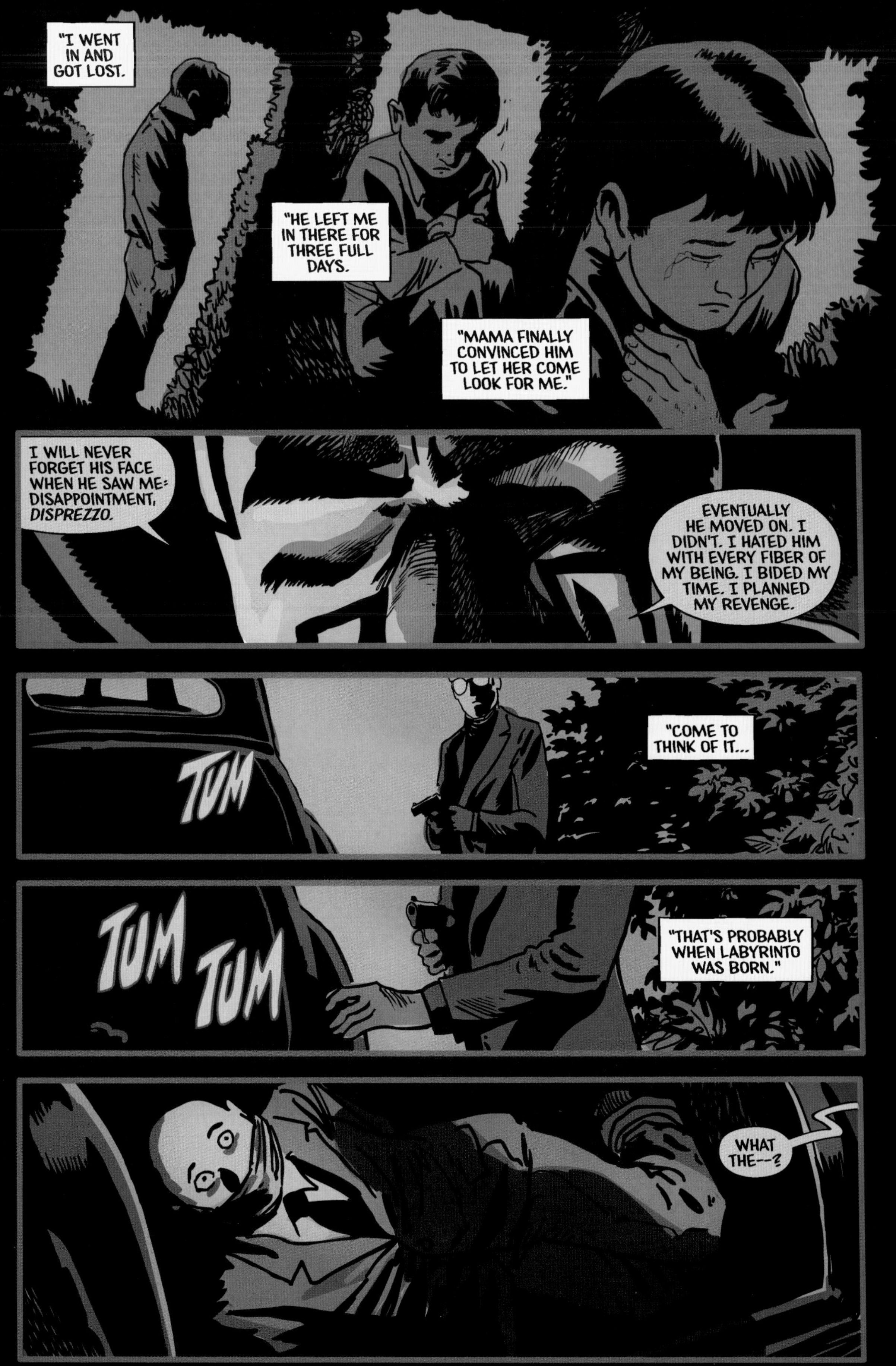

"I WENT IN AND GOT LOST.
"HE LEFT ME IN THERE FOR THREE FULL DAYS.
"MAMA FINALLY CONVINCED HIM TO LET HER COME LOOK FOR ME."
I WILL NEVER FORGET HIS FACE WHEN HE SAW ME: DISAPPOINTMENT, *DISPREZZO.*
EVENTUALLY HE MOVED ON. I DIDN'T. I HATED HIM WITH EVERY FIBER OF MY BEING. I BIDED MY TIME. I PLANNED MY REVENGE.
TUM
"COME TO THINK OF IT...
TUM TUM
"THAT'S PROBABLY WHEN LABYRINTO WAS BORN."
WHAT THE--?

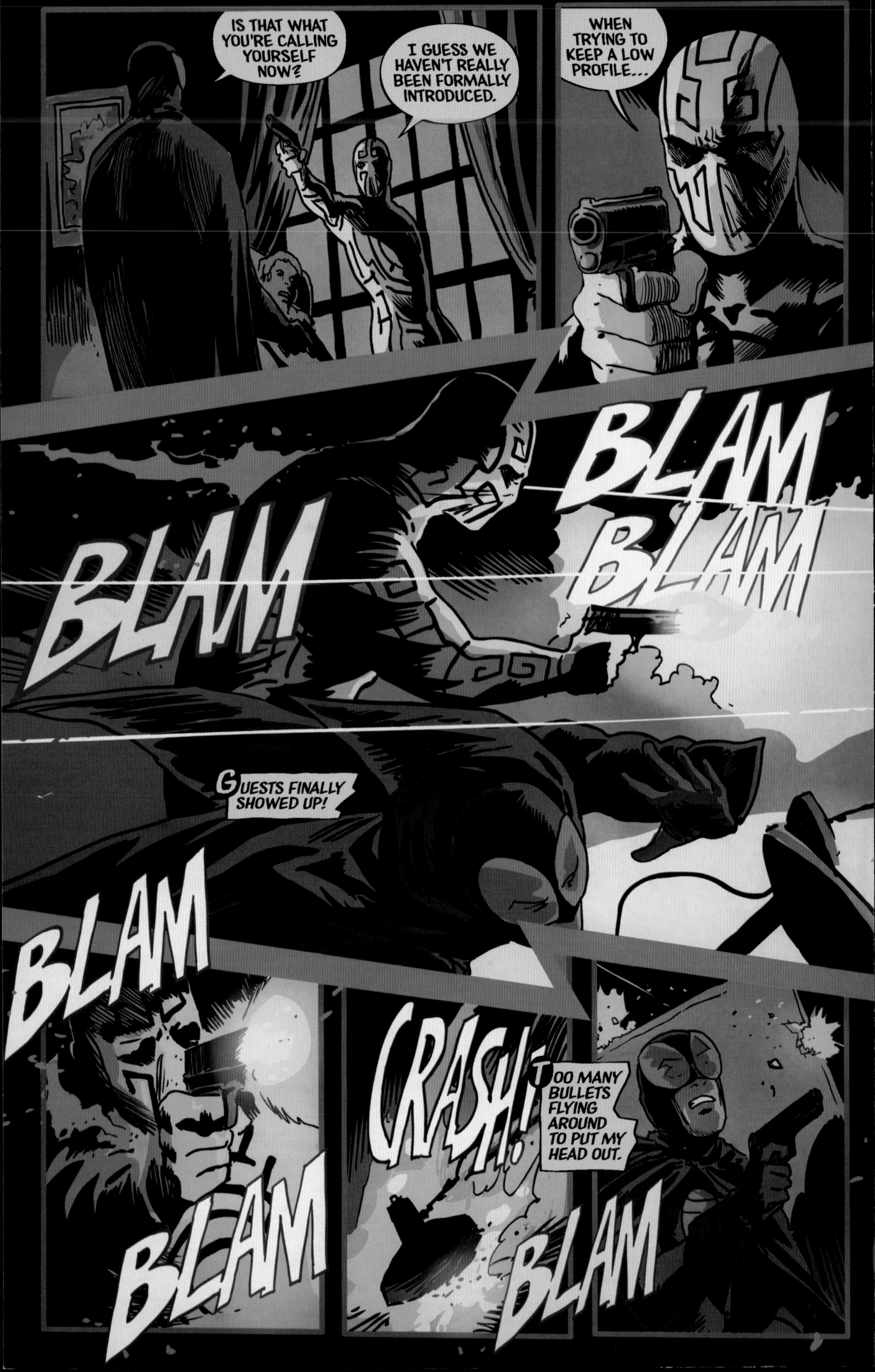
IS THAT WHAT YOU'RE CALLING YOURSELF NOW?
I GUESS WE HAVEN'T REALLY BEEN FORMALLY INTRODUCED.
WHEN TRYING TO KEEP A LOW PROFILE...
BLAM
BLAM
BLAM
GUESTS FINALLY SHOWED UP!
BLAM
BLAM
CRASH!
TOO MANY BULLETS FLYING AROUND TO PUT MY HEAD OUT.
BLAM

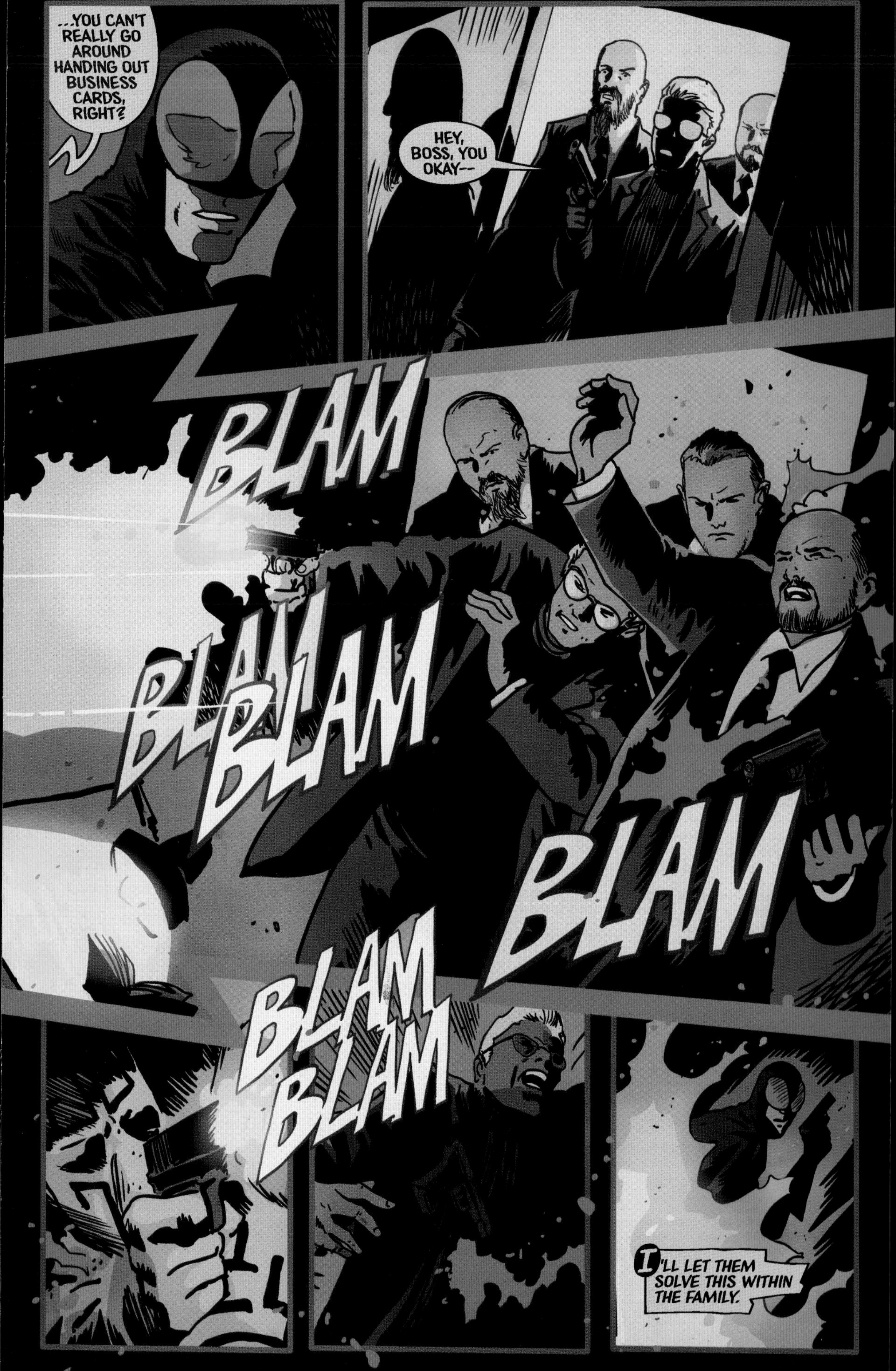
...YOU CAN'T REALLY GO AROUND HANDING OUT BUSINESS CARDS, RIGHT?
HEY, BOSS, YOU OKAY--
BLAM
BLAM
BLAM
BLAM
BLAM
BLAM
BLAM
I'LL LET THEM SOLVE THIS WITHIN THE FAMILY.

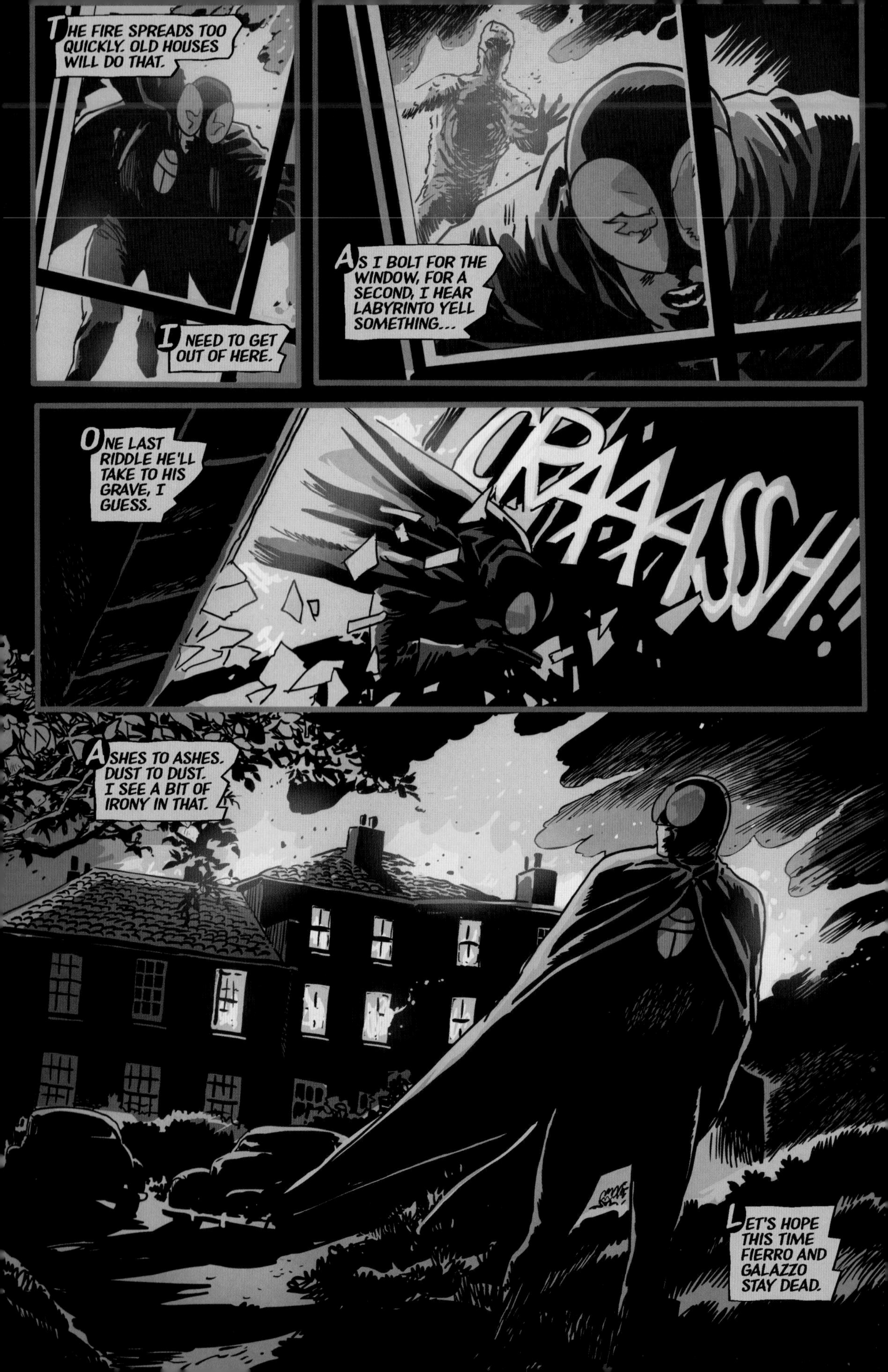

THE FIRE SPREADS TOO QUICKLY. OLD HOUSES WILL DO THAT.
I NEED TO GET OUT OF HERE.
AS I BOLT FOR THE WINDOW, FOR A SECOND, I HEAR LABYRINTO YELL SOMETHING...
ONE LAST RIDDLE HE'LL TAKE TO HIS GRAVE, I GUESS.
CRAAAASSH!!!
ASHES TO ASHES. DUST TO DUST. I SEE A BIT OF IRONY IN THAT.
LET'S HOPE THIS TIME FIERRO AND GALAZZO STAY DEAD.

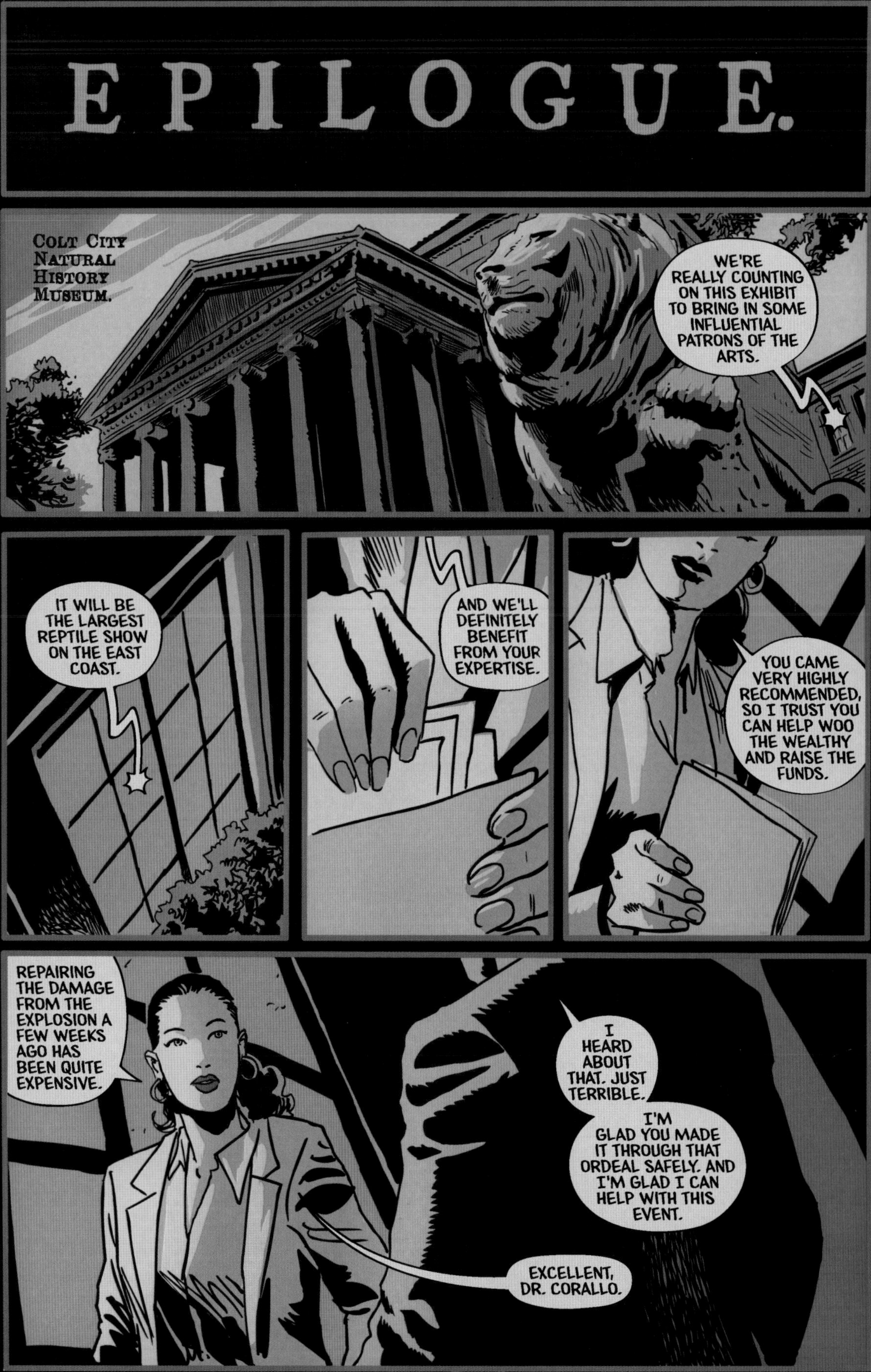
EPILOGUE.
COLT CITY NATURAL HISTORY MUSEUM.
WE'RE REALLY COUNTING ON THIS EXHIBIT TO BRING IN SOME INFLUENTIAL PATRONS OF THE ARTS.
IT WILL BE THE LARGEST REPTILE SHOW ON THE EAST COAST.
AND WE'LL DEFINITELY BENEFIT FROM YOUR EXPERTISE.
YOU CAME VERY HIGHLY RECOMMENDED, SO I TRUST YOU CAN HELP WOO THE WEALTHY AND RAISE THE FUNDS.
REPAIRING THE DAMAGE FROM THE EXPLOSION A FEW WEEKS AGO HAS BEEN QUITE EXPENSIVE.
I HEARD ABOUT THAT. JUST TERRIBLE.
I'M GLAD YOU MADE IT THROUGH THAT ORDEAL SAFELY. AND I'M GLAD I CAN HELP WITH THIS EVENT.
EXCELLENT, DR. CORALLO.

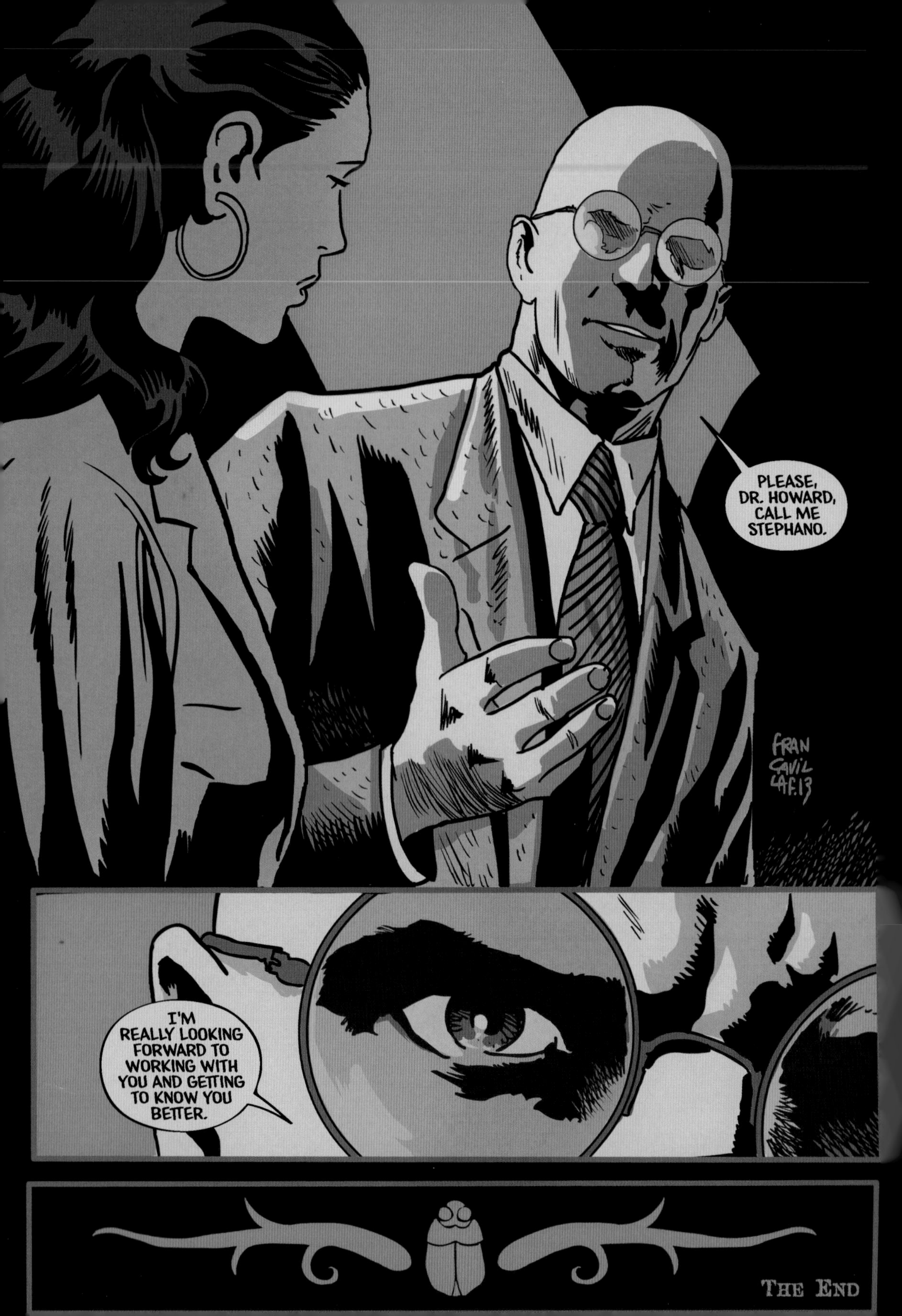
PLEASE, DR. HOWARD, CALL ME STEPHANO.
I'M REALLY LOOKING FORWARD TO WORKING WITH YOU AND GETTING TO KNOW YOU BETTER.
THE END

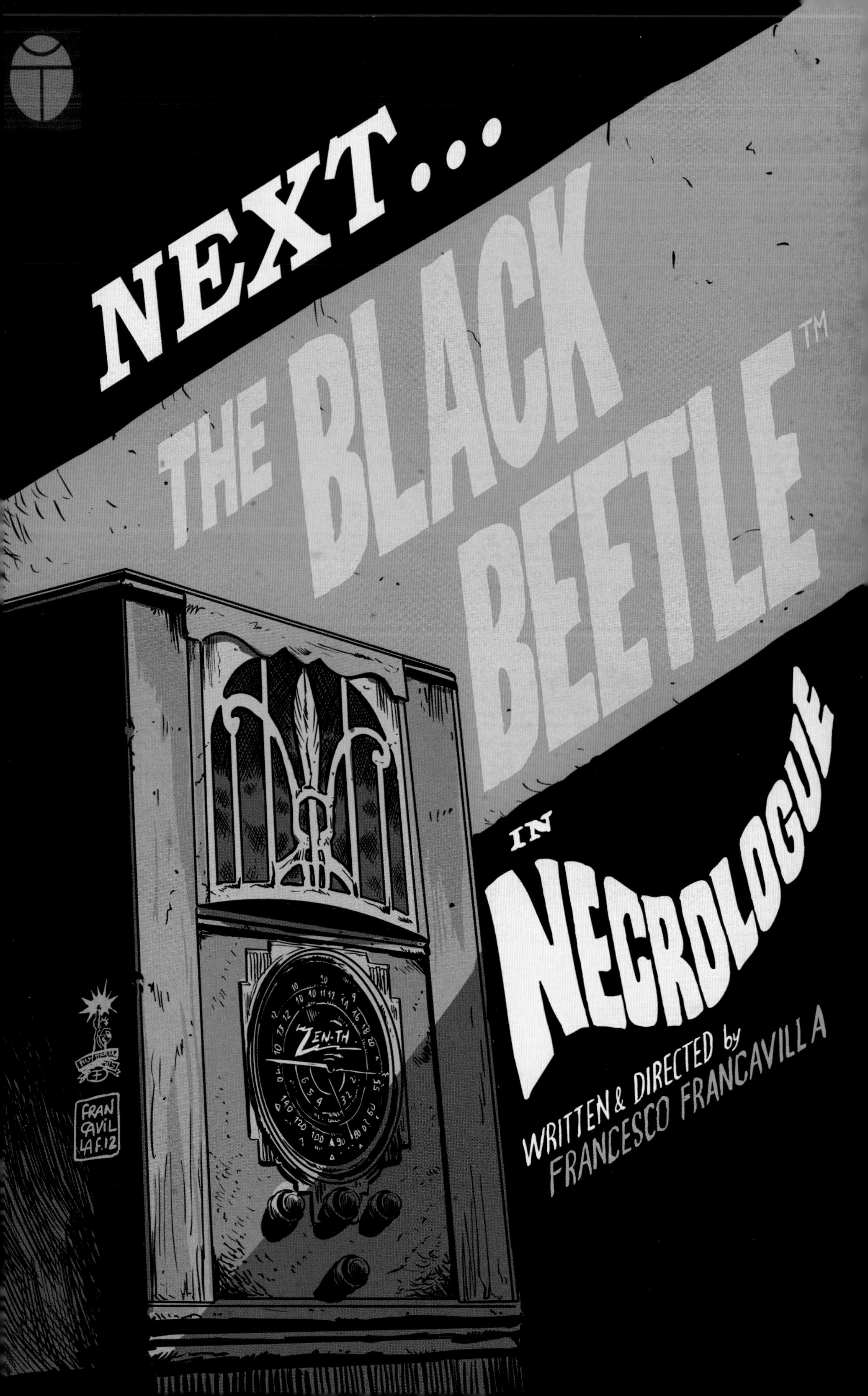
NEXT...
THE BLACK BEETLE™
IN
NECROLOGUE
WRITTEN & DIRECTED by
FRANCESCO FRANCAVILLA
FRANCAVILLA F.12

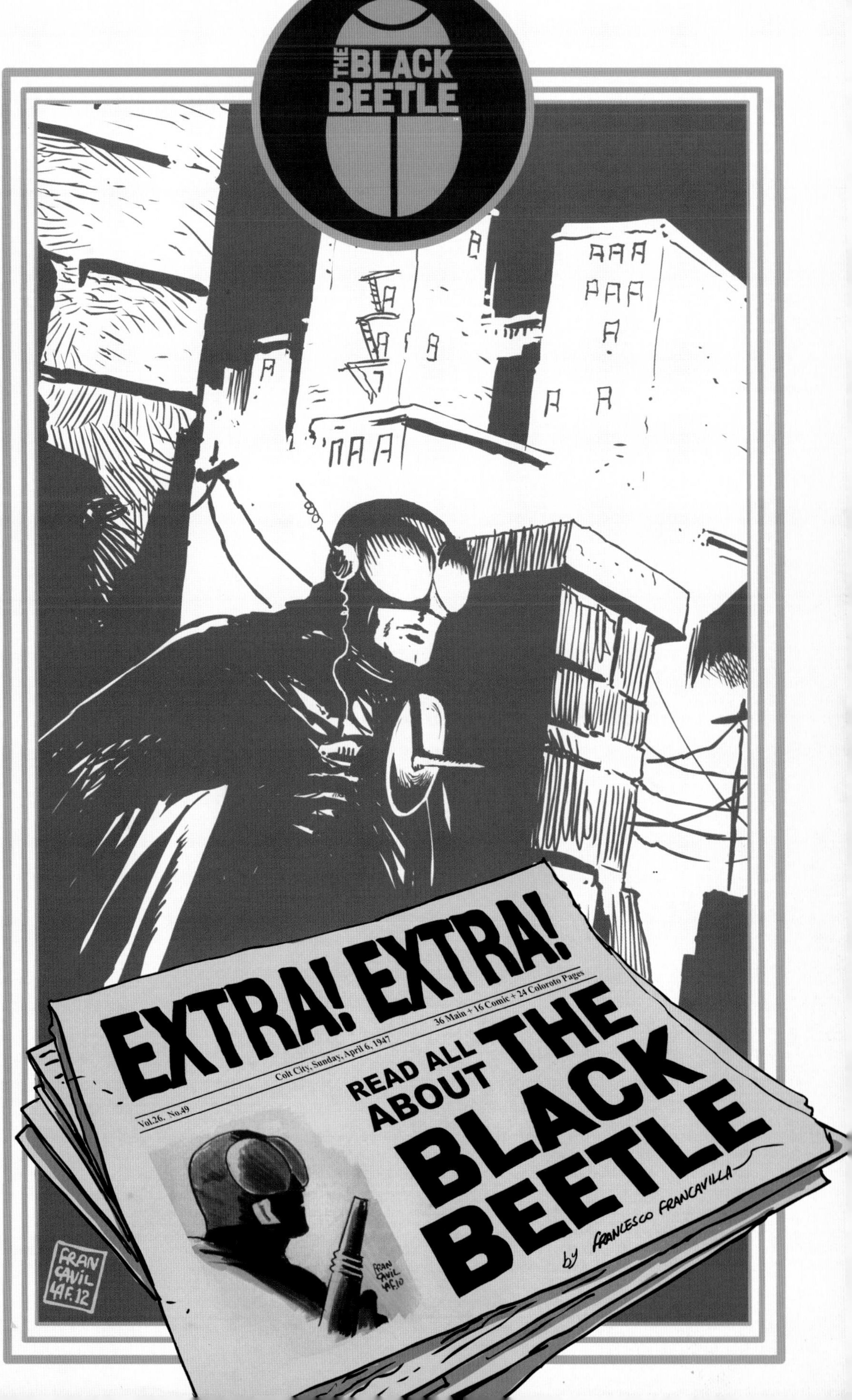
THE BLACK BEETLE
EXTRA! EXTRA!
36 Main + 16 Comic + 24 Coloroto Pages
Colt City, Sunday, April 6, 1947
Vol.26. No.49
READ ALL ABOUT THE BLACK BEETLE
by FRANCESCO FRANCAVILLA
FRAN CAVIL LA F.12

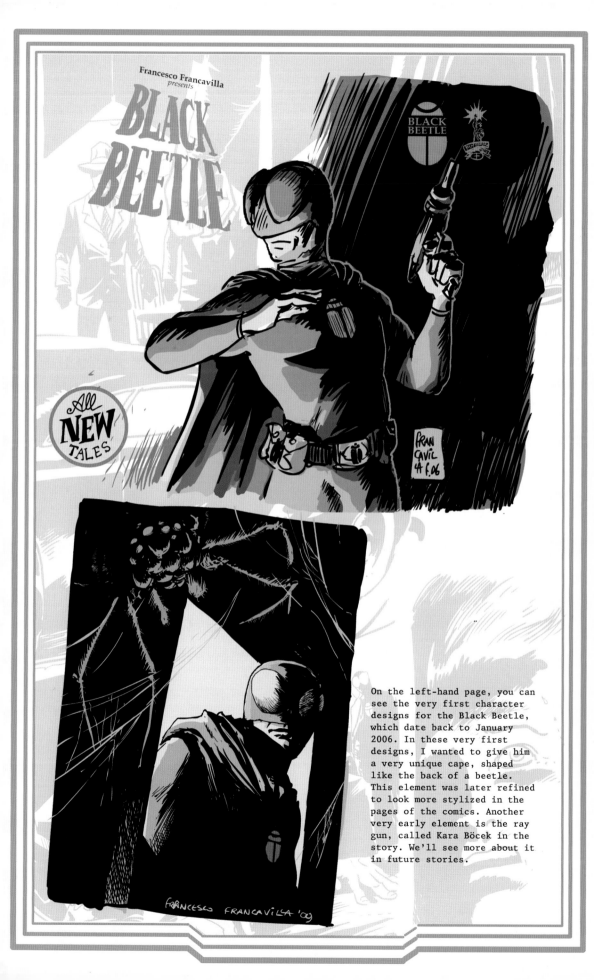

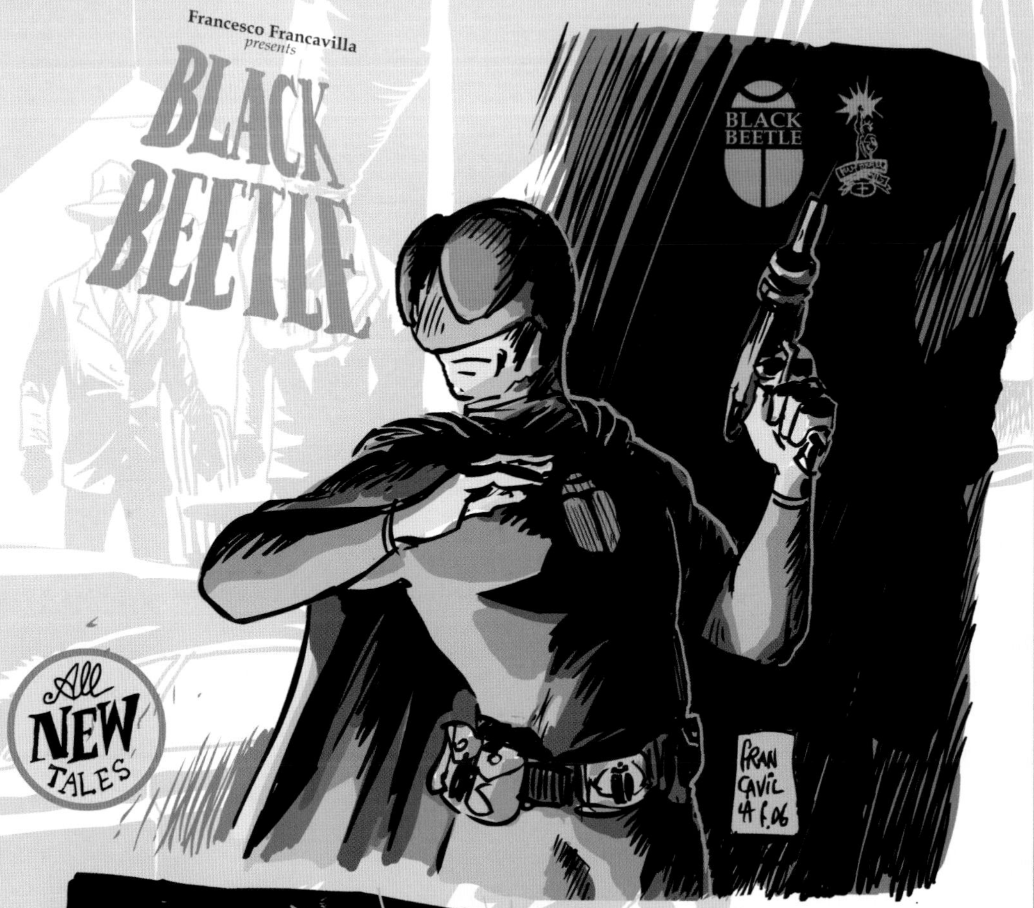
Francesco Francavilla
presents
BLACK
BEETLE
BLACK
BEETLE
All
NEW
TALES
FRAN
CAVIL
LA F.06

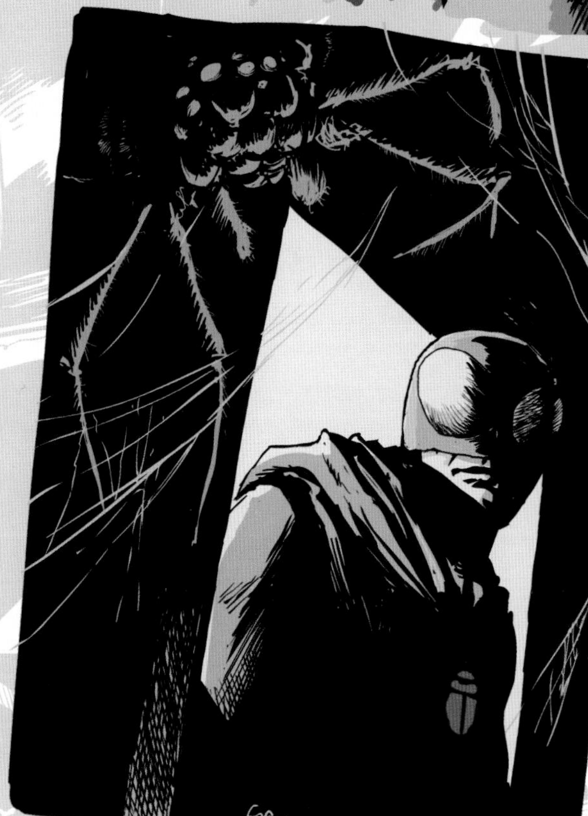
FRANCESCO FRANCAVILLA '09

On the left-hand page, you can see the very first character designs for the Black Beetle, which date back to January 2006. In these very first designs, I wanted to give him a very unique cape, shaped like the back of a beetle. This element was later refined to look more stylized in the pages of the comics. Another very early element is the ray gun, called Kara Böcek in the story. We'll see more about it in future stories.

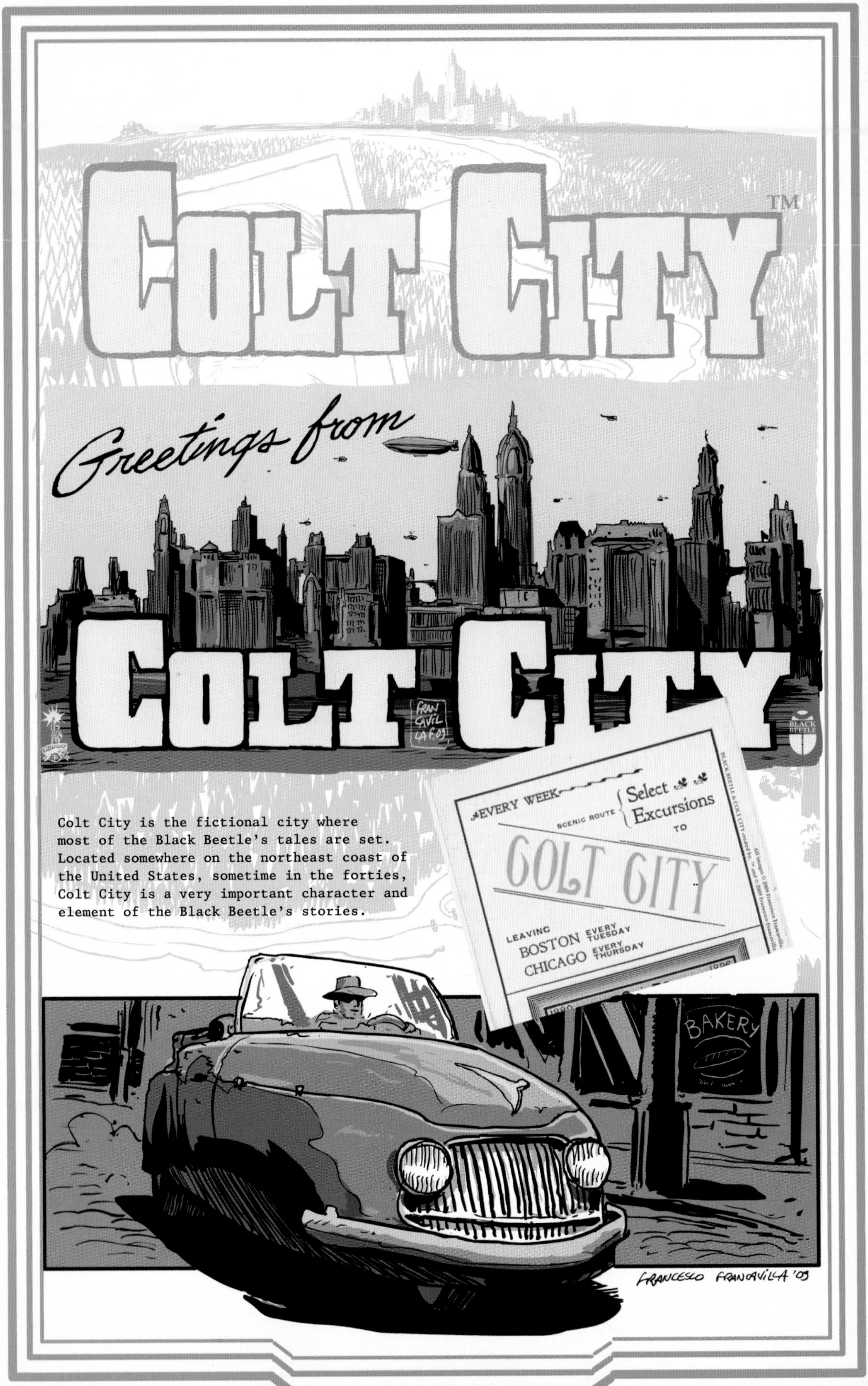
COLT CITY™
Greetings from
COLT CITY
FRAN CAVIL LA f.09
BLACK BEETLE
EVERY WEEK
SCENIC ROUTE
Select Excursions
TO
COLT CITY
LEAVING
BOSTON EVERY TUESDAY
CHICAGO EVERY THURSDAY
BAKERY
FRANCESCO FRANCAVILLA '09

Colt City is the fictional city where most of the Black Beetle's tales are set. Located somewhere on the northeast coast of the United States, sometime in the forties, Colt City is a very important character and element of the Black Beetle's stories.

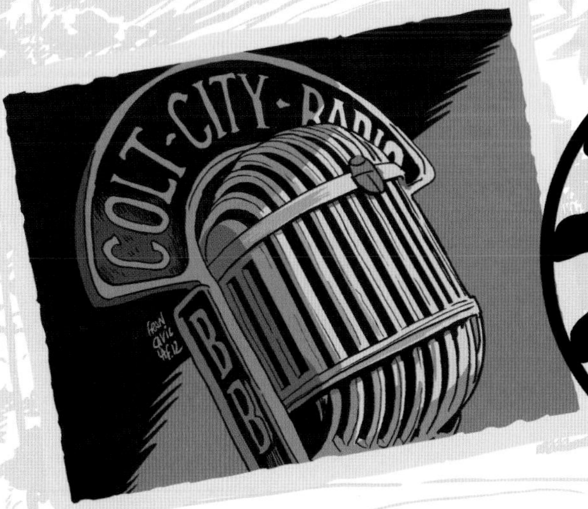
COLT-CITY-
BB

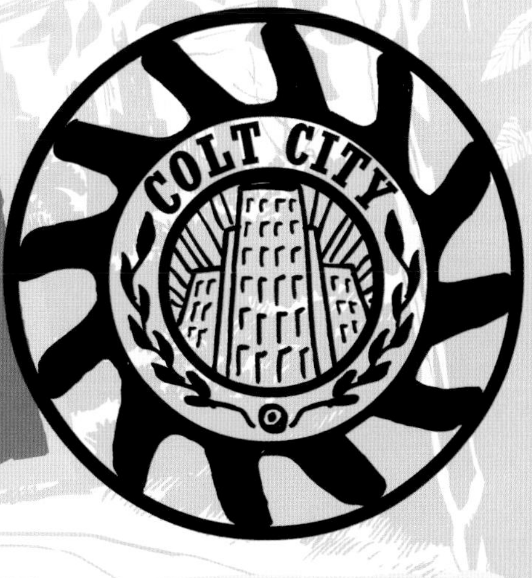
COLT CITY

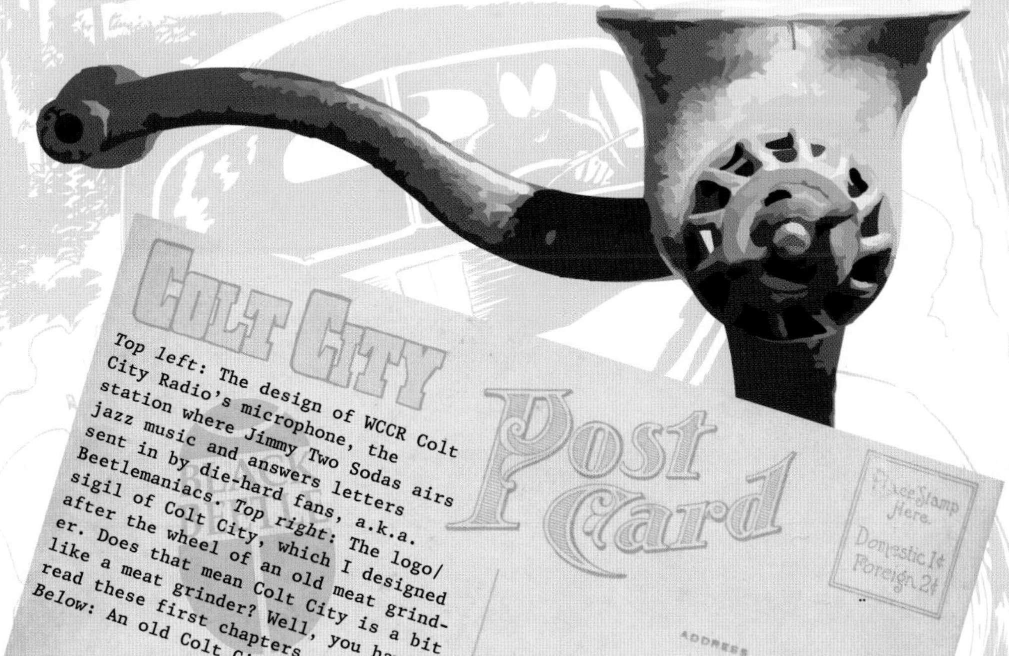
COLT CITY
Post Card
Place Stamp Here.
Domestic 1¢
Foreign 2¢
ADDRESS

Top left: The design of WCCR Colt City Radio's microphone, the station where Jimmy Two Sodas airs jazz music and answers letters sent in by die-hard fans, a.k.a. Beetlemaniacs. Top right: The logo/sigil of Colt City, which I designed after the wheel of an old meat grinder. Does that mean Colt City is a bit like a meat grinder? Well, you have read these first chapters . . . Below: An old Colt City postcard.

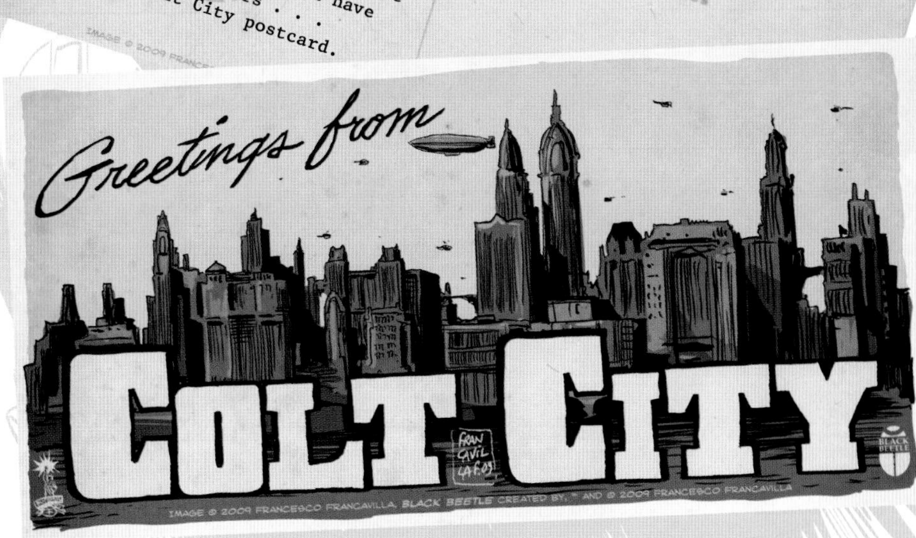
Greetings from
COLT CITY
IMAGE © 2009 FRANCESCO FRANCAVILLA. BLACK BEETLE CREATED BY, ™ AND © 2009 FRANCESCO FRANCAVILLA

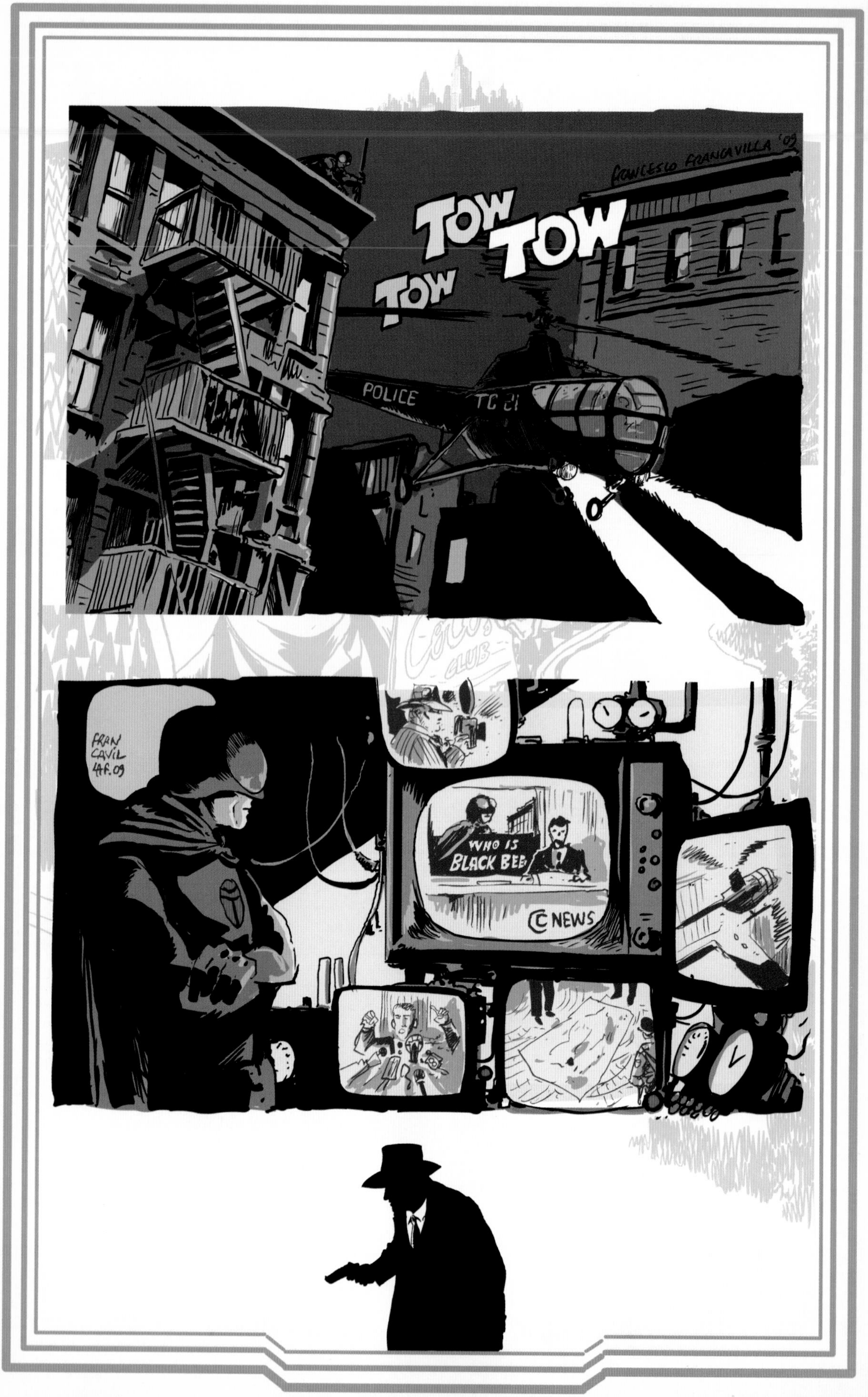
FRANCESCO FRANCAVILLA '09
TOW
TOW
TOW
POLICE
WHO IS
BLACK BEE
NEWS

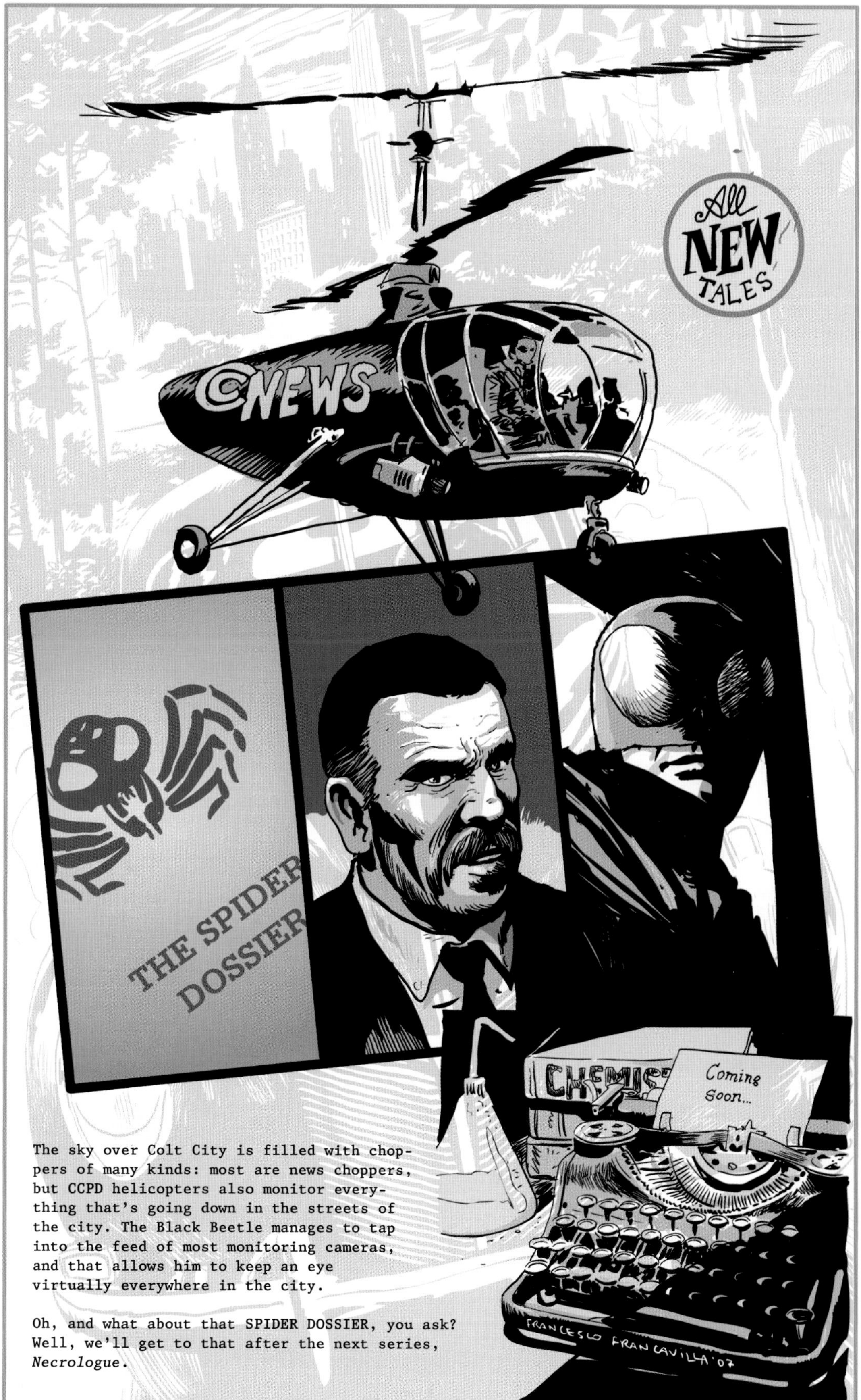

NEWS
All NEW TALES
THE SPIDER DOSSIER
CHEMIS
Coming Soon...
FRANCESCO FRANCAVILLA '07

The sky over Colt City is filled with choppers of many kinds: most are news choppers, but CCPD helicopters also monitor everything that's going down in the streets of the city. The Black Beetle manages to tap into the feed of most monitoring cameras, and that allows him to keep an eye virtually everywhere in the city.

Oh, and what about that SPIDER DOSSIER, you ask? Well, we'll get to that after the next series, *Necrologue*.

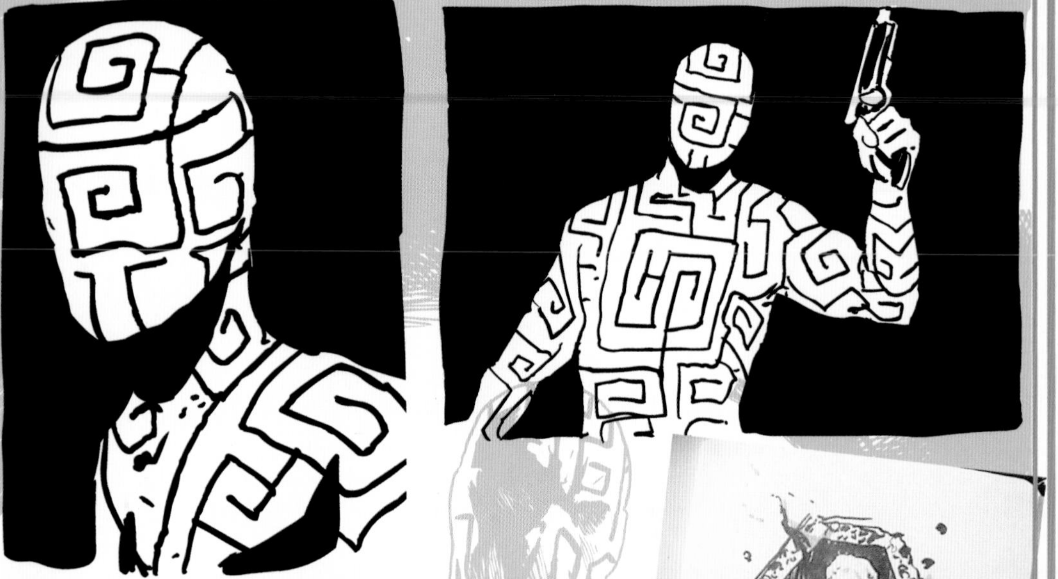

LABYRINTO

Above: The very first appearance of Labyrinto . . . on paper! As you can see, I changed the design of the maze a bit from its original incarnation. Evolution of any design happens all the time. You start with a rough concept and then you polish it until it's ready to be used.

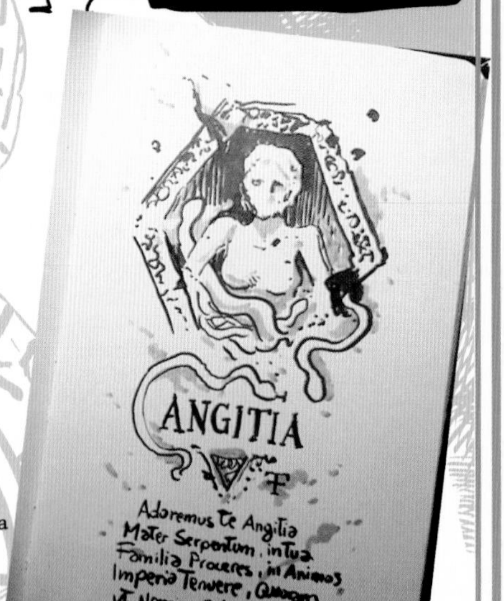
ANGITIA
Adoremus te Angitia
Mater Serpentum, in Tua
Familia Proceres, in Animos
Imperia Tenere, Quorum
ut Nomina Celebramus,

On the right: The first sketch of the mysterious Angitia sculpture we saw in *No Way Out*.

Below: An early lobby card announcing Night Shift, the very first Black Beetle story, which appeared in the pages of *Dark Horse Presents*.

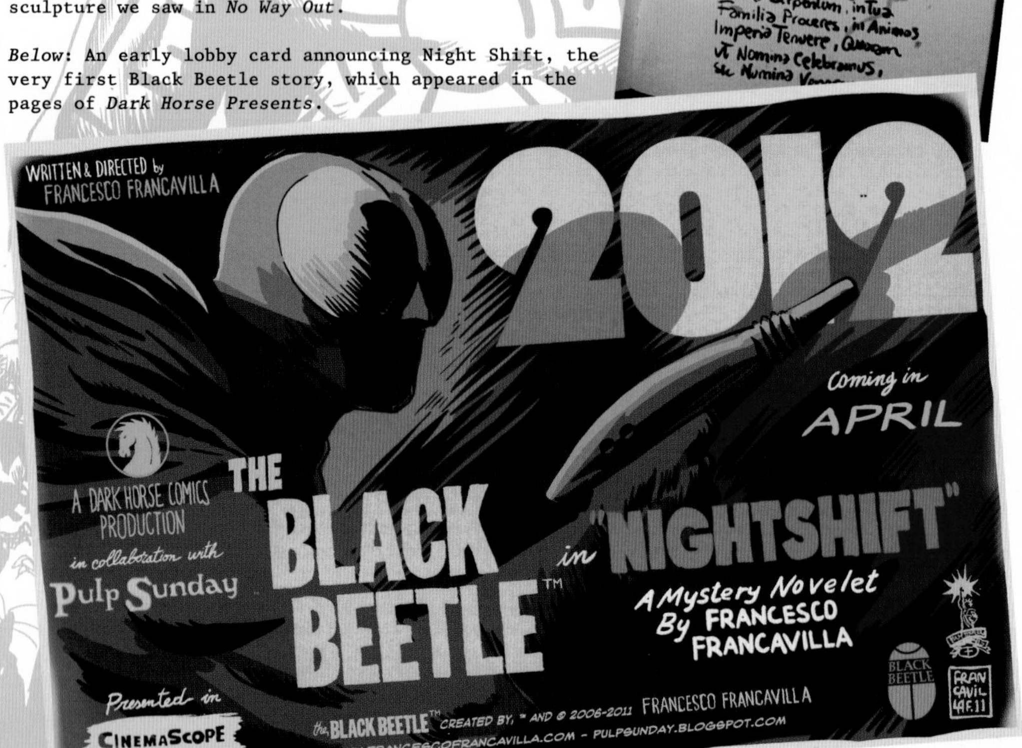
WRITTEN & DIRECTED by
FRANCESCO FRANCAVILLA
2012
Coming in
APRIL
A DARK HORSE COMICS PRODUCTION
in collaboration with
Pulp Sunday
THE
BLACK
BEETLE™
in "NIGHTSHIFT"
A Mystery Novelet
By FRANCESCO
FRANCAVILLA
BLACK BEETLE
FRAN CAVIL LAF.11
Presented in
CINEMASCOPE
TECHNICOLOR
the BLACK BEETLE™ CREATED BY, ™ AND © 2006-2011 FRANCESCO FRANCAVILLA
WWW.FRANCESCOFRANCAVILLA.COM - PULPSUNDAY.BLOGSPOT.COM

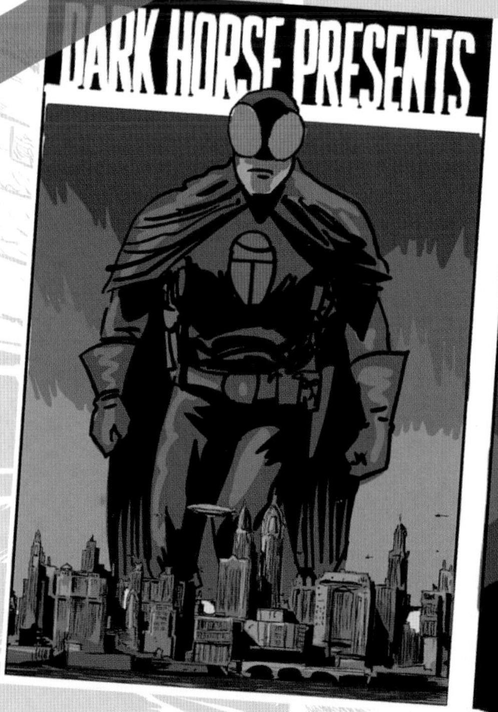
DARK HORSE PRESENTS

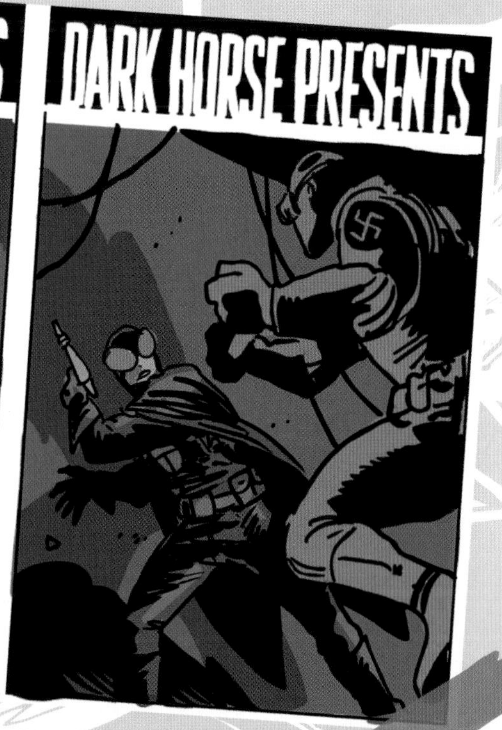
DARK HORSE PRESENTS

Layouts and concepts
for the first Black Beetle cover (for *Dark Horse Presents* #11). After a round of notes, we decided to go with the bottom right.

On the next few pages, you can see some of the layouts from *No Way Out*, mostly related to those double-page spreads that seem to be so popular among readers.

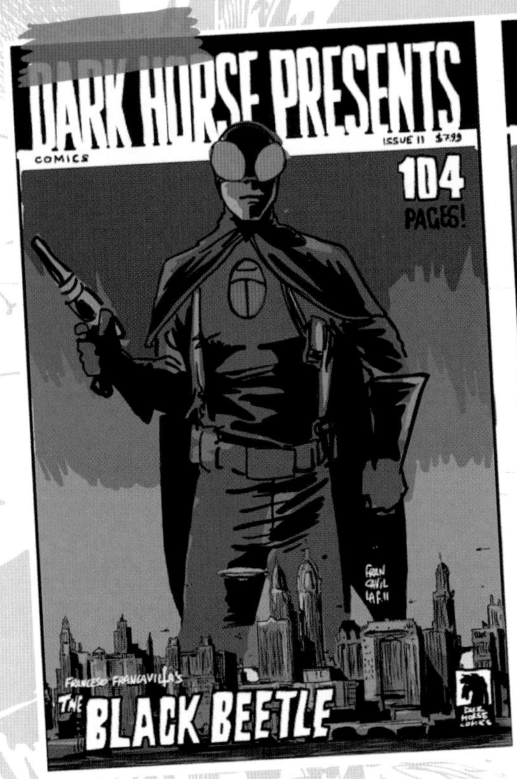
DARK HORSE PRESENTS
COMICS
ISSUE 11 $7.99
104
PAGES!
FRANCESCO FRANCAVILLA'S
THE
BLACK BEETLE

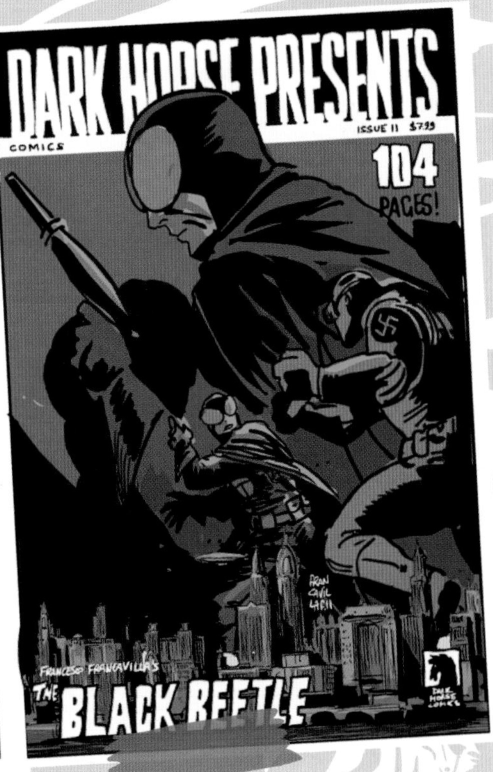
DARK HORSE PRESENTS
COMICS
ISSUE 11 $7.99
104
PAGES!
FRANCESCO FRANCAVILLA'S
THE
BLACK BEETLE

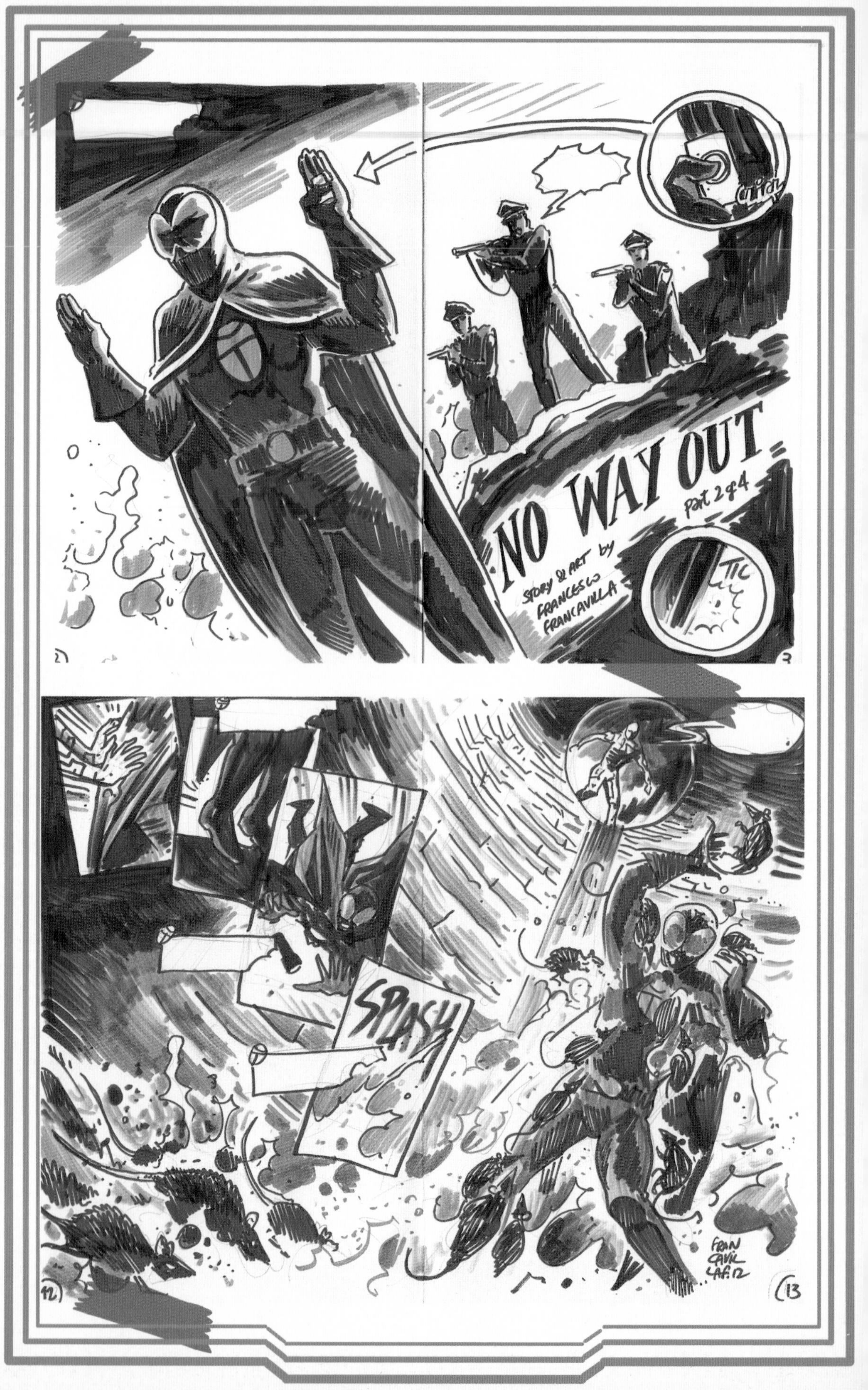
NO WAY OUT
part 2 of 4
STORY & ART by
FRANCESCO
FRANCAVILLA
TIC
SPLASH
FRAN
CAVIL
LAF.12

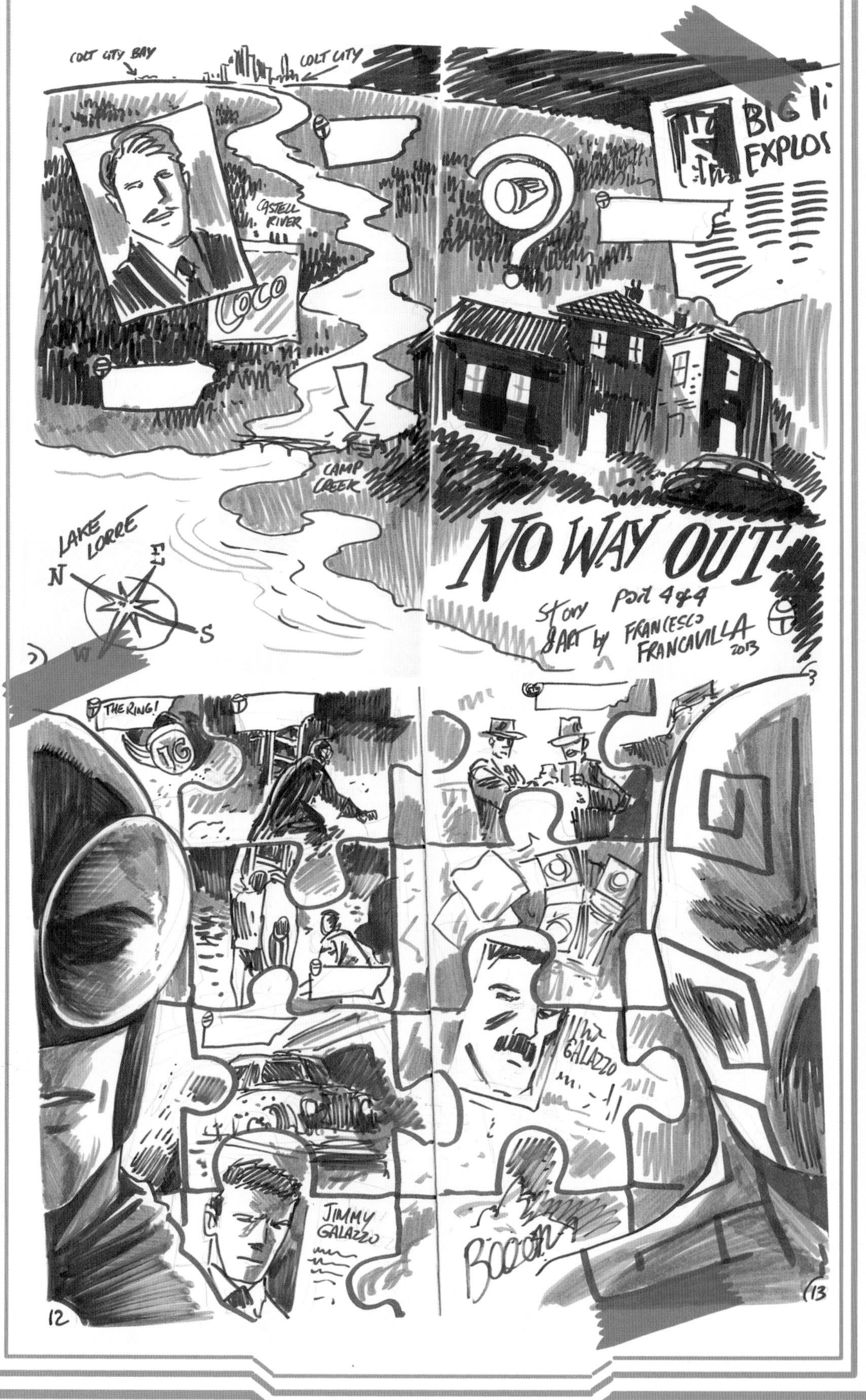

COLT CITY BAY
COLT CITY
CASTELL RIVER
COCO
CAMP CREEK
LAKE LORRE
N
E
S
W
BIG
EXPLOS
NO WAY OUT
Story part 4 of 4
& ART by FRANCESCO FRANCAVILLA 2013
THE RING!
TG
GALAZZO
JIMMY GALAZZO
BOOOM
12
13

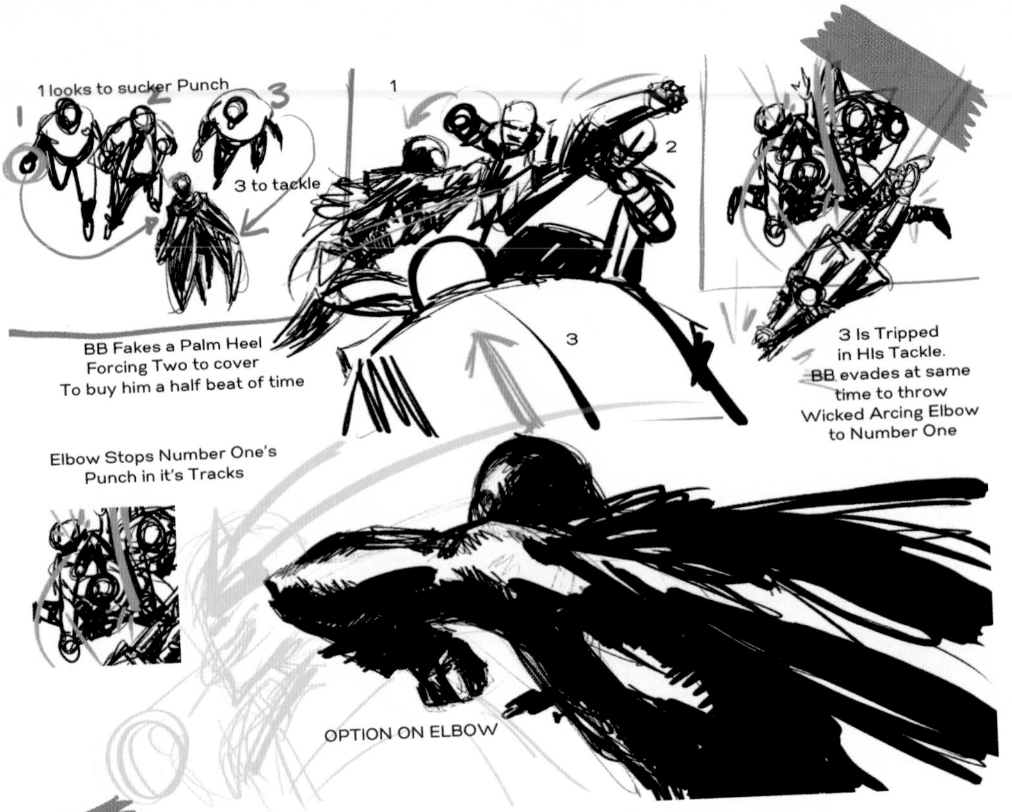
1 looks to sucker Punch
1
2
3
3 to tackle
BB Fakes a Palm Heel
Forcing Two to cover
To buy him a half beat of time
1
2
3
3 Is Tripped
in HIs Tackle.
BB evades at same
time to throw
Wicked Arcing Elbow
to Number One
Elbow Stops Number One's
Punch in it's Tracks
OPTION ON ELBOW

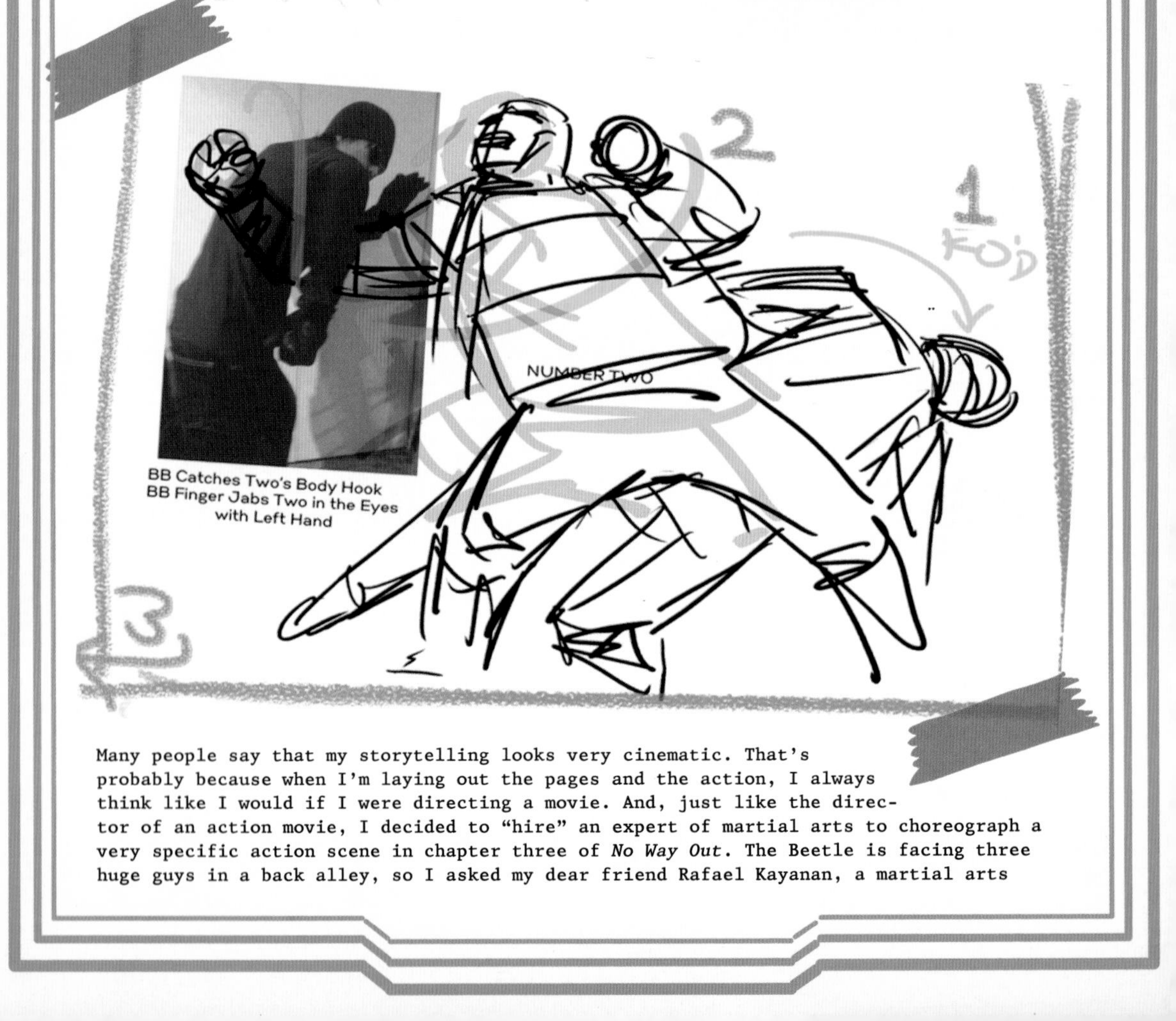
2
1
KO'D
NUMBER TWO
BB Catches Two's Body Hook
BB Finger Jabs Two in the Eyes
with Left Hand
3

Many people say that my storytelling looks very cinematic. That's probably because when I'm laying out the pages and the action, I always think like I would if I were directing a movie. And, just like the director of an action movie, I decided to "hire" an expert of martial arts to choreograph a very specific action scene in chapter three of *No Way Out*. The Beetle is facing three huge guys in a back alley, so I asked my dear friend Rafael Kayanan, a martial arts

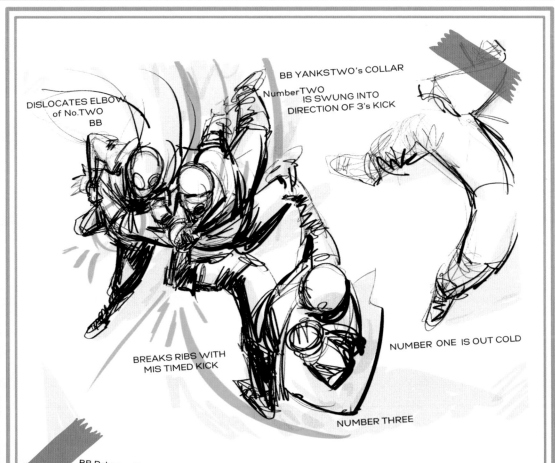

DISLOCATES ELBOW
of No.TWO
BB

BB YANKSTWO's COLLAR

NumberTWO IS SWUNG INTO DIRECTION OF 3's KICK

BREAKS RIBS WITH MIS TIMED KICK

NUMBER ONE IS OUT COLD

NUMBER THREE

BB Releases the broken elbow of Two

BB Dives, Elbows Two's Knee sideways.
And Uses the knee as leverage to Double Kick the
Incoming Number Three.

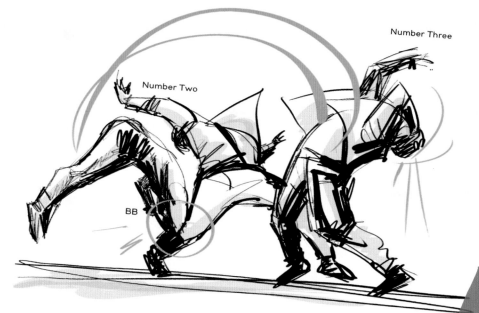

Number Three

Number Two

BB

and combat fight expert (he actually gets hired by the Hollywood types for
training actors in movies and TV shows), as well as a talented artist, to help
me with the choreography. The result was a stunning six-page fight sequence
that was praised by critics and fans alike. Success! Thanks, Rafa!

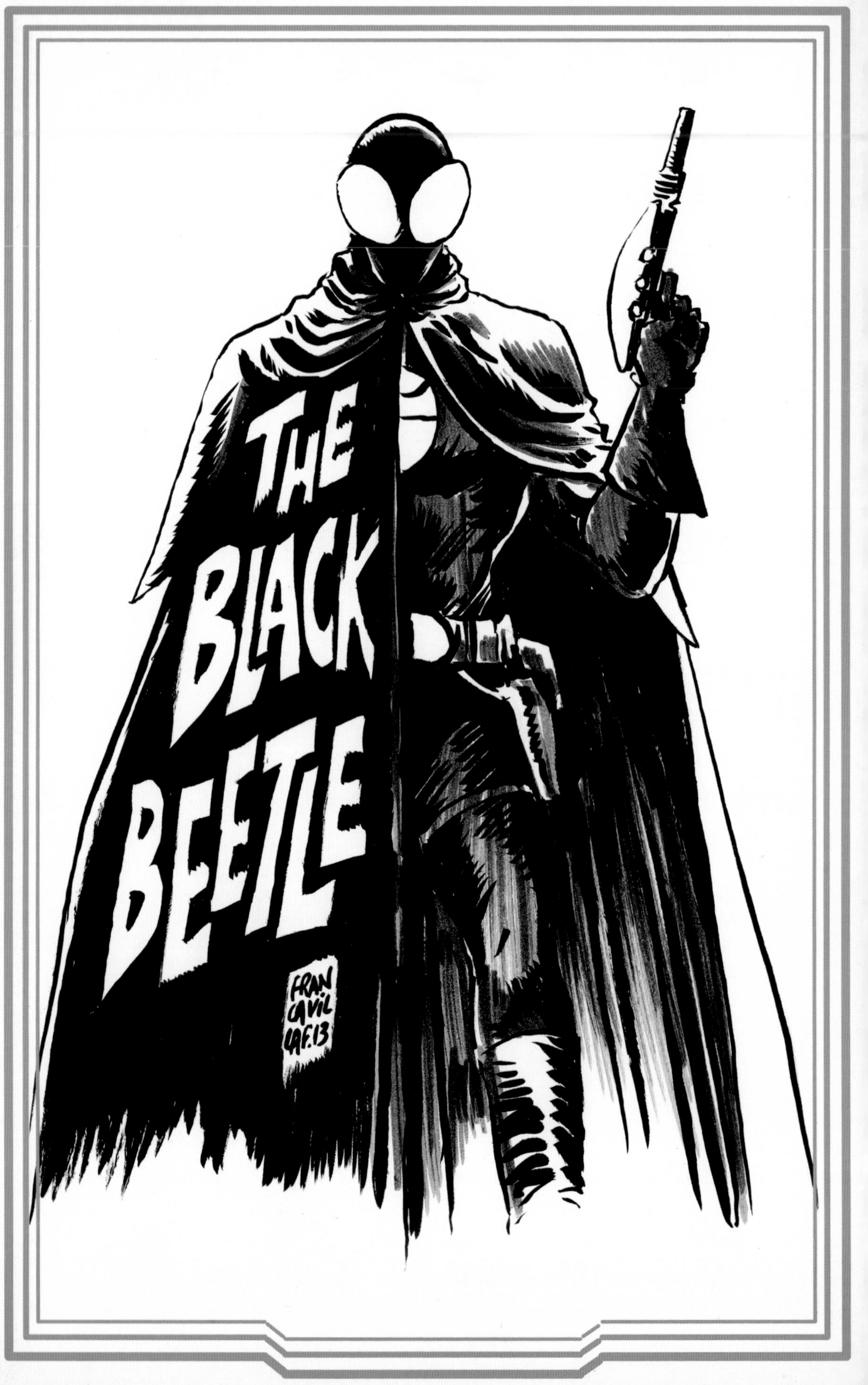
THE
BLACK
BEETLE
FRAN
CAVIL
LAF.13

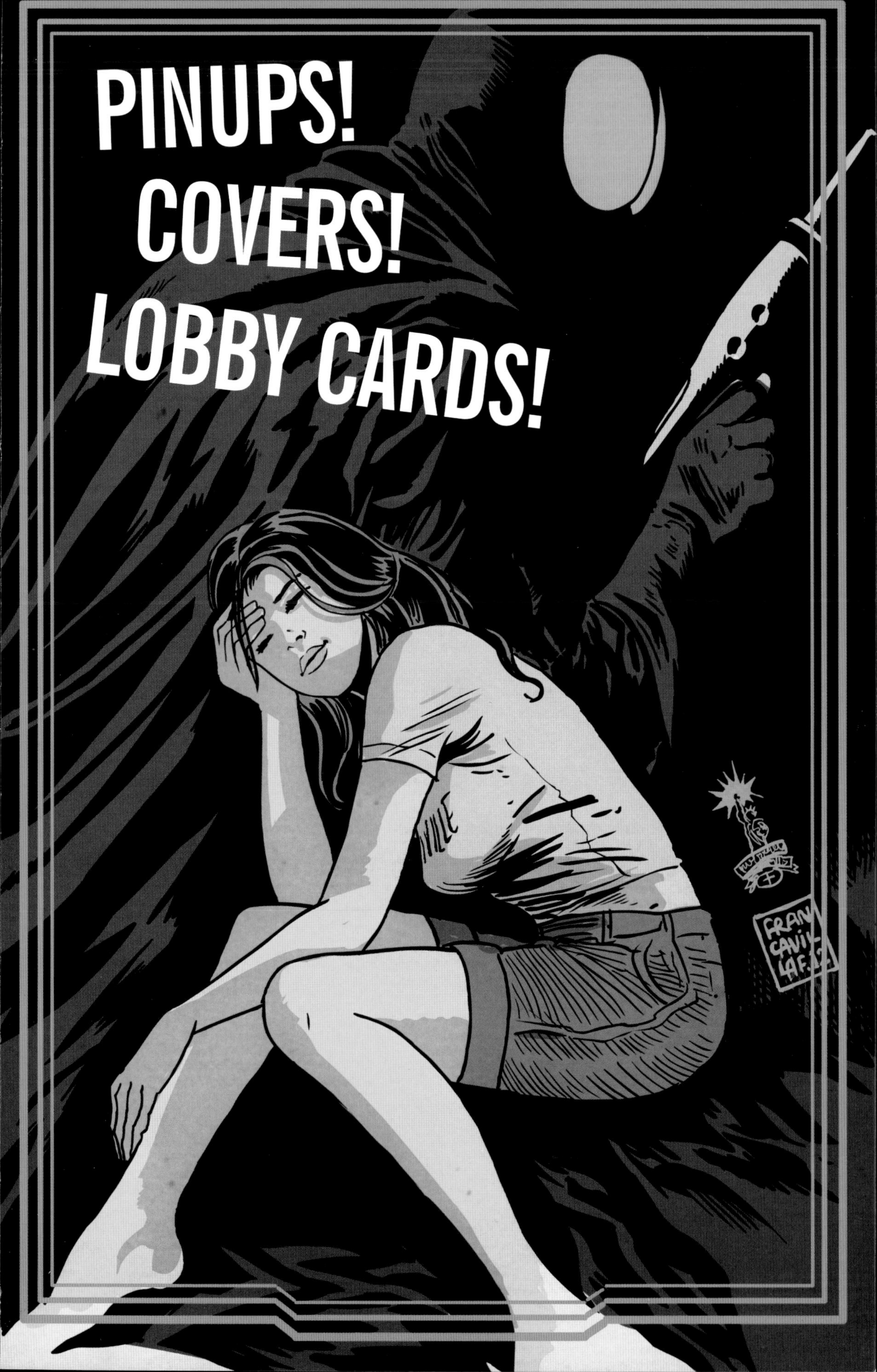
PINUPS!
COVERS!
LOBBY CARDS!

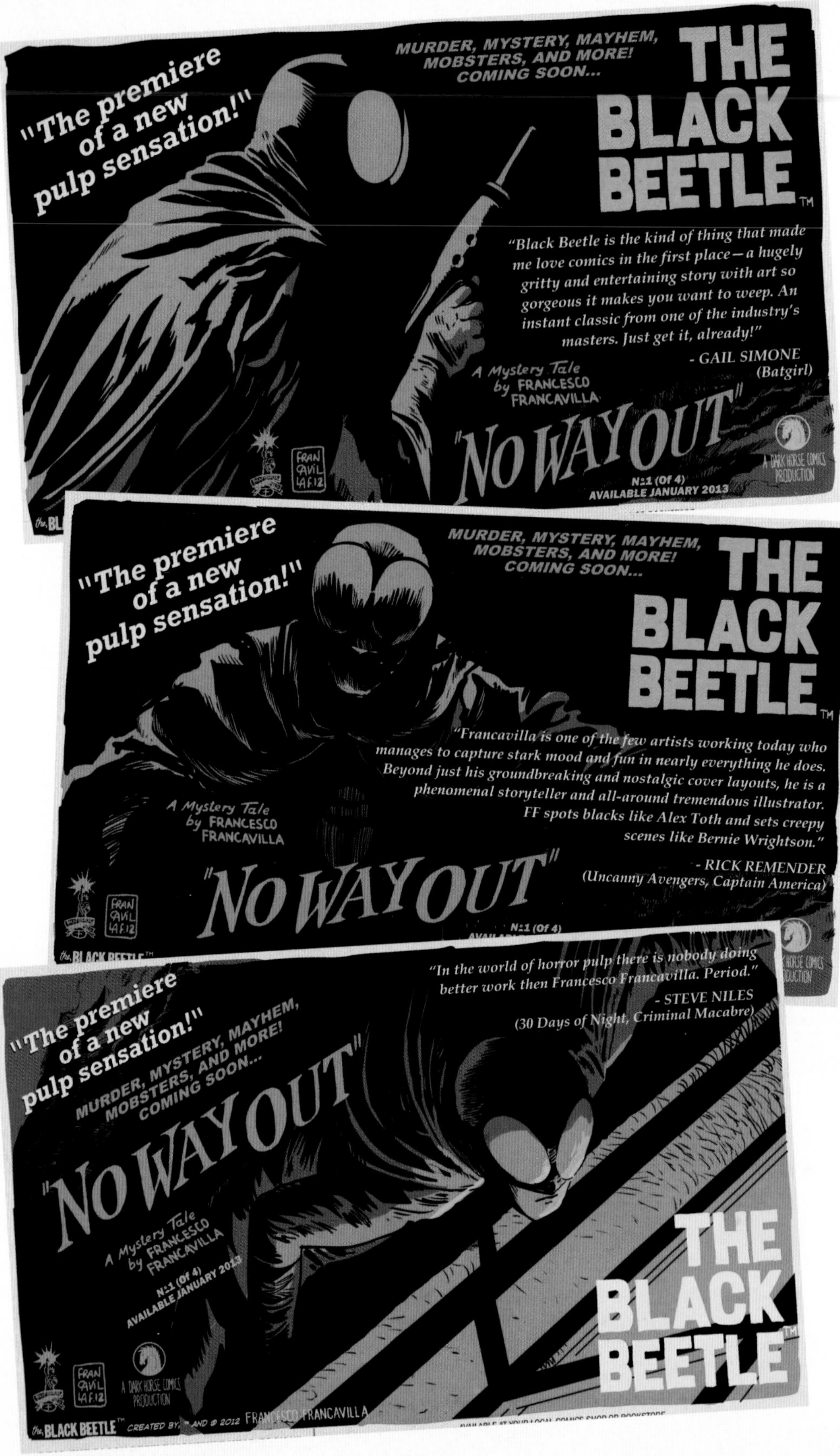
"The premiere of a new pulp sensation!"
MURDER, MYSTERY, MAYHEM, MOBSTERS, AND MORE! COMING SOON...
THE BLACK BEETLE™
"Black Beetle is the kind of thing that made me love comics in the first place—a hugely gritty and entertaining story with art so gorgeous it makes you want to weep. An instant classic from one of the industry's masters. Just get it, already!"
- GAIL SIMONE (Batgirl)
A Mystery Tale by FRANCESCO FRANCAVILLA
"NO WAY OUT"
N.1 (Of 4) AVAILABLE JANUARY 2013
A DARK HORSE COMICS PRODUCTION
FRAN CAVIL LA F.12
"The premiere of a new pulp sensation!"
MURDER, MYSTERY, MAYHEM, MOBSTERS, AND MORE! COMING SOON...
THE BLACK BEETLE™
"Francavilla is one of the few artists working today who manages to capture stark mood and fun in nearly everything he does. Beyond just his groundbreaking and nostalgic cover layouts, he is a phenomenal storyteller and all-around tremendous illustrator. FF spots blacks like Alex Toth and sets creepy scenes like Bernie Wrightson."
- RICK REMENDER (Uncanny Avengers, Captain America)
A Mystery Tale by FRANCESCO FRANCAVILLA
"NO WAY OUT"
N.1 (Of 4)
FRAN CAVIL LA F.12
the BLACK BEETLE™
"In the world of horror pulp there is nobody doing better work then Francesco Francavilla. Period."
- STEVE NILES (30 Days of Night, Criminal Macabre)
"The premiere of a new pulp sensation!"
MURDER, MYSTERY, MAYHEM, MOBSTERS, AND MORE! COMING SOON...
"NO WAY OUT"
A Mystery Tale by FRANCESCO FRANCAVILLA
N.1 (Of 4) AVAILABLE JANUARY 2013
THE BLACK BEETLE™
FRAN CAVIL LA F.12
A DARK HORSE COMICS PRODUCTION
the BLACK BEETLE™ CREATED BY, ™ AND © 2012 FRANCESCO FRANCAVILLA

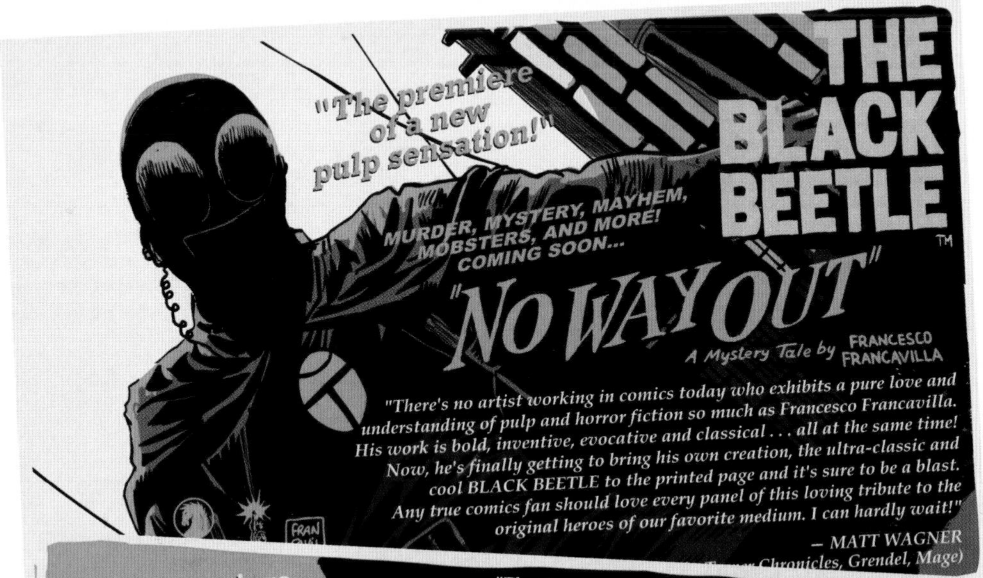
THE BLACK BEETLE™
"The premiere of a new pulp sensation!"
MURDER, MYSTERY, MAYHEM, MOBSTERS, AND MORE! COMING SOON...
"NO WAY OUT"
A Mystery Tale by FRANCESCO FRANCAVILLA
"There's no artist working in comics today who exhibits a pure love and understanding of pulp and horror fiction so much as Francesco Francavilla. His work is bold, inventive, evocative and classical . . . all at the same time! Now, he's finally getting to bring his own creation, the ultra-classic and cool BLACK BEETLE to the printed page and it's sure to be a blast. Any true comics fan should love every panel of this loving tribute to the original heroes of our favorite medium. I can hardly wait!"
— MATT WAGNER
Chronicles, Grendel, Mage)

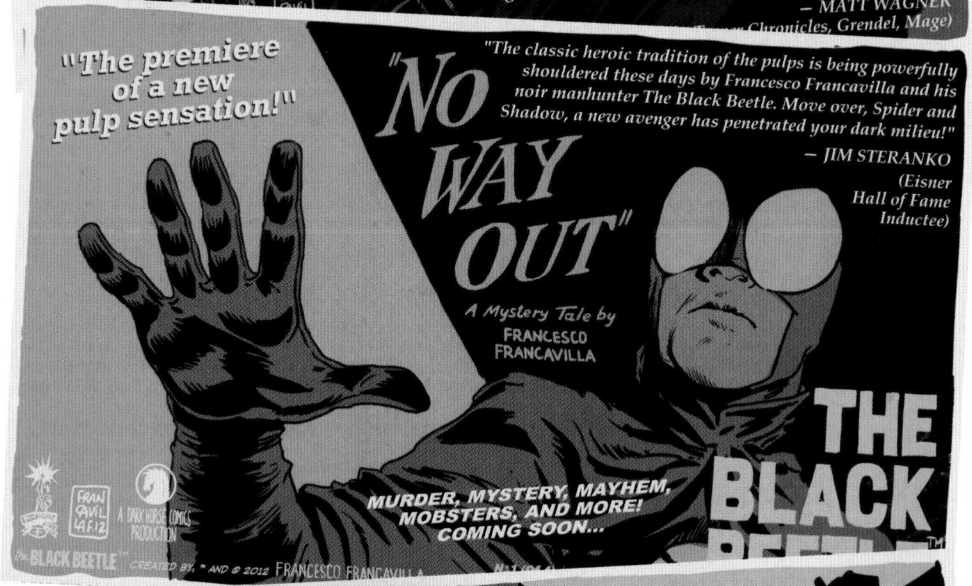
"The premiere of a new pulp sensation!"
"The classic heroic tradition of the pulps is being powerfully shouldered these days by Francesco Francavilla and his noir manhunter The Black Beetle. Move over, Spider and Shadow, a new avenger has penetrated your dark milieu!"
— JIM STERANKO
(Eisner Hall of Fame Inductee)
"NO WAY OUT"
A Mystery Tale by FRANCESCO FRANCAVILLA
THE BLACK
MURDER, MYSTERY, MAYHEM, MOBSTERS, AND MORE! COMING SOON...
FRAN CAVIL LA F.12
A DARK HORSE COMICS PRODUCTION
the BLACK BEETLE™ CREATED BY, ™ AND © 2012 FRANCESCO FRANCAVILLA

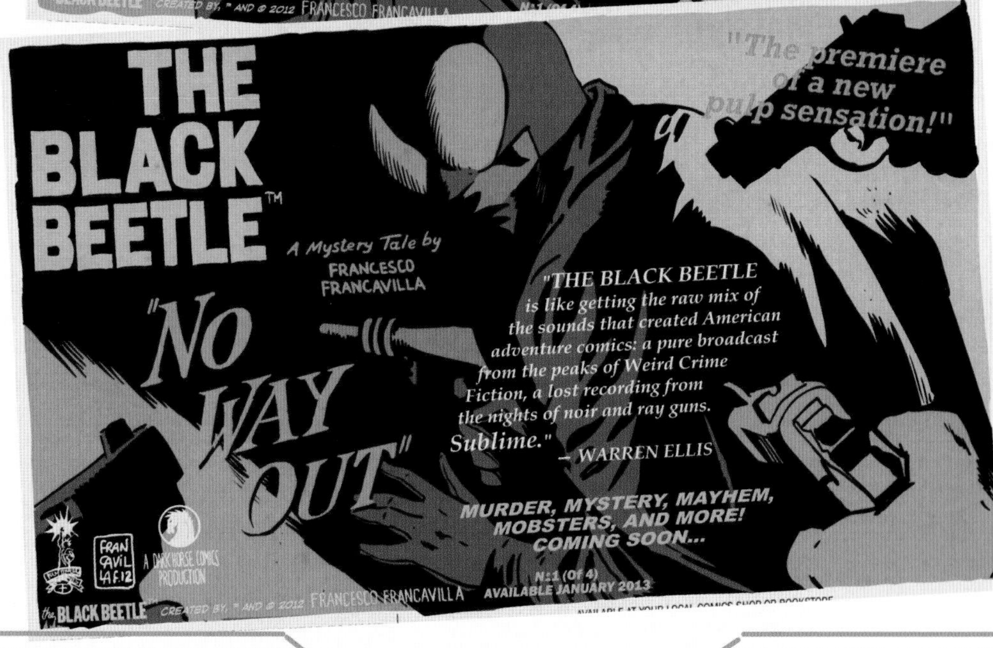
THE BLACK BEETLE™
"The premiere of a new pulp sensation!"
A Mystery Tale by FRANCESCO FRANCAVILLA
"NO WAY OUT"
"THE BLACK BEETLE is like getting the raw mix of the sounds that created American adventure comics: a pure broadcast from the peaks of Weird Crime Fiction, a lost recording from the nights of noir and ray guns. Sublime."
— WARREN ELLIS
MURDER, MYSTERY, MAYHEM, MOBSTERS, AND MORE! COMING SOON...
FRAN CAVIL LA F.12
A DARK HORSE COMICS PRODUCTION
N:1 (Of 4)
AVAILABLE JANUARY 2013
the BLACK BEETLE CREATED BY, ™ AND © 2012 FRANCESCO FRANCAVILLA

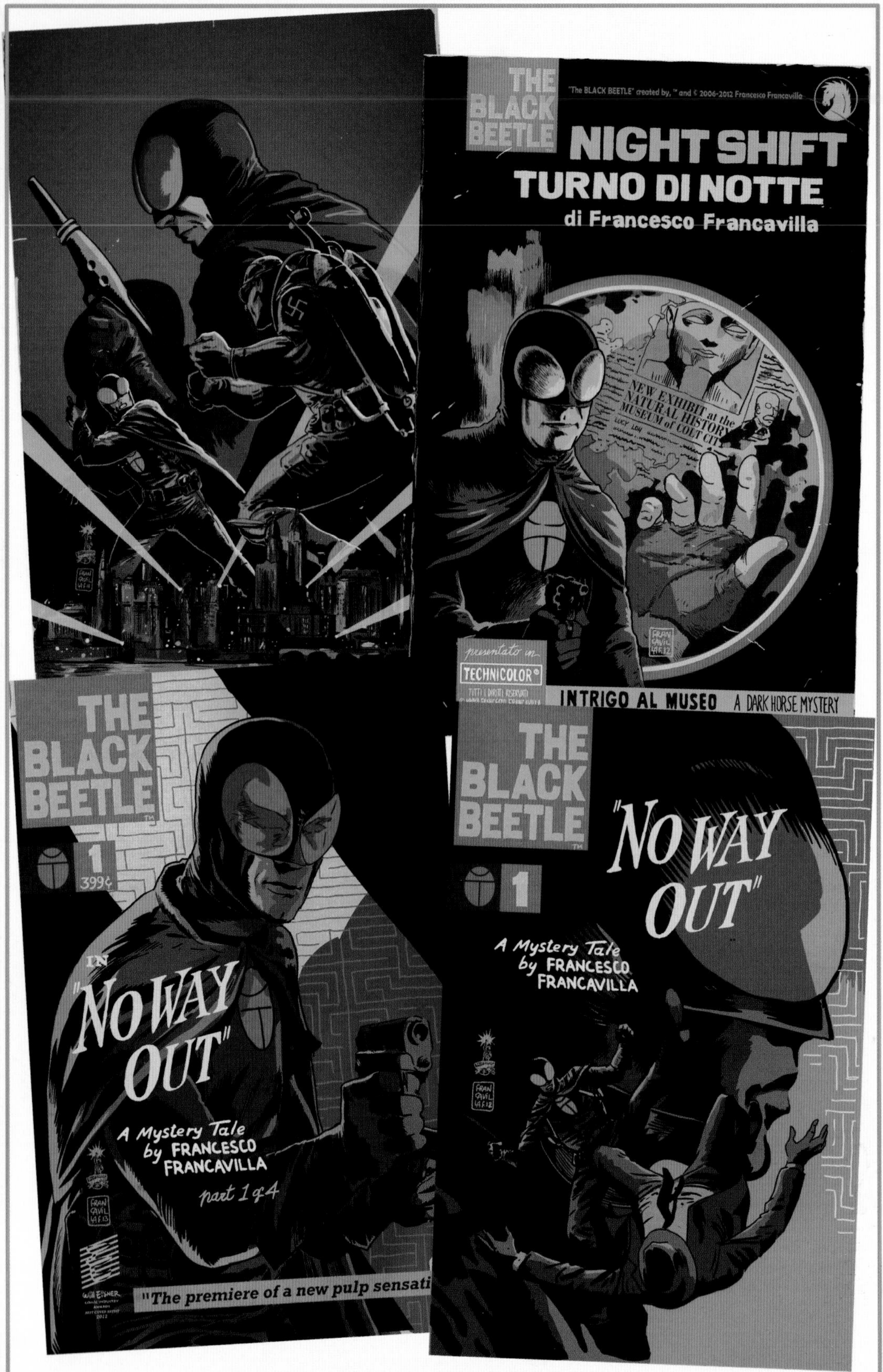
THE BLACK BEETLE
"The BLACK BEETLE" created by, ™ and © 2006-2012 Francesco Francavilla
NIGHT SHIFT
TURNO DI NOTTE
di Francesco Francavilla
NEW EXHIBIT at the NATURAL HISTORY MUSEUM of OUT CITY
presentato in
TECHNICOLOR
INTRIGO AL MUSEO
A DARK HORSE MYSTERY
THE BLACK BEETLE
1
"NO WAY OUT"
A Mystery Tale by FRANCESCO FRANCAVILLA
THE BLACK BEETLE
1
399¢
IN
"NO WAY OUT"
A Mystery Tale by FRANCESCO FRANCAVILLA
part 1 of 4
"The premiere of a new pulp sensati

Clockwise from top left: The cover to *Dark Horse Presents* #11, a signing card for San Diego Comic-Con International 2012, the second-printing cover for #1, and the Exclusive ComicsPro cover for #1.

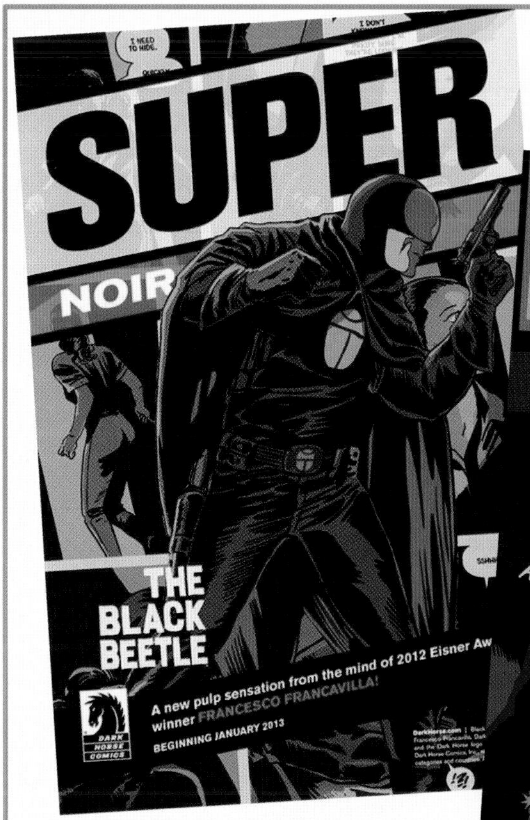
I NEED TO HIDE.
SUPER
NOIR
THE BLACK BEETLE
winner FRANCESCO FRANCAVILLA!
BEGINNING JANUARY 2013

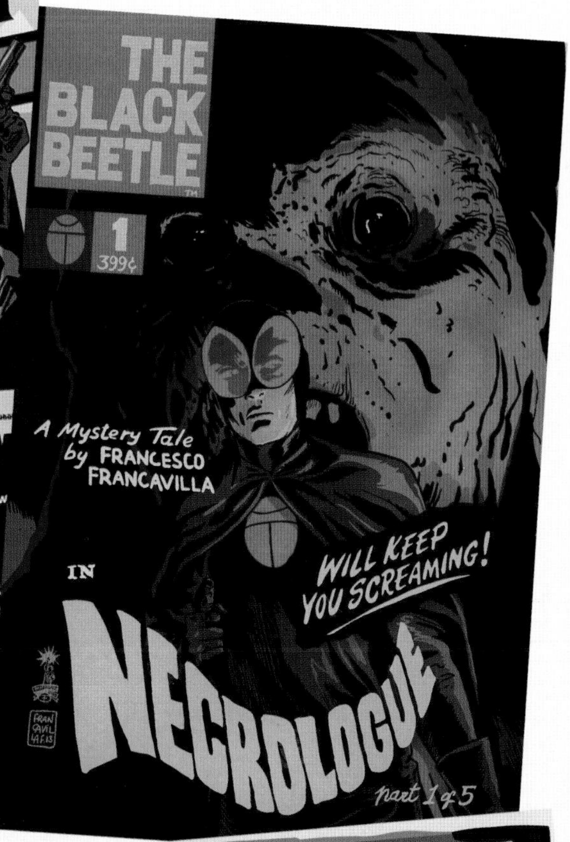
THE BLACK BEETLE
1
399¢
A Mystery Tale by FRANCESCO FRANCAVILLA
WILL KEEP YOU SCREAMING!
IN
NECROLOGUE
part 1 of 5

Clockwise from top left: A poster designed by Dark Horse Comics to promote *The Black Beetle* as SUPER NOIR, the cover for the upcoming *Necrologue* #1, and a lobby card for *Necrologue*.

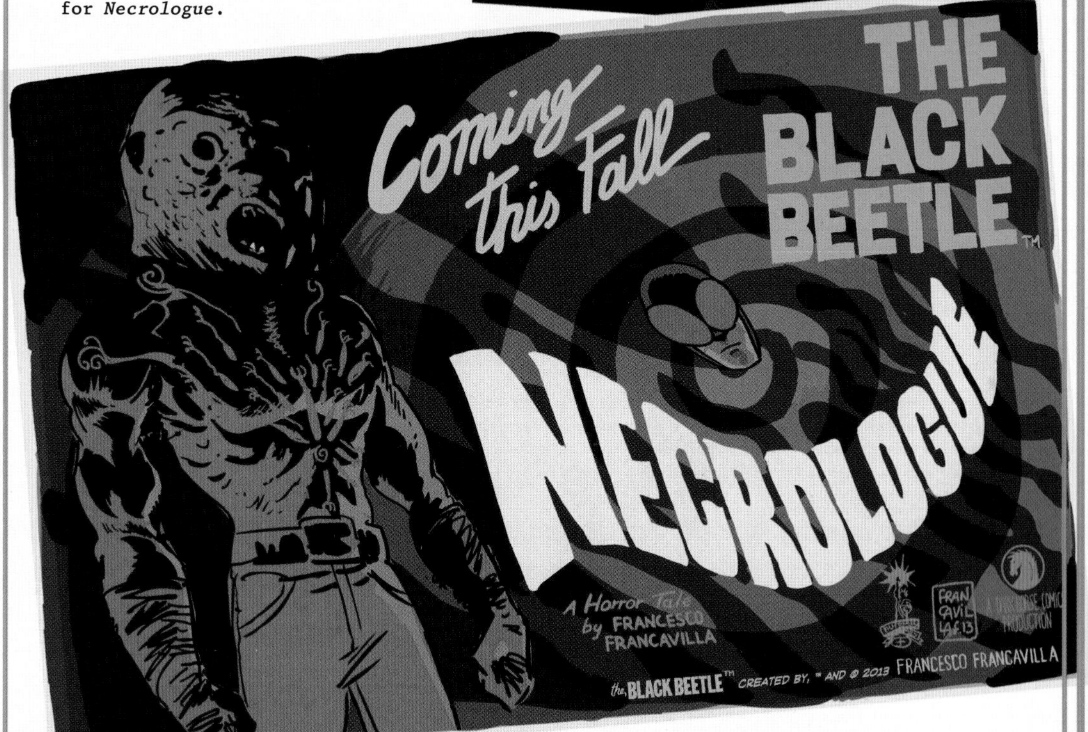
Coming this Fall
THE BLACK BEETLE
NECROLOGUE
A Horror Tale by FRANCESCO FRANCAVILLA
A DARK HORSE COMICS PRODUCTION
the BLACK BEETLE™ CREATED BY, ™ AND © 2013 FRANCESCO FRANCAVILLA

THE BLACK BEETLE™

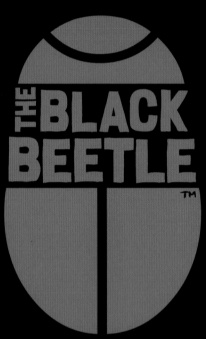